RATEMAKING IN INTERNATIONAL AIR TRANSPORT

RATEMAKING IN INTERNATIONAL AIR TRANSPORT

A LEGAL ANALYSIS OF INTERNATIONAL AIR FARES AND RATES

PETER P. C. HAANAPPEL

KLUWER – THE NETHERLANDS – 1978

To my Mother

ISBN 90 268 0979 4

SUMMARY

Ratemaking in international air transport is a matter of vital importance for airlines, consumers and Governments. For airlines, because the level of international air fares and rates forms one of the bases of their profit-making ability. For consumers, because that level determines whether they can afford the use of international air transport. For Governments, because they, as the guardians of the interests of both the airlines and the consumers, have the task to strike a just balance between those interests.

International air fares and rates are of two kinds: scheduled and non-scheduled. The International Air Transport Association (IATA), the trade association of the world's scheduled international airlines, determines, under Governmental supervision and control, uniform fares and rates for scheduled international air services. These services account for approximately seventy-five percent of total international air traffic. The remaining twenty-five percent consists of non-scheduled, or charter international air services. International charter air fares and rates are by and large set by the free forces of the marketplace, and compete with scheduled international (IATA) air fares and rates. This book studies both scheduled and charter international air fares and rates. It examines the role of airlines, airline associations and Governments in the international ratemaking process. Furthermore, it analyses the competitive relationship between charter and scheduled international air fares and rates.

The book's originality lies in the fact that it is the first comprehensive legal study of ratemaking in international air transport, encompassing both the scheduled and charter aspects. In addition, the inquiry takes into account not only the interests of the airlines and the wishes of their respective Governments, but also and especially, the interests of the consumer, the user of international air transport.

ACKNOWLEDGEMENTS

The author wishes to thank the Faculty of Law of McGill University for their financial assistance in preparing the manuscript of this book. He also wishes to express his gratitude to Professor Ivan A. Vlasic, who supervised the work on the doctoral dissertation which forms the basis of this book.

ABOUT THE AUTHOR:

Dr. Haanappel was born in the Netherlands in 1949 and has lived in Canada since 1972. He received his first legal training at the Faculty of Law of the Free University of Amsterdam, from which he graduated in 1972. He is also a graduate of the International Faculty for the Teaching of Comparative Law in Strasbourg. His aerospace studies at the Institute of Air and Space Law of McGill University in Montreal led to a Master of Laws (LL.M.) degree in 1974 and a Doctor of Civil Law (D.C.L.) degree in 1976. "Ratemaking in International Air Transport" is a slightly modified and updated version of the author's doctoral dissertation. In June 1976, Dr. Haanappel was appointed Assistant Professor of Law at the Faculty of Law of McGill University. He also teaches at McGill's Institute of Air and Space Law and is consultant - research adviser to the Centre for Research of Air and Space Law.

The author's previous air law publications include:

- The IATA Conditions of Contract and Carriage for Passengers and Baggage, IX European Transport Law 650-684 (1974);
- Deregulation of the United States System of Government Regulation of Domestic Civil Aviation in Light of the Overall Structure of International Civil Aviation, 9 Akron Law Review 651-660 (1976);
- Background of the Dutch-American Aviation Conflict, I Annals of Air and Space Law 63-81 (1976);
- International Air Transport Association: Quo Vadis? in: International Air Transport: Law, Organization and Policies for the Future, Ed. by N.M. Matte, Carswell/Toronto, Pedone/Paris 67-78 (1977).

ABBREVIATIONS

AACO	Arab Air Carriers Organization
AAFRA	Association of African Airlines
ABC	Advance Booking Charter
ACAP	Aviation Consumer Action Project
ACCA	Air Carriers Charter Association
AEA	Association of European Airlines
AFCAC	African Civil Aviation Conference
AGM	Annual General Meeting
APA	Airline Passengers Association
APEX	Advance Purchase Excursion (Fare)
ASDA/SVLR	Association Suisse de Droit Aérien/ Schweizerische Vereinigung für Luftrecht
ASTA	American Society of Travel Agents
ATA	Air Transport Association of America
ATAC	Air Transport Association of Canada
ATAF	Association des Transporteurs de la Zone Franc
ATC	Air Transport Committee
AVI	Aviation Cases
AWST	Aviation Week and Space Technology
BEA	British European Airways
CAA	Civil Aviation Authority
CAAC	Civil Aviation Administration of China
CAB	Civil Aeronautics Board
CCH	Commerce Clearing House, Inc.
CFR	Code of Federal Regulations
CNR	Canadian National Railways
CP Air	Canadian Pacific Airlines
CTC	Canadian Transport Commission
DOT	Department of Transportation
EARB	European Airlines Research Bureau
EC	Executive Committee
ECAC	European Civil Aviation Conference
ECSC	European Coal and Steel Community
EEC	European Economic Community
FCC	Federal Communications Commission
FMC	Federal Maritime Commission
IACA	International Air Carrier Association
IATA	International Air Transport Association
ICAO	International Civil Aviation Organization
ICC	Interstate Commerce Commission
ICEO	International Charter Enforcement Organization
ICRC	International Committee of the Red Cross
IMF	International Monetary Fund
INTELSAT	International Telecommunications Satellite Organization
ITA	Institut de Transport Aérien

ITC	Inclusive Tour Charter
IUV	International Unit of Value
JALC	Journal of Air Law and Commerce
JT	Joint Traffic Conference
KLM	KLM - Royal Dutch Airlines
LJ	Law Journal
LR	Law Review
NACA	National Air Carrier Association
NSIT	Non-Scheduled and Inclusive Tour Study Group
OAA	Orient Airlines Association
OCA	Office of the Consumer Advocate
OPEC	Organization of Petroleum Exporting Countries
OTC	One-Stop-Inclusive Tour Charter
Pan Am	Pan American World Airways
PICAO	Provisional International Civil Aviation Organization
PL	Public Law
RFDA	Revue Française de Droit Aérien
RGA	Revue Générale de l'Air
RSC	Revised Statutes of Canada
RTKLS	Revenue Tonne Kilometres
SAS	Scandinavian Airlines System
SDR	Special Drawing Rights
SEC	Special Event Charter
TC	Traffic Conference
TC Res.	Traffic Conference Resolution
TGC	Travel Group Charter
TIA	Trans International Airlines
TIAS	Treaties and Other International Acts Series
TS	Treaty Series
TWA	Trans World Airlines
UK	United Kingdom of Great Britain and Northern Ireland
UNCTAD	United Nations Conference on Trade and Development
UNO	United Nations Organization
UPU	Universal Postal Union
USA	United States of America
USC	United States Code
USCA	United States Court of Appeals
USDC	United States District Court
USSR	Union of Socialist Soviet Republics
UTA	Union de Transports Aériens

TABLE OF CONTENTS

INTRODUCTION

Ratemaking in international air transport is a matter of vital importance for airlines, consumers and Governments. For airlines, because the level of international air fares and rates forms one of the bases of their profit-making ability. For consumers, because the level of international air fares and rates decides whether they can afford the use of international air transport. For Governments, because they, as the guardians of the interests of both the airlines and the consumers, have the task to strike a just balance between those interests.

A fundamental distinction should be made between ratemaking in scheduled and in non-scheduled international air transport. Just under three-fourths of the total international air traffic is carried on scheduled and the rest on non-scheduled flights. Statistics for the year 1972, for instance, show that in that year a total of 27.620 million tonne-kilometres was flown on scheduled international air services. Estimated total tonne-kilometres performed on non-scheduled international air services amounted to 10.600 million in 1972.(1) Thus, in 1972, approximately twenty-eight percent of the total international air traffic was carried on non-scheduled flights, and the remainder, approximately seventy-two percent, on scheduled flights. Uniform fares and rates for almost all scheduled international air services are set on an inter-carrier basis through the ratemaking machinery of the International Air Transport Association (IATA). By contrast, fares and rates for non-scheduled international air services are generally set by the free forces of the marketplace, by the forces of supply and demand.

The fact that almost three-fourths of the total international air traffic is carried on scheduled flights and that virtually all fares and rates for those flights are set through the IATA ratemaking machinery, explains the great importance of IATA with respect to the subject of international ratemaking. IATA is the trade association of the world's scheduled international airlines and it is one of the largest and most significant organizations in the field of international civil aviation. In importance it is probably only exceeded by the International Civil Aviation Organization (ICAO). ICAO is an intergovernmental organization created by the Chicago Convention of 1944. (2) It is a specialized agency of the United Nations Organization (UNO), and it performs a multitude of functions in international civil aviation. These functions lie mainly, although certainly not exclusively, in the technical field of civil aviation. In the legal field ICAO is, among other things, involved in the preparation of international air law conventions. As shall be seen below, in the economic field, ICAO is at the present time actively involved in a study of international fares and rates. (3)

Whereas ICAO is thus an intergovernmental organization, whose members are States, IATA is a private international organization, whose members are airlines, namely, the world's scheduled international airlines. IATA was founded by the International Air Transport Operators Conference held at Havana (Cuba) in April 1945. It is a corporate body under Canadian law and its headquarters are located at Montreal. The variety of functions which IATA performs in international civil aviation is very wide. To some extent ICAO's and IATA's functions overlap each other. As far as IATA is concerned, this book will concentrate on the legal aspects of IATA's ratemaking function. Some of the economic aspects of IATA's ratemaking function will also be taken into account. Further, the book will deal with the legal, and again with some of the economic aspects of non-IATA ratemaking, especially as far as non-scheduled international air transport is concerned.

The statement, made above, that IATA is a private international organization, needs some correction or refinement. For the reasons set out below, IATA is sometimes called a 'quasi-public' rather than a private organization. The first reason for calling IATA 'quasi-public' lies in the composition of the IATA member airlines. This composition shows a 'public' characteristic in that more than one half of the IATA member airlines is either entirely or more than fifty percent State-owned. This means that those airlines, which form a majority in IATA, are in fact State-controlled, and when acting in IATA, they can be regarded as acting under State supervision and control. Furthermore, a certain number of privately-owned IATA airlines are so strictly controlled by their respective Governments, that they too can be regarded as behaving in accordance with the will of their Governments, when acting in IATA. The second reason lies in the character of a number of functions performed by IATA. These functions, often called IATA's 'quasi-public' functions, have been delegated to the Association by a majority of States through their bilateral air transport agreements. The most important of these 'quasi-public' functions - at the same time probably the most important and the most controversial function of IATA as a whole - is IATA's above-mentioned ratemaking function, pursuant to which IATA sets fares and rates for scheduled international air transport. Because of the composition of its member airlines, and because of the 'quasi-public' nature of some of its functions, especially its ratemaking function, it is understandable that IATA is often looked upon as a 'quasi-public' organization, or at least, as a private organization with 'public' characteristics.

IATA is not just _an_ association of scheduled international airlines. It is _the_ association of scheduled international airlines. Almost all major scheduled international air carriers belong to it. Of the total of 31.670 million tonne-kilometres performed in _scheduled_ international air services in 1973, 29.689 million, or approximately ninety-four percent, were performed on the flights of IATA airlines. For all those flights IATA seeks to set the rates and fares. Only the fares and rates for the relatively small number of scheduled international flights, performed by airlines which are not members of IATA - totalling approximately six percent of the tonne-kilometres performed on all scheduled international air services in 1973 - remain outside the IATA ratemaking system.(4)

As noted before, over one-fourth of total international air traffic is performed on non-scheduled, or as they are often called, charter flights. Fares and rates for these flights are, apart from a limited amount of Government intervention, set by the free forces of the marketplace, i.e. by the forces of supply and demand. Charter flights can be performed both by scheduled air carriers, most of which, of course, are IATA members; and by charter only air carriers. In fact, most IATA member airlines nowadays perform both scheduled and charter flights. Of the total international passenger air traffic in 1973, twenty-two four-tenth percent was carried by charter only airlines, and eight four-tenth percent was carried on the charter flights of IATA airlines.(5) A number of charter only airlines are wholly or partially owned by IATA airlines. Notwithstanding the fact that most IATA airlines thus perform both scheduled and non-scheduled air services, membership in IATA is only open to scheduled air carriers. Membership of the scheduled air carriers in IATA does not prevent them from performing charter services besides their scheduled services, but membership in the Association remains closed to those air carriers which only perform charter air services. Those airlines, exclusively providing charter air services, have created their own trade associations: the National Air Carrier Association (NACA), the International Air Carrier Association (IACA) and the Air Carriers Charter Association (ACCA). NACA is the trade association of a number of independent U.S. supplemental airlines.(6) IACA is the trade association of a number of independent charter operators from the U.S.A., Canada and Europe.(7) Finally, ACCA is the trade association of a number of charter operators, all of them European, which are affiliates or subsidiaries of IATA airlines.(8) These three associations are all much younger than IATA and their activities are not nearly as comprehensive as those of IATA. Furthermore, whereas membership of the scheduled international air carriers in IATA is almost universal, this is not so in the case of these three charter associations. Perhaps the most important difference between IATA on the one hand, and NACA, IACA and ACCA on the other, is that the latter have never tried to set fares and rates for international charter air services, whereas IATA has always done this with respect to scheduled international air services. International charter fares and rates, including those for charter flights performed by IATA airlines, have so far almost exclusively been set by the three forces of the marketplace. Although IATA has thus never set charter fares and rates for the non-scheduled flights performed by its member airlines, it has always tried to somewhat limit the right of its members to perform charter air services.

Due to a number of economic circumstances, charter air carriers have always been able to offer air transport to the public at considerably lower fares and rates than scheduled air carriers. Over the years, charter competition has become a real threat to IATA and its member airlines. This threat has had an important influence on the IATA tariff structure, since the Association and its members had to find ways to combat the every growing charter competition. Several unsuccessful attempts have been undertaken to bring the charter only airlines within the institutional framework of IATA.

IATA, NACA, IACA and ACCA are not the only existing airline associations. Eight other associations should be mentioned: the Arab Air Carriers Association (AACO), the Association of African Airlines (AAFRA), the Association of European Airlines (AEA), the Air Transport Association of America (ATA), the Air Transport Association of Canada (ATAC), the Association des Transporteurs de la Zone Franc (ATAF), the Berlin Agreement Carriers and the Orient Airlines Association (OAA).(9) Of these associations, AEA and ATA are especially important. AEA is the trade association of the European scheduled airlines. It is a follow-on organization to the former European Airlines Research Bureau (EARB). ATA is the trade association of the (domestic) U.S. scheduled airlines. None of these eight associations is involved in ratemaking.

IATA was preceded by another association of scheduled international airlines, the International Air Traffic Association, bearing the same initials as the present IATA. It is usually referred to as the old or pre-war IATA. This pre-war IATA was founded at The Hague on August 28, 1919, by six young European airline companies, of which only one, the Dutch company KLM, is still in operation. By 1939, the membership of the old IATA had increased to twenty-nine. There are two very significant differences between the pre-war and the present IATA. In the first place, whereas the present IATA is really a worldwide organization, the old IATA was mainly a European affair. Most members of the old IATA were European airlines. The only North American airline that ever joined the old IATA was Pan American Airways. It joined the Association in 1938, but it never actively took part in its activities due to the outbreak of the Second World War in 1939. In the second place, and this is very important, the old IATA was not, at least not formally, involved in international ratemaking, whereas ratemaking is precisely the most significant function of the present IATA. Although the so-called Timetable and Accountancy Conferences of the old IATA, unlike the Traffic Conferences of the present IATA, were not formally authorized by their parent body or by Governments to set international air fares and rates, they did give airline representatives the opportunity to discuss and to agree upon uniform fares and rates along many routes on an informal basis. Formally, however, the old IATA had no ratemaking power.

The activities of the pre-war IATA were interrupted by the Second World War. The thirty-ninth General Meeting of the Association, which was to be held at New York City in 1939, never took place due to the outbreak of the war. Informally, however, some of IATA's activities were carried on during the war, and also during this period, plans were thought out to replace the old IATA by a new, worldwide organization of scheduled international airlines. This new worldwide organization would be the present IATA, founded at Havana (Cuba) in April, 1945. At a meeting in London on September 17, 1945, the members of the old IATA decided that the organization should be liquidated and that its documents of interest should be transferred to the new IATA. Formally, there are no legal connections between the old and the present IATA.[10]

Whereas, as can be seen from the above, airlines, both scheduled and charter, are well organized in trade associations this does not hold true for their counterpart, the consumer or the user of air transport. There is only one really active association of airline users, the Aviation Consumer Action Project (ACAP). The Washington D.C. based ACAP was set up by consumer advocate Ralph Nader in 1971. Its first executive director was Dr. K.G.J. Pillai.[11]

At the end of this introduction a few words should be said about the terminology to be used in this book. Throughout the work the terms "fares", "rates", "tariffs" and "ratemaking" will appear frequently. The term "fares" relates to the prices to be paid for the air transportation of passengers and their baggage, whereas the term "rates" relates to the prices to be paid for the air transportation of cargo. In practice, however, the two terms are often used interchangeably. The wider term "tariffs" means the prices to be paid for the air transportation of passengers, baggage and cargo, and the condition under which those prices apply, often including prices and conditions for agency and other auxiliary services.(12) The term "ratemaking" means the method of determining fares and rates for air transportation. Finally, the term "charter only airlines" means those airline companies which exclusively perform charter or non-scheduled air services. ICAO usually refers to charter only airlines as "independent charter operators". In the U.S.A. they are most often called "supplemental airlines".

(1) These figures exclude China and the U.S.S.R. See Review of the Economic Situation of Air Transport (1963-1973), ICAO Circ. 122-AT/32 (1974) at 57 and 21.

(2) ICAO Doc.2187, p.39 et seq.

(3) See, e.g., Survey of International Air Transport Fares and Rates, ICAO Circ. 123-AT/33 (1974). About ICAO in general see: Schenkman, International Civil Aviation Organization, Diss. Geneva, 1955; Buergenthal, Law-Making in the International Civil Aviation Organization, Syracuse Univ. Press, Syracuse, N.Y., 1969.

(4) These figures exclude China and the U.S.S.R. See, The State of the Air Transport Industry, IATA Publ., 30th Annual General Meeting, Montreal, 1974, Appendices 7 and 8. The largest non-IATA scheduled (international) airline is the U.S.S.R. flag carrier, Aeroflot: see infra, Ch. VI, para. I.

(5) See, The State of the Air Transport Industry, op.cit., Chart 12.

(6) Members of NACA in 1976: Evergreen International Airlines, McCulloch International Airlines, Overseas National Airways, Saturn Airways, Trans International Airlines and World Airways. (See NACA Annual Report 1976)

(7) Members of IACA include: Air Spain, Aviogenex, A/S Conair, Euralair, Inex Adria Airways, Maersk, Overseas National Airways (also NACA member), Pomair, SATA, Saturn Airways (also NACA member), Spantax, Sterling Airways, TAE, Transavia Holland, Trans International Airlines (also NACA member), Wardair Canada, World Airways (also NACA member). At IACA's June 1973 Annual General Meeting, it was announced that the Association would amend its statutes so as to permit scheduled air carriers engaged in charter activities, or their affiliates, to become IACA members. See ICAO Bull., May 1974, at 29.

(8) Members of ACCA include: Aéromaritime (affiliated with UTA), Air Charter International (affiliated with Air France), Aviaco (affiliated with Iberia), Balair (affiliated with Swissair), BEA Airtours (affiliated with British Airways), Condor (affiliated with Lufthansa), Kar-Air (affiliated with Finnair), Martinair (affiliated with KLM), Scanair (affiliated with SAS) and Sobelair (affiliated with Sabena).

(9) Source: The State of the Air Transport Industry, op.cit., at 24.

(10) On the old IATA see: 2 IATA Bull., Dec. 1945; Hildred, International Air Transport Association, 1 Air Affairs 277 at 278-279 (1946-1947); IATA: The First Three Decades. A Record of Thirty Years of International Cooperation by the Airlines of the World in the Interest of the Public, 9 IATA Bull., 11 (July 1949); Chuang, The International Air Transport Association. A Case Study of a Quasi-Governmental Organization, A.W. Sijthoff, Leiden at 20-21 (1972).

(11) Pillai is the author of The Air Net, The case against the world aviation cartel, Grossman Publishers, New York, 1969. The Airline Passengers' Association (APA), a Dallas (Texas) based organization is more a commercial enterprise than a consumers' association. Two Governmental aviation authorities have created special consumer affairs departments. The U.S. Civil Aeronautics Board has created the Office of the Consumer Advocate (OCA) and the British Civil Aviation Authority has created the Airline Users Committee.

(12)Cf. definition of "tariff" in Article 2(1) of the 1967 *International Agreement on the Procedure for the Establishment of Tariffs for Scheduled Air Services*, ICAO Doc. 8681. See also *infra*, Ch.I, para. III.

CHAPTER I: THE REGULATORY FRAMEWORK OF INTERNATIONAL RATEMAKING

The basis of the regulatory framework of postwar international civil aviation was laid by the International Civil Aviation Conference, held at Chicago in 1944.(1) This Conference, a great success in the technical field of civil aviation, left many economic questions of postwar international civil aviation unresolved. Among these questions was the problem of international air fares and rates. The Conference not being able to agree on an international ratemaking system, the airlines themselves took the initiative, created IATA in 1945, and equipped this new Association with a ratemaking machinery, generally known as IATA's Traffic Conference machinery. This IATA ratemaking machinery came to be recognized by the American and British Governments in their Bermuda Agreement of 1946.(2) In this bilateral air transport agreement, the U.S.A. and the U.K. delegated to the IATA ratemaking machinery the task of setting fares and rates for scheduled air services between their respective territories, subject to Government approval. The great majority of bilateral air transport agreements, concluded after the Bermuda Agreement, follow this example and delegate international ratemaking to IATA, again subject to Government approval. In this fashion the system emerged, whereby fares and rates for scheduled international air services are set by IATA, under Government authority - given in the bilateral air transport agreements - and under Government control - retained in those bilaterals. The IATA ratemaking system is a worldwide one, and can as such be regarded as a "multilateral" system. Paradoxically, it derives its authority from a bilateral system, the existing network of bilateral air transport agreements.

The IATA ratemaking system only covers fares and rates for scheduled international air services. With a few exceptions, the present network of bilateral air transport agreements only covers scheduled flights. Non-scheduled international flights are usually performed outside that network, mostly on the basis of unilaterally issued Government permits. As was pointed out in the Introduction, fares and rates for non-scheduled international air services have by and large been determined by the free forces of the marketplace. IATA is not, at least not yet, equipped with a machinery to set fares and rates for international charter air services. In some instances national aviation authorities have determined certain minimum international charter prices, either on a per seat-mile basis, or as a percentage of scheduled IATA fares. There are a few recently concluded bilateral air charter service agreements between various Governments, which do contain ratemaking provisions, but none of these agreements contains a delegation of international charter ratemaking to IATA or any other association of airlines.

During the Chicago Conference and thereafter, several largely unsuccessful attempts were undertaken to produce a multilateral agreement on the international exchange of commercial aviation rights.

These attempts at multilateralism have, in the field of international ratemaking, led to the conclusion of one multilateral agreement, the 1967 International Agreement on the procedure for the establishment of tariffs for scheduled air services.(3) This Agreement is in force between a large number of States, members of the European Civil Aviation Conference (ECAC). It is also open for accession by non-ECAC States which are either members of the UNO or of one of its specialized agencies.(4) The Agreement delegates the determination of tariffs for air transportation between States, parties to the Agreement, to IATA, again subject to Government approval.

A recent step towards multilateralism in the field of international ratemaking was made by the ICAO Assembly during its Twenty-First Session, held at Montreal in September and October, 1974. The Assembly directed the ICAO Council to instruct the Secretariat to "undertake a study of existing bilateral tariff clauses with a view to exploring the feasibility and relative benefits of either an international ICAO standard tariff clause or an international agreement embodying such a clause."(5)

I. The Chicago Conference and the Establishment of IATA

The Chicago Conference, convened by U.S. President Roosevelt, was held from November 1 until December 7, 1944, and was attended by representatives from fifty-four nations. The purpose of the Conference was to design a blueprint for the worldwide regulation of postwar international civil aviation. Whereas the Conference encountered relatively few problems in the technical field of civil aviation, it was largely unsuccessful in its attempts to reach agreement on the economic regulation of postwar international civil aviation. In this field the views of the key nations, represented at Chicago, were too far apart to make an agreement possible.

The main documents produced by the Chicago Conference are the following: the Convention on International Civil Aviation, which among other things, created ICAO; the Interim Agreement on International Civil Aviation, which created PICAO, the provisional ICAO;(6) the International Air Services Transit Agreement; the International Air Transport Agreement; the Draft Technical Annexes to the Convention, and a Standard Form of Agreement for Provisional Air Routes.(7)

In the economic field the main purpose of the Chicago Conference was to reach a multilateral agreement on the exchange of commercial rights for international civil aviation. This purpose was only partially realized. The Chicago Convention, the Transit Agreement and the Transport Agreement do indeed contain provisions of an economic nature, but at the same time they leave many other important economic questions unsettled. None of the three agreements, for instance, contains any provision in the ratemaking field.

Most of the economic discussions at Chicago focussed on the concept of "freedom of the air" in its commercial sense. The words "in its commercial sense" should be stressed as there was no doubt at Chicago that in the political, in the public international law field, the air would not be free. In Article 1 of the Chicago Convention the following principle of customary international law was laid down:

> "The contracting States recognize that every State has complete and exclusive sovereignty over the airspace above its territory."

Article 2 of the Convention then continues to define "territory" as including the territorial waters of each State. The Convention, however, says nothing about sovereignty over the airspace above the high seas. The high seas themselves being "free", it should also be concluded that the airspace above those high seas is "free". This last principle was later incorporated in another Convention, the 1958 Convention on the High Seas.(8)

The sovereignty principle of Article 1 of the Chicago Convention had already been enunciated in the three pre-war Conventions on air navigation, the Paris, Madrid and Havana Conventions.(9)

The economic consequence of the sovereignty principle is that every State can close its airspace to commerce with other nations, if it so wishes. As stated above, the Chicago Conference now tried, within the framework of the sovereignty principle, to reach a multilateral understanding between States on the exchange of commercial aviation rights, on a certain commercial "freedom of the air".

The concept of commercial "freedom of the air" is usually divided into five separate "freedoms", the so-called "Five Freedoms of the Air".(10) For the aircraft of State A, these freedoms are:

- Freedom 1. The privilege of flying over the territory of State B without landing.
- Freedom 2. The privilege of landing in State B for technical reasons only, i.e. for such purposes as refuelling but not to pick up or set down any passengers, cargo or mail.
- Freedom 3. The privilege to set down in State B traffic (i.e. passengers, cargo or mail) picked up in State A.
- Freedom 4. The privilege of picking up in State B traffic destined for State A. This is closely linked with the third freedom.
- Freedom 5. The privilege of picking up or setting down in State B traffic which is destined for or has come from State C.

The first and second freedoms are usually known as the "technical rights", whereas the third, fourth and fifth freedoms are usually known as the "traffic rights". Although the first twc freedoms are perhaps not really commercial rights, they very often form an important prerequisite for the existence of the other, the purely commercial rights. Perhaps it should be noted that, in view of the sovereignty principle of Article 1 of the Chicago Convention, it would be linguistically better to speak of "privileges" than of "rights".

Sometimes not five, but six "Freedoms of the Air" are distinguished. The term "sixth freedom traffic" then applies to that type of fifth freedom traffic which passes from one foreign country to another via the country of nationality of the aircraft. Sixth freedom traffic can also be regarded as a combination of third and fourth freedoms traffic.(11)

Very different views were expressed at Chicago as to how commercial rights for postwar international civil aviation should be exchanged.(12) The position of the U.S.A. was that air routes should be agreed on bilaterally between States, but that, in addition, there should be as little international economic regulation as possible. Instead of regulation, the U.S.A. wanted a system of free competition. The U.K. on the other hand, was opposed to free competition, and advocated the concept of "order in the air". It wanted to exchange the first four freedoms of the air on a multilateral basis, but at the same time wanted the exercise of the traffic rights, embodied in these freedoms, to be strictly controlled by an international organization, an International Air Authority. This International Air Authority should be empowered to determine air routes, capacity, frequency and tariffs. In its principles, the Canadian position at Chicago was almost identical to the British. Canada's concrete proposals, however, were much more precise than the British. Australia and New Zealand came to Chicago with the radical idea of creating one internationally owned airline company for the exploitation of the world's trunk air routes. The British proposal for "order in the air" was supported by most European States, except the Netherlands and Sweden, which supported the American "free competition" proposal. This proposal was also supported by most Latin American States. Australia's and New Zealand's joint proposal found very little support at Chicago.

The British and American proposals reflected very well the economic situation of the airline industry in the U.K. and in the U.S.A. at the end of the war. The British airline industry, like that of most other European countries had been almost completely destroyed during the war, whereas the American airline industry could at the end of the war dispose of large numbers of readily available aircraft, in particular military transport planes, which could easily be converted into civil aircraft. A system of free competition would definitely favour the U.S. airlines, and it was exactly this competition which the British feared. They intended to protect their own, weakened airline industry through an international regulatory machinery which would give each country a "fair share" of the international air traffic. The British and American positions at Chicago were exactly the reverse of what they had been before the war. Then Britain was the champion of the free competition concept, whereas, at that time, the U.S.A. took a rather protectionist attitude.

Thus, as far as international ratemaking is concerned, the British favoured the system of international air fares and rates being determined on an intergovernmental basis through the International Air Authority. The U.S.A. while opposed to ratemaking by an International Air Authority, was not against a system, whereby the airlines themselves through an "operators' conference" would achieve uniform minimum fares and rates. The system which the U.S.A. had in mind followed the example of the already existing Shipping Conferences, groups of liners operating on routes with basic agreements to charge uniform rates.(13) The ratemaking system that Canada proposed at Chicago contained elements of both the American and British proposals. The airlines themselves would initially determine their tariffs. They would have to file these tariffs with their so-called Regional Councils, subdivisions of the International Air Authority. Any Government would have the right to file objections against such filed tariffs. The Regional Council in question would then hold hearings and would have the right to modify the tariff complained of. The standard to be followed by the Regional Council would be that a rate should be set so that the lowest-cost operator would cover the full cost and obtain a reasonable profit. Decisions by the Regional Council could be appealed to the International Air Authority.(14)

Whereas the differences of opinion between the above-mentioned nations concerning international ratemaking could perhaps have been bridged at Chicago, if international ratemaking were an isolated problem, this was not possible, since it was interconnected with other economic issues, such as frequencies, capacity and fifth freedom traffic. During the Conference, the Canadian delegation went a long way in trying to reconcile the contrasting economic views of the U.S.A. and the U.K., but it was finally the problem of fifth freedom traffic - whether this traffic should be included in a multilateral agreement and how to determine fifth freedom capacity - that caused the breakdown. On December 4, 1944, the Chicago Conference decided to refer all unsettled economic problems, including those of capacity, fifth freedom traffic and ratemaking, to PICAO for further study.(15)

As shall be seen later, PICAO, and also the later ICAO were unable to solve these problems. Consequently States turned away from the idea of exchanging commercial rights for international civil aviation on a multilateral basis, and started to exchange those commercial rights on a bilateral basis.

The most important principles adopted by the Chicago Conference in the economic field of international civil aviation are the following. First of all Article 1 of the Chicago Convention: although the sovereignty principle laid down in this Article is in essence not an economic principle, but rather a political, public international law principle, it has an important economic consequence, namely, that every State has the right ot close its airspace to commerce with other nations, if it so wishes. Therefore, in order to make international civil aviation possible, multilateral or bilateral agreements between States, exchanging commercial aviation rights, are necessary.

Article 5 of the Chicago Convention makes an exception to the sovereignty principle of Article 1 and exchanges on a multilateral basis commercial rights for aircraft engaged in non-scheduled international air services. It grants these commercial rights, however, under numerous restrictions. The Article reads:

> "Each contracting State agrees that all aircraft of the other contracting States, being aircraft not engaged in scheduled international air services shall have the right, subject to the observance of the terms of this Convention, to make flights into or in transit non-stop across its territory and to make stops for non-traffic purposes without the necessity of obtaining prior permission, and subject to the right of the State flown over to require landing. Each contracting State nevertheless reserves the right, for reasons of safety of flight, to require aircraft desiring to proceed over regions which are inaccessible or without adequate air navigation facilities to follow prescribed routes, or to obtain special permission for such flights.
> Such aircraft, if engaged in the carriage of passengers, cargo or mail for remuneration or hire on other than scheduled international air services, shall also, ..., have the privilege of taking on or discharging passengers, cargo or mail, subject to the right of any State where such embarkation or discharge takes place to impose such regulations, conditions or limitations as it may consider desirable."

The first paragraph of Article 5 thus exchanges on a multilateral basis the first and second freedoms of the air, the "technical rights", for non-scheduled international air services under certain restrictions of minor importance. The second paragraph of Article 5 then continues to exchange the third, fourth and fifth freedoms, the "traffic rights", for non-scheduled international air services, but this time under the important restrictions enumerated at the end of the paragraph. Most States have interpreted these restrictions so widely that they require prior permission for the performance of virtually all international charter flights. For this reason, the second paragraph of Article 5 has almost become inoperative, notwithstanding the fact that the ICAO Council, in 1952, warned States not to interpret the restrictions in question

> "in such a way as to render the operation of this important form of air transport /i.e. non-scheduled air transport/ impossible or non-effective".(16)

In practice it can be said that the effect of Article 5 is limited to a multilateral exchange of the first two freedoms of the air for non-scheduled international air services.

Article 6 of the Chicago Convention expressly denies any multilateral grant of commercial rights for scheduled international air services. The Article reads:

> "No scheduled international air service may be operated over or into the territory of a contracting State, except with the special permission or other authorization of that State, and in accordance with the terms of such permission or authorization."

Other important provisions of an economic nature can be found in the Transit and Transport Agreements, also enunciated by the Chicago Conference. The Transit Agreement contains a multilateral exchange of the first two freedoms of the air for scheduled international air services. It has, like the Chicago Convention itself, been widely ratified. For the many countries which are parties to both the Chicago Convention and the Transit Agreement, Article 5 of the Convention and Article 1, Section 1 of the Agreement together form a multilateral exchange of the first two freedoms of the air for all international air services, scheduled and non-scheduled.

The Transport Agreement, also called the "Five Freedoms Agreement", exchanges on a multilateral basis all the five freedoms of the air. It is a reflection of the free competition concept of the U.S.A. Due to lack of ratification the Agreement has virtually become a dead letter.(17) The U.S.A. itself signed and accepted the Agreement, but decided to withdraw from it, as soon as it became clear that it would not receive general acceptance. The withdrawal of the U.S.A. became effective on July 25, 1947.(18)

Altogether the economic results of the Chicago Conference can be taken as a large-scale multilateral exchange of the first two freedoms of the air, the "technical rights", without a further exchange of the other three freedoms, the "traffic rights". The Chicago Conference did not adopt any provisions in the international ratemaking field.

It did, however, reach agreement on a "Form of Standard Agreement for Provisional Air Routes".(19) This Standard Form was meant as a model for bilateral agreements to be concluded between States. It was not meant to be binding on ICAO contracting States. The Form of Standard Agreement itself does not determine routes and does not indicate which commercial rights are exchanged. These important items were to be included in annexes to the agreements. The Form of Standard Agreement contains no provisions in the ratemaking field. Immediately after the Chicago Conference, the U.S.A. concluded a rather large number of these so-called Standard "Chicago" Agreements.(20) Most of them were soon to be replaced by Bermuda-type bilateral air transport agreements. The latter, and especially the ratemaking provisions contained therein, will be discussed in the following paragraph.

On December 6, 1944, almost at the end of the Chicago Conference, thirty-four airline representatives who had attended the Conference as members of, or as advisers to their national delegations, held a separate meeting in view of the failure of the Conference to reach agreement on important economic issues. At this meeting, it was decided to set up IATA and to equip it with a ratemaking machinery which would take, more or less, the form of the "operators conference" as indicated by the U.S.A. A committee under the Chairmanship of John Cobb Cooper, Vice-President of Pan American World Airways, was then appointed to draft Articles of Association for the new IATA. Within a week the committee was able to send out draft Articles and to call the airlines into conference to consider them. This Conference, the International Air Transport Operators Conference, was held at Havana (Cuba), April 16-19, 1945, and was attended by airline representatives from thirty-one nations. At the end of the Conference IATA's Articles of Association were enacted. Article VIII(5) of the Articles of Association provided for the possibility of creating an IATA ratemaking machinery. The first Annual General Meeting of IATA was held at Montreal, from October 16-18, 1945. The Meeting confirmed Sir William P. Hildred as Director General of IATA.[21] By unanimous vote of all the members present, the Meeting adopted the Provisions for the Regulation and Conduct of the IATA Traffic Conferences. These provisions created IATA's ratemaking machinery, usually called IATA's Traffic Conference machinery. This machinery will be discussed in more detail in Chapter III. On December 18, 1945, Royal Assent was given to a special Act of the Canadian Parliament incorporating IATA in Canada.[22]

II. The Bermuda and Subsequent Bilateral Air Transport Agreements

To summarize, the situation at the end of 1945 was as follows. The Chicago Conference had failed to reach agreement on a multilateral exchange of third, fourth and fifth freedom traffic rights and the related problems of capacity, frequency of flights and ratemaking. In the meantime, the scheduled international air carriers had on their own initiative, through their new trade association, IATA, devised a system, the Traffic Conference machinery, to set fares and rates for scheduled international air transport.

Since the multilateral way of exchanging commercial aviation rights was not working, States turned away from multilateralism and started to exchange commercial aviation rights on a bilateral basis. As mentioned above, shortly after the Chicago Conference a number of Standard "Chicago" Bilateral Agreements was concluded. It was, however, not the Standard "Chicago" Agreement that became the model for the network of bilateral air transport agreements which would eventually cover the world, but rather the Bermuda Agreement, the bilateral air transport agreement between the U.S.A. and the U.K. of February 1946.[23]

Already before the Second World War commercial aviation rights had frequently been exchanged in bilateral agreements. Some of these agreements were concluded between Governments, others between airlines and the Governments of the countries to which these airlines wished to fly. Some of the agreements included tariff provisions. However, pre-war international air routes were not always operated pursuant to bilateral agreements: many international air routes were in fact operated on an informal basis.[24]

Both for the U.S.A. and for the U.K. the Bermuda Agreement constituted a mutually acceptable compromise between the economic views which the two countries held at the time of the Chicago Conference. For the British the compromise represented a retreat from their previous demand for predetermination of capacity and frequencies of flights. For the Americans the compromise amounted to a departure from their previous objection against Government control of international ratemaking. The reason why, at the time of the Bermuda Conference, the attention of the two Governments was focussed on international tariff control, probably lies in the fact that in the fall of 1945 Pan American announced that it would reduce its North Atlantic air fares substantially. This proposed fare-cut met with fierce resistance from the British and the French. For them international tariff control now became a vital point. The British and French insistence on such control also forced the American Government to pay attention to the subject. The outcome was that, at Bermuda, the U.S.A. was willing to give in in the ratemaking field, and accept a form of international tariff control, in return for which Britain was willing to give in in the field of capacity and frequencies, and abandon its insistence on predetermination of capacity and frequencies of flights.(25)

Instead of a priori determination of capacity and frequencies the Bermuda Agreement adopted the system of ex post facto review of capacity and frequencies. Initially the airlines themselves would determine the capacity to be offered and the frequencies of their services, whereby

> "there shall be a fair and equal opportunity for the carriers of the two nations to operate on any route between their respective territories."(26)

With regard to fifth freedom traffic capacity should be related

> "a. to traffic requirements between the country of origin and the countries of destination;
> b. to the requirements of through airline operation; and
> c. to the traffic requirements of the area through which the airline passes after taking account of local and regional services."(27)

Only if one or both Governments were dissatisfied with the capacity offered and the frequencies of the services, could they require intergovernmental consultations on the subject in order to rectify the situation.(28)

The ratemaking provisions of the Bermuda Agreement are contained in Annex II to the Agreement. Paragraph (a) of Annex II establishes the principle that rates and fares for air services between the territories of the respective contracting States shall be subject to Government approval. The paragraph reads:

> "Rates to be charged by the air carriers of either Contracting Party between points in the territory of the U.S. and points in the territory of the U.K. ... shall be subject to the approval of the Contracting Parties within their respective constitutional powers and obligations ..."

Paragraph (b) then continues to delegate the determination of international air fares and rates to the IATA ratemaking machinery. The paragraph reads:

> "The Civil Aeronautics Board of the United States having announced its intention to approve the rate conference machinery of the International Air Transport Association (hereinafter called "IATA"), as submitted, for a period of one year beginning in February, 1946, any rate agreements concluded through this machinery during this period and involving United States air carriers will be subject to approval by the Board."

The text of the paragraph is perhaps not very clear. The idea behind it, however, is definitely a delegation by both the U.S.A. and the U.K. to IATA to set rates and fares for air transportation between the two countries, subject to Government approval. The delegation of ratemaking power by the U.K. can be said to be implicit in this article. The delegation by the U.S.A., on the other hand, is explicit. It had to be explicit, as the approval of the IATA ratemaking machinery by the U.S. Civil Aeronautics Board (CAB) was required in order to relieve IATA's rate-fixing activities from the operation of the U.S. antitrust laws.(29) The U.S. CAB is an independent regulatory agency charged with the economic regulation of civil aviation.(30) Its approval of the IATA ratemaking machinery was obtained on February 19, 1946,(31) only a few days after the close of the Bermuda Conference. This approval was valid for one year. It was renewed in 1947, 1948, 1950, 1951, 1952 and 1954. In 1955 the approval was finally made permanent.(32) It should be noted that the approval by the CAB of the IATA ratemaking machinery is not tantamount to an approval of actual IATA fares and rates. As can be seen at the end of paragraph (b), all IATA agreed rates and fares have to be submitted to the CAB for individual approval.

Paragraph (c) of Annex II reads:

> "Any new rate proposed by the air carrier or air carriers of either Contracting Party shall be filed with the aeronautical authorities of both Contracting Parties at least thirty days before the proposed date of introduction; provided that this period of thirty days may be reduced in particular cases if so agreed by the aeronautical authorities of both Contracting Parties."

The provisions of this paragraph are meant to give the aeronautical authorities in question a reasonable time to review IATA agreed fares and rates, and to give them the opportunity to disapprove such fares and rates, if they wish to do so.

In paragraph (d) of Annex II it was agreed

> "that where
> (1) during the period of the Board's approval of the IATA rate conference machinery, either any specific rate agreement is not approved within a reasonable time by either Contracting Party or a conference of IATA is unable to agree on a rate, or
> (2) at any time no IATA machinery is applicable, or
> (3) either Contracting Party at any time withdraws or fails to renew its approval of that part of the IATA rate conference machinery relevant to this provision,
>
> the procedure described in paragraphs (e), (f) and (g) hereof shall apply."

The provisions contained in the above-mentioned paragraphs (e), (f) and (g) will, together with the related paragraph (j), be discussed below in Chapter IV, paragraph III. A good understanding of these paragraphs presupposes a thorough knowledge of U.S. aviation legislation.

Paragraph (h) finally gives some guidelines for the level at which fares and rates should be set. The paragraph reads:

> "The rates to be agreed in accordance with the above paragraphs shall be fixed at reasonable levels, due regard being paid to all relevant factors, such as cost of operation, reasonable profit and the rates charged by any other air carriers."

This paragraph should be read in conjunction with paragraph (1) of the Final Act of the Bermuda Conference. The first sentence of this paragraph reads:

> "That the two Governments desire to foster and encourage the widest possible distribution of the benefits of air travel for the general good of mankind at the cheapest rates consistent with sound economic principles."

The above guidelines are rather vague. It is, however, clear that they do not permit IATA and its member carriers, or any other air carriers to set fares and rates at the highest level that the traffic will bear. Rates and fares should rather cover the costs of operation, and allow a certain margin for reasonable profits.

The Bermuda Agreement served as an example for the majority of bilateral air transport agreements which were subsequently concluded between the U.S.A., the U.K. and third countries, and also between third countries among themselves. On September 19, 1946, the U.S.A. and the U.K. had issued a joint statement proclaiming the Bermuda Agreement as the standard pattern for all bilateral air transport agreements concluded or to be concluded by the two countries.(33)

As far as international ratemaking is concerned, most presently existing bilateral air transport agreements explicitly delegate the determination of fares and rates for scheduled international air services covered by those agreements, to IATA, but virtually always under the reservation that such rates and fares shall be subject to Government approval. Very seldom, however, do these agreements make the use of the IATA ratemaking machinery mandatory. Practically all bilateral agreements which explicitly delegate ratemaking to the IATA Traffic Conference machinery state that rates and fares shall be determined by the airlines designated under the agreements in question, and that "where possible" the IATA machinery shall be used for that purpose.

A rather small number of bilateral air transport agreements implicitly delegates international ratemaking to IATA. These agreements delegate international ratemaking, again mostly "subject to Government approval" and "where possible", to "<u>an</u> association of air carriers" or "<u>an</u> international air transport association."(34)

Besides a certain number of bilateral air transport agreements which do not touch upon ratemaking at all, there are also some bilateral agreements which delegate international ratemaking directly to the airlines which fly the routes covered by the bilateral agreements, without mentioning IATA or any other air carrier association. This is the case with respect to most bilateral air transport agreements concluded by the few countries, whose national air carriers are not members of IATA. Aeroflot, for instance, the national air carrier of the U.S.S.R., is not an IATA member, and consequently the bilateral air transport agreements concluded between the U.S.S.R. and other States do not mention the IATA ratemaking machinery and generally delegate ratemaking directly to the airlines designated under the agreements - for the U.S.S.R. this airline is Aeroflot - subject to Government approval. In this context, it should be noted that where a bilateral agreement does not touch upon ratemaking at all, or where a bilateral agreement delegates ratemaking to the airlines flying the routes covered by the agreement in question, the use of the IATA ratemaking machinery is still possible, provided that the airlines concerned are members of IATA and provided that interested Governments do not oppose such a practice.

Many bilateral air transport agreements also provide that where no IATA machinery is available, where that machinery is unable to agree on rates and fares, where airlines designated under the agreements are unable to agree on rates and fares, or where any agreed rates and fares are disapproved by Governments, the Governments concerned shall start consultations with each other and shall try to agree on rates and fares among themselves. When Governments are also unable to agree on the rates and fares in question, many bilateral agreements then refer the dispute to an arbitrator or arbitrators, either within ICAO or outside thereof, for an advisory opinion or for a decision. Furthermore, many bilateral agreements provide that pending such a dispute the old fares and rates shall remain in force until such time as new ones have been established.

A complicating factor in all this is that, when dealing with delegation of ratemaking to IATA or with ratemaking in general, some bilateral air transport agreements use the terms "rates" and/or "fares", whereas others use the wider, but more vague term "tariffs", sometimes without defining this term.(35)

Thus, by far the most bilateral air transport agreements, in one way or another, delegate international ratemaking to IATA. It is from these agreements that IATA derives its ratemaking authority, which according to the same agreements, it should exercise subject to Government approval. With a few exceptions bilateral air transport agreements only cover scheduled international air services. Commercial rights for non-scheduled international air services are usually not exchanged on a bilateral basis, but are rather obtained on a unilateral basis through a system of unilaterally issued Government permits. These permits can be issued on an *ad hoc* basis, i.e., for each individual charter flight, or they can be issued for a certain series of charter flights, for certain types of charter flights or for certain carriers. Only to a very limited extent are commercial rights for non-scheduled air services exchanged either on a multilateral or on a bilateral basis. As noted before, non-scheduled international air fares and rates are usually set through the free forces of the marketplace, except for a certain amount of unilateral Government intervention. As yet IATA does not dispose of a rate-fixing machinery for international charter air services, and as yet none of the trade associations of international charter airlines is involved in charter rate-fixing.

In addition to the above-discussed provisions of Article 5 of the Chicago Convention, there are two regional multilateral agreements which exchange commercial rights for non-scheduled air services: the *Multilateral Agreement on Commercial Rights of Non-Scheduled Air Services in Europe*, usually called the 1956 Paris Agreement, and the *1971 Multilateral Agreement on Commercial Rights of Non-Scheduled Air Services Among the Association of South East Asian Nations*.(36) The importance of these two agreements is limited. The 1956 Paris Agreement was reached within the framework of ECAC and geographically its scope is restricted to Europe. The 1971 Agreement was reached within the framework of the Association of South East Asian Nations and its geographical scope is limited to South East Asia. Furthermore, both agreements only exchange commercial rights for certain types of non-scheduled flights, thereby leaving aside other, perhaps more important types of charter flights.(37) Neither of the two agreements contains any ratemaking provisions.(38)

In recent years, and in view of the growing importance of charter flights, a number of bilateral non-scheduled air service agreements and memoranda of understanding on the operation of charter air services has been concluded between the U.S.A. and several other countries.(39) Recent U.S. policy to conclude such bilateral agreements covering non-scheduled international air services is in conformity with the 1970 U.S. *Statement on International Air Transportation Policy*, approved by President Nixon on June 22, 1970.(40) The relevant part of the Statement reads:

> "..... intergovernmental agreements covering the operation of charter services should be vigorously sought, distinct, however, from agreements covering

scheduled services. In general, there should be no trade-off as between scheduled service rights and charter service rights. In negotiating charter agreements, the continuation of and the nature of the charter rights of foreign carriers will be at issue."(41)

A draft U.S. standard bilateral agreement for charter air services was developed by the CAB, the State Department and the Department of Transportation.(42) By and large this draft was followed in concluding the three non-scheduled air service agreements which were signed by the U.S.A. so far: the Non-Scheduled Air Service Agreements between the Government of the U.S.A. and the Government of the Socialist Federal Republic of Yugoslavia,(43) the Government of Canada(44) and the Government of the Hashemite Kingdom of Jordan.(45) They are of an indefinite duration.

Memoranda of understanding on the operation of charter air services have been concluded between the U.S.A. and the following countries: Austria,(46) Belgium,(47) France,(48) Germany,(49) Ireland,(50) the Netherlands,(51) Switzerland,(52) and the U.K.(53) Some of the Memoranda only cover the so-called Advance Booking or Travel Group Charters (ABCs and TGCs). Others also cover other types of charters, such as affinity charters and Special Event Charters (SECs).(54)

Most of these Memoranda expired either on March 31, or on December 31, 1976. They were not expected to be extended into the year 1977 with the exception of the Memorandum with the U.K., which was extended until March 31, 1978.

Four of the eight Memoranda of understanding contain provisions in the ratemaking field. The Memoranda of understanding with France and Germany provide:

"To assure that prices are neither unreasonably high or low taking into account all relevant costs, each Party shall require the filing of tariffs or price schedules (as applicable) and enforce conformity to tariff or price schedules on all flights operated."

The Memoranda of understanding with Ireland(55) and the Netherlands go a little further and stipulate:

"... the regulatory authorities of each Party shall: ... Consult with the appropriate authorities of the other Party about uneconomical, unreasonable or unjustly discriminatory charter rates charged or proposed to be charged for services conducted pursuant to this understanding and, in the event of no resolution by consultation, may take appropriate action to prevent the inauguration or continuation of uneconomical, unreasonable, or unjustly discriminatory rates."

The three full-scale bilateral non-scheduled air service agreements also contain ratemaking provisions. Article XI of the Agreement with Yugoslavia provides:

"(A) The rates charged by each carrier shall be reasonable, considering all the relevant factors bearing upon the economic characteristics of prescribed non-scheduled air services. Such rates shall be subject to the approval of the aeronautical authorities of the Contracting Parties, who shall act in accordance with their obligations under this Agreement, within the limits of their legal competence.

(B) Any rate proposed to be charged by a carrier of

either Contracting Party for carriage to or from the territory of the other Contracting Party shall, if so required, be filed by such carrier with the aeronautical authorities of the other Contracting Party at least thirty (30) days before the proposed date of introduction unless the Contracting Party with whom the filing is to be made permits filing on shorter notice. The aeronautical authorities of each Contracting Party shall use their best efforts to insure that the rates charged and collected conform to the rates filed with either Contracting Party, and that no carrier rebates any portion of such rates by any means, directly or indirectly, including the payment of excessive sales commissions to agents.

(C) If one Party, upon review of the rates charged or practices followed by a carrier of the other Party, finds these rates or practices are or will be uneconomical, unjust, unreasonable, or unjustly discriminatory, or unduly preferential or unduly prejudicial, it may so notify the other Party and thereafter the Parties shall endeavour to reach agreement on resolution of the complaint.

(D) In the event that agreement is reached pursuant to paragraph (C), each Party will exercise its best efforts to insure its implementation.

(E) In the event that the complained is not resolved pursuant to paragraphs (C) and (D), each Party may take whatsoever steps it considers necessary to prevent the inauguration or continuation of the objectionable rates or practices, provided, however, that the Party taking such action shall not require the rate to be charged by the carrier of the other Party to be higher than the rate charged by its own carriers for comparable service."

Article XI of the Agreement with Canada prescribes:

"1. The rates to be charged by the carriers of either Contracting Party for carriage to or from the territory of the other Contracting Party shall be reasonable, considering all relevant factors bearing upon the economic characteristics of prescribed non-scheduled air services.

2. If the aeronautical authorities of one Contracting Party are dissatisfied with a proposed or existing rate of a carrier or carriers of the other Contracting Party, that other Contracting Party shall be so informed and the Contracting Parties shall exercise their best efforts to resolve the matter through prior consultations. Each Contracting Party shall retain the right to apply its laws and regulations with respect to such rates.

3. The aeronautical authorities of each Contracting Party shall exercise their best efforts to insure that the rates charged and collected conform to the rates filed and in effect with each Contracting Party, and that no carrier rebates any portion of such rates by any means, directly or indirectly, including the payment of excessive sales commissions to agents."

Finally, Article XI of the Agreement with Jordan stipulates:

"A. The rates to be charged by the carriers of either Contracting Party for carriage to or from the territory of the other Contracting Party shall be reasonable, considering all relevant factors bearing upon the economic characteristics of prescribed non-scheduled air services provided for in this Agreement.

B. Any rate proposed to be charged by a carrier of one Contracting Party for carriage to or from the territory of the other Contracting Party shall, if so required, be filed by such carrier with the aeronautical authorities of the other Contracting Party at least thirty (30) days before the proposed date of effectiveness, unless the aeronautical authorities of the Contracting Party with whom the filing is to be made allows that filing to be made on shorter notice. Such rate shall not come into force unless approved or permitted by the aeronautical authorities of that Contracting Party.

C. If the aeronautical authorities of one Contracting Party, upon review of the filing referred to in paragraph B above, are dissatisfied with the rate proposed, the other Contracting Party shall be so informed prior to the expiration of the first fifteen (15) days of the thirty (30) days period referred to in paragraph B above, and the Contracting Parties shall endeavour to reach agreement on the appropriate rate.

If the procedure set forth in this paragraph is not utilized, the rate shall be deemed to be approved or permitted by the aeronautical authorities of the Contracting Party receiving the filing and shall be allowed to come into force on the proposed date of the effectiveness.

D. If the aeronautical authorities of one Contracting Party, upon review of an existing rate charged for carriage to or from the territory of that Contracting Party by a carrier or carriers of the other Contracting Party, are dissatisfied with that rate, the other Contracting Party shall be so notified and the Contracting Parties shall endeavour to reach agreement on the appropriate rate.

E. In the event that an agreement is reached pursuant to the provisions of paragraph C or D, each Contracting Party will exercise its best efforts to put such rate into effect.

F. If:

1) under the circumstances set forth in paragraph C, no agreement can be reached prior to the date that such proposed rate would otherwise become effective; or

2) under the circumstances set forth in paragraph D, no agreement can be reached prior to the expiration of sixty (60) days from the date of notification, then the Contracting Party raising the objection may take whatever steps it considers necessary to prevent the inauguration or continuation of the rate with which it is dissatisfied: provided, however, that except with respect to unjustly discriminatory rates, such steps will deal only with traffic enplaned in its own territory.

G. The aeronautical authorities of each Contracting Party shall use their best efforts to insure that the rates charged and collected conform to the rates filed and in effect with each Contracting Party, and that no carrier rebates any portion of such rates by any means, directly or indirectly, including the payment of excessive sales commissions to agents."

The four above-mentioned Memoranda of understanding and the three bilateral agreements thus leave charter ratemaking in the first instance to the carriers concerned. Only in the event of dissatisfaction with the tariffs charged by those carriers, do the Memoranda and the agreements provide for the possibility of Government intervention. No mention is made of the use of any rate-fixing machinery.

Due to the growing importance of international charter air services - they were almost non-existent at the time of the Bermuda Agreement, whereas today they constitute over one fourth of the total international air traffic - bilateral air transport agreements of the future might cover both scheduled and non-scheduled international air services.(56) This opinion is, for instance, defended by Sir Peter Masefield, one of the signatories of the Bermuda Agreement. According to him, the Bermuda Agreements should again be taken as an example for these new bilateral air transport agreements covering both scheduled and non-scheduled international air services.(57)

In the ratemaking field these bilateral air transport agreements could provide that all rates and fares shall be subject to Government approval. They could further provide that rates and fares shall be determined in the first instance by the air carriers concerned, and that, where possible, the ratemaking machinery of an association of international air carriers or associations of international air carriers shall be used for this purpose. This would give the air carriers concerned the opportunity to use the IATA ratemaking machinery for the determination of scheduled international air fares and rates. Furthermore, it would give the international charter airlines the possibility of creating their own ratemaking machinery, and it would also give IATA the possibility of extending its ratemaking machinery to the determination of international charter fares and rates. The desirability of charter ratemaking through an association of international charter airlines or through an extended IATA ratemaking machinery will be discussed in Chapters VI and VIII. The possibility of including the proposed ratemaking provisions in a multilateral agreement will be discussed below in paragraph III of this Chapter.

Alternatively, if bilateral air transport agreements covering both scheduled and non-scheduled international air services prove unfeasible, the future could show a worldwide network of two sorts of bilateral agreements, one for scheduled, the other for non-scheduled international air services, both containing similar tariff provisions.

III. Attempts at Multilateralism

When it became clear that the Chicago Conference would not be able to agree on such important economic matters as the multilateral exchange of third, fourth and fifth freedom traffic rights, and the problems of capacity, frequencies and ratemaking, the Conference decided to refer all these unsettled issues to PICAO for further study.(58)

During the latter part of 1945, and during the first months of 1946, the PICAO Secretariat prepared a Draft Multilateral Agreement on Commercial Rights in International Air Transport. This Draft was submitted to the first PICAO Assembly in the spring of 1946. The Assembly rejected the Draft. Hereafter, a new draft was prepared by the PICAO Secretariat and circulated in March, 1947. The 1947 Draft was accompanied by a dissenting Minority Report. Both the 1947 Draft and the Minority Report were submitted to the first ICAO Assembly in May, 1947. The Assembly decided to refer the matter to a special commission, the Commission on Multilateral Agreement on Commercial Rights in International Civil Air Transport. The Commission met at Geneva in November 1947, but was unable to reach agreement. As at Chicago, one of the biggest stumbling-blocks proved to be whether or not fifth freedom traffic should be included in a multilateral agreement on the exchange of commercial rights for civil aviation.(59)

After 1947, still further attempts were undertaken within ICAO to reach a multilateral agreement on the exchange of commercial rights for international civil aviation, but none of these attempts was successful. In 1953, the Seventh Session of the ICAO Assembly adopted a Resolution stating that

> "There is no present prospect of achieving a universal multilateral agreement." (60)

Attempts at exchanging commercial rights for civil aviation on a multilateral basis, after 1953, resulted in two regional agreements containing such an exchange, but only for non-scheduled international flights: the above-mentioned 1956 Paris Agreement and the 1971 South Asian Agreement.(61)

Of all the above-mentioned PICAO and ICAO proposals, the rejected 1946 PICAO Draft was the only one which contained interesting innovations in the ratemaking field. All the other drafts were based on the existing system of ratemaking for scheduled international air transport: scheduled international fares and rates were, whenever possible, to be agreed upon through the IATA ratemaking machinery, subject to Government approval.(62) None of the drafts touched upon the question of non-scheduled international ratemaking.

In many respects the ratemaking proposals contained in the 1946 PICAO Draft, resembled those put forward by Canada at the Chicago Conference.(63) According to Article 21 of the 1946 Draft,(64) airlines or an airline conference, such as IATA, or a Government or Governments, would initiate rates and fares or changes in rates and fares. In the event of a State objecting to a certain fare or rate, that State would consult with other affected States. If no agreement was possible, any State would have the right to refer the dispute to the International Civil Air Transport Board, an organ which would be created under Article 27 of the Draft.(65) The Board would then decide the dispute and its decision would be binding, subject to the right of each State to appeal the decision to the ICAO Council. In its ratemaking decisions the Board would be guided by the principle laid down in Article 20 of the Draft:

> "Rates shall be deemed to be unreasonable if they are found by the Board to depart unduly from the level indicated by the costs of the most economic comparable operator, plus a profit reasonable in the circumstances."(66)

The only multilateral agreement which was ever reached in the international ratemaking field is the 1967 International Agreement on the procedure for the establishment of tariffs for scheduled air services.(67) The Agreement was reached within the framework of ECAC, but its geographical scope is in principle not limited to Europe. The Agreement is open for signature and ratification on behalf of any ECAC member State.(68) Since its date of entry into force, the Agreement is, furthermore, open for accession by non-ECAC States, which are members of the U.N.O., or one of its specialized agencies.(69) Although the geographical scope of the Agreement is thus not restricted to Europe, non-ECAC States have so far failed to adhere to it.

The Agreement is firmly committed to the existing method of ratemaking for scheduled international air transport through IATA, subject to Government approval. The key provisions of the Agreement are contained in paragraphs (3) and (4) of Article 2:

> "(3) The tariffs referred to in paragraph 2 of this Article(70) shall, if possible, be agreed by the airlines concerned of both Parties, after consultation with the other airlines operating over the whole or part of the route, and such agreement shall, wherever possible, be reached by the use of the procedures of the International Air Transport Association for the working out of tariffs.
> (4) The tariffs so agreed shall be submitted for approval of the aeronautical authorities of both Parties at least ninety days before the proposed date of their introduction. In special cases, this period may be reduced, subject to the agreement of the said authorities."

When a tariff cannot be agreed upon in accordance with Article 3(3) or when a Government disapproves a certain tariff, the aeronautical authorities of the States involved shall try to determine the tariff by mutual agreement.(71) In the event that such mutual agreement cannot be reached, the 1967 Agreement provides for certain methods to resolve the dispute.(72) Pending the dispute the old fares and rates remain in force for at least twelve months after the date on which they would otherwise have expired.(73) In the event of the existence of a bilateral air transport agreement between two States, Parties to the Agreement, the tariff provisions of the Agreement shall replace those of the relevant bilateral agreements.(74)

The importance of the 1967 Agreement does not lie in an innovation of new ratemaking methods for scheduled international air transport - the Agreement is, as noted before, based on the existing ratemaking system - but rather in a multilateral "codification", harmonization and unification of tariff clauses in existing bilateral air transport agreements.

The latest impulse towards multilateralism in the internationa ratemaking field was initiated by the Twenty-First Session of the ICAO Assembly, held at Montreal in September and October, 1974. During the Assembly, a proposal was put forward by Sweden and Switzerland to under take a study of existing tariff clauses in bilateral air transport agreements with a view to explore the feasibility and relative benefits of either an international ICAO standard tariff clause or an international agreement embodying such a clause.(75) The joint Swedish-Swiss proposal made reference to the 1967 ECAC Agreement as a possible example for the future ICAO standard tariff clause or agreement. This reference was deleted in the Resolution which was finally adopted by the Assembly.(76) It reads:

> "The procedure for the establishment of tariffs for scheduled air services.
> WHEREAS tariffs for scheduled air services should be established on the basis of uniform principles and procedures;
> and
> WHEREAS ICAO has not yet developed any standard bilateral tariff clause and existing bilateral tariff clauses vary considerably from each other;

> THE ASSEMBLY:
> DIRECTS the Council to instruct the Secretary General to undertake a study of existing bilateral tariff clauses with a view to exploring the feasibility and relative benefits of either an international ICAO standard tariff clause or an international agreement embodying such a clause."

Although the reference to the 1967 Agreement was thus deleted in the Resolution, it is clear from its text that the study and the possible ICAO standard tariff clause or agreement have the same aim as the ECAC Agreement: to bring uniformity and harmony in existing bilateral tariff clauses. Innovations in the international ratemaking field do not come within the scope of the study, clause or agreement. Upon the recommendation of the Air Transport Committee, the ICAO Council contracted the study out to the Institut de Transport Aérien (ITA) in Paris. The study was completed in May 1975. It concludes ..... that there does not exist

> "enough favourable evidence ..... for a really useful multilateral agreement on tariff clauses to be adopted by a large majority of States."(77)

However,

> "The development of a standard clause is a less ambitious but more realistic objective. An agreement seems possible on a series of points." (78)

On the basis of the ITA study ICAO's Air Transport Committee is presently developing such a standard clause, which will then be submitted to ICAO's forthcoming Assembly Meeting in the fall of 1977. Again, the standard clause should be viewed more as a harmonization of existing bilateral tariff clauses then as an innovation in scheduled international ratemaking procedures. The clause only envisages scheduled international air tariffs.

It is submitted that an ideal regulatory framework of international ratemaking would be based on an ICAO standard tariff clause or agreement covering tariffs not only for scheduled but also for non-scheduled international air services.(79) Between contracting States such a clause or agreement would replace existing tariff clauses in their bilateral air transport agreements. The reason why a standard tariff clause or agreement should not only cover scheduled international air services, but also non-scheduled international air services, is above all that it has become increasingly difficult to make a real and useful distinction between the two kinds of air services.(80) Furthermore, non-scheduled international air services are now only to a very limited extent covered by bilateral agreements. Unimportant as international charter air services may have been at the time of the Chicago Conference and the Bermuda Agreement, they have nowadays become so significant and widespread, that their regulation in general and the regulation of their tariffs in particular, cannot be left to unilateral Government regulation.

It is, therefore, proposed that a future ICAO standard tariff clause or agreement would delegate international ratemaking for both scheduled and non-scheduled air transport to the airlines concerned, under Government approval. As is the case under the regime of most existing bilateral air transport agreements, the airlines themselves would, in the first instance, decide on the level of international rates and fares, whereas Governments would thereafter review that level in accordance with their task to protect both the airlines' and the consumers' interests. The ICAO standard clause or agreement could further provide that, whenever possible and desirable, the airlines will, in establishing fares and rates, make use of the ratemaking machinery or machineries of an existing air carrier association or associations. A provision as outlined above will - as was also pointed out at the end of paragraph II - afford airlines the possibility of a continuing use of the IATA ratemaking machinery. It will afford charter international airlines the possibility to create their own ratemaking machinery, if desirable. Finally, it will enable IATA to extend its ratemaking activities to the determination of international charter tariffs. The advantage of not mentioning IATA specifically as an association of air carriers in the clause or agreement is, that the clause or agreement would then be more acceptable to States, whose national air carriers are not members of IATA. In the event that airlines or an association or associations of air carriers are unable to agree on certain fares and rates, or in the event that such fares and rates are disapproved by a Government or Governments, the ICAO standard tariff clause should provide that Governments must try to determine the rates and fares in question among themselves. As a second best solution, ICAO could adopt two similar standard clauses or agreements, one for scheduled, one for non-scheduled international air services.

In concluding this Chapter, it should perhaps be noted that the above-mentioned ICAO study of existing bilateral tariff clauses is not the only ICAO study in the ratemaking field. Pursuant to Resolution A 18-17, adopted by the Eighteenth Session of the ICAO Assembly in 1971, the ICAO Secretariat started a general fares and rates study(81) which, i.a., resulted in the publication of the already mentioned Survey of International Air Transport Fares and Rates.(82) During the Twenty-First Session of the ICAO Assembly, in 1974, it was decided that in the future this Survey would be issued annually.(83)

While the ICAO Secretariat worked on its first Survey, IATA decided to publish its own rates and fares study: "Agreeing Fares and Rates".(84) Frequent references to both the ICAO and IATA studies will be made in this book.

During the Twenty-First Session of the ICAO Assembly it was also decided that before the next Session of the Assembly in 1977, a small panel of experts would meet to examine the machinery for the establishment of international fares and rates. That panel could then

> "make recommendations to the (ICAO) Council for submission to the Assembly concerning possible improvements of that machinery, taking into account not only the legitimate interests of the international air carriers, but also the legitimate interests of the users of international air transport."(85)

The first meeting of the panel took place from 6 to 17 December, 1976.(86)

Finally, the question of international fares and rates was brought up during a special ICAO Air Transport Conference, held from 13 to 26 April, 1977, concerning present worldwide air transport problems.(87)

The ICAO rates and fares studies and the convening of a panel of experts and of a full-scale Air Transport Conference, are all signs of growing ICAO involvement in the problem of international ratemaking. This ICAO involvement will be further studied in Chapter VIII, paragraph II.

(1) *International Civil Aviation Conference*, Chicago, Nov. 1 - Dec. 7, 1944, ICAO Doc. 2187; *hereinafter* cited as the Chicago Conference.

(2) *Air Services Agreement between the Government of the United States of America and the Government of the United Kingdom of Great Britain and Northern Ireland*, Feb. 11, 1946. Annexes and Final Act of the Civil Aviation Conference, held at Bermuda, Jan.15 - Feb.11, 1946. TIAS 1507.

(3) Agreement of July 10, 1967, ICAO Doc. 8681.

(4) Article 8 of the Agreement, *cit. supra*.

(5) Res. A21-27 ICAO Ass., 21st Sess., Montreal, Sept./Oct. 1974.

(6) PICAO functioned from June 6, 1945, until April 4, 1947.

(7) See *International Civil Aviation Conference*, Chicago, Nov. 1 - Dec. 7, 1944, Final Act and Appendices, ICAO Doc. 2187. As of Sept. 1974, 129 States were parties to the Convention on International Civil Aviation, *hereinafter* the Chicago Convention; 86 States were parties to the International Air Services Transit Agreement, *hereinafter* the Transit Agreement, and 12 States were parties to the International Air Transport Agreement, *hereinafter* the Transport Agreement. For the proceedings of the Chicago Conference, see *Proceedings of the International Civil Aviation Conference*, Chicago, Ill., Nov. 1 - Dec. 7, 1944; Washington 1948, Dept. of State Publ. 2820; 2 Vols., XVI - 774 pp. and XVII - 734 pp.

(8) *Convention on the High Seas*, adopted by the U.N. Conference on the Law of the Sea, April 29, 1958 (U.N. Doc. A/Conf. 13/L53, Article 2(4).

(9) *Convention Relating to the Regulation of Aerial Navigation* (Paris, 1919); *Ibero-American Convention Relating to Aerial Navigation* (Madrid, 1926); *Convention on Commercial Aviation* (Havana, 1928). Many European States were party to the Paris Convention, whereas the U.S.A. and a large number of Latin American States were party to the Havana Convention. The Madrid Convention stayed, due to lack of ratification, virtually a dead letter. See also: Lee, *The International Flying Convention and the Freedom of the Air*, 33 Harvard Law Review 23 (1919); Latchford, *A Comparison of the Chicago Air Convention with the Paris and Havana Conventions*, 12 Dept. of State Bull., 411 (1945); Johnson, *The Paris Convention*, in *Rights in Air Space*, Manchester Univ. Press, Manchester at 33 (1965); *Explorations in Aerospace Law, Selected Essays* by John Cobb Cooper, Ed. by Ivan A. Vlasic, Part III: The Evaluation of the Modern Principle of State Sovereignty in Airspace, McGill Univ. Press, Montreal, at 104 (1968).

(10) The terminology seems to have originated with the Canadian delegation at Chicago.

(11) Source: *British Air Transport in the Seventies*: Report of the Committee of Inquiry into Civil Air Transport (The Edwards Report), Her Majesty's Stationery Office, London, at 284 (1969).

(12) See, i.a.: de la Pradelle, *La Conférence de Chicago, 1 novembre - 7 décembre 1944, Sa place dans l'évolution politique, économique et juridique du monde*, 9 RGA 107 (1946); Warner, *The Chicago Air Conference, Accomplishments and Unfinished Business*, 23 Foreign

Affairs 406 (1945), in French: 9 RGA 168 (1946); Berle, The Freedom of the Air, Dept. of State Publ. 2.348-Conf. Series 70, US Govt. Printing Off., Washington, 1945, in French: 9 RGA 190 (1946); Burden, Opening the Sky. American Proposals at Chicago, Dept. of State Publ. 2.348-Conf. Series 70, US Govt. Printing Off., Washington, 1945, in French: 9 RGA 214 (1946); Verdurand, Transports aériens internationaux. Les conséquences de la Conférence de Chicago, 9 RGA 224 (1946). Cribbett, Some International Aspects of Air Transport, 54 Journal of the Royal Aeronautical Society 669 (1950); Johnson, op.cit., at 58 et seq; O'Connor, Economic Regulation of the World's Airlines. A Political Analysis, Praeger Publishers, New York, at 16 (1971).

(13) See, The Liner Conference System, UNCTAD Report, UN Doc. TD/B/C.4/62/Rev. 1 (1970).

(14) About the Canadian ratemaking proposal at Chicago see, O'Connor, op.cit., at 26-27.

(15) See, Resolution X, Final Act Chicago Conference, ICAO Doc. 2187, at 22.

(16) See, Definition of a Scheduled International Air Service, ICAO Doc. 7278 - C/841, May 10, 1952, at 12.

(17) At present, twelve States, none of them important "air powers", are still parties to the Transport Agreement: Bolivia, Burundi, Costa Rica, El Salvador, Ethiopia, Greece (with reservation), Honduras, Liberia, Kingdom of the Netherlands, Paraguay, Sweden and Turkey (with reservation). For ratifications, see also supra, nt. 7.

(18) See, Dept. of State Press Release, no. 510, July 25, 1946.

(19) See ICAO Doc. 2187, at 19 et seq.

(20) E.g. with Canada, Denmark, Iceland, Ireland, Norway, Portugal, Spain, Sweden and Switzerland. The Agreement with Canada exchanged the first four freedoms of the air, whereas the other Agreements exchanged all five freedoms. See Waldo, Sequels to the Chicago Aviation Conference, 11 Law and Contemporary Problems 609 at 624, nt. 32 (1946).

(21) Sir William P. Hildred was Director General of IATA from 1945 until 1966, when he was succeeded by the present Director General, Mr. Knut Hammarskjöld.

(22) 9 - 10 Geo. VI, Chap. 51 (1945).

(23) TIAS 1507. At the end of June 1976 the U.K. announced its intention to withdraw from the Bermuda Agreement, effective June 1977. See infra Postscriptum.

(24) See Meyer, Freiheit der Luft als Rechtsproblem, Aeroverlag, Zürich at 155, 189 (1944); Cribbett, op.cit., at 671 - 673; Chuang, op.cit., at 19.

(25) Cf. Baker, The Bermuda Plan as the Basis for a Multilateral Agreement, lecture delivered at McGill University, Montreal, April 18, 1947, reprinted in part in Chayes, Ehrlich and Lowenfeld, International Legal Process: Materials for an Introductory Course, Little, Brown & Co., Boston, Vol. I at 498-499 (1968).

(26) Para. 5, Final Act of the Civil Aviation Conference, held at Bermuda, Jan. 15 - Feb. 11, 1946, cit.supra.

(27) Ibidem, para. 6.

(28) See Cribbett, op.cit., at 678-681. Although the Bermuda Agreement served as an example for the majority of all postwar bilateral air transport agreements, some of these agreements later returned to a system of full or partial predetermination of capacity: see, e.g., Handbook on Capacity Clauses in Bilateral Air Transport Agreements, ICAO Circ., 72-AT/9 at 27 (1965). The present dispute between

the U.K. and the U.S.A. over the Bermuda Agreement (see supra nt.23) is almost entirely related to the capacity provisions of the Agreement. The British now advocate an a priori sharing of capacity between U.S. and U.K. airlines on the air routes between the two countries.

(29) See infra, Ch.II, para.II.

(30) See infra, Ch.IV, para.III.

(31) 6 CAB Reports 639 (1946), Agreement no.493.

(32) CAB Orders E-269 (1947); E-706 (1947); E-1227, 9 CAB Reports 222 (1948); E-3888 (1950); E-5709 (1951); E-6390 (1952); E-8023 (1954); E-9305 (1955).

(33) See, Wassenbergh, Postwar International Civil Aviation and The Law of the Air, Nijhoff, The Hague at 18 (1957); O'Connor, op.cit., at 48.

(34) Underlining supplied.

(35) For definitions of "fares", "rates" and "tariffs" see supra Introduction. On the subject of tariff provisions in bilateral air transport agreements see: Handbook on Administrative Clauses in Bilateral Air Transport Agreements, ICAO Circ. 63-AT/6 at 99-109 (1962); Chuang, op.cit., at 35-42; Tariff Clauses in Bilateral Agreements, ICAO Doc. AT-WP/1207, Attachment (1975).

(36) The 1956 Paris Agreement was signed at Paris on April 13, 1956, ICAO Doc. 7695. The 1971 South East Asian Agreement was signed at Manila on March 13, 1971, (Agreement not registered with ICAO).

(37) Article 2 of the Paris Agreement; article 2 of the 1971 Agreement.

(38) For literature on the 1956 Paris Agreement see: Heere, International Bibliography of Air Law 1900-1971, Sijthoff/Oceana, Leiden/Dobbs Ferry, N.Y. at 194 (1972).

(39) The only countries which before that time, around 1950, concluded a number of bilateral air charter service agreements were France and the U.K. The agreements are no longer in force. The agreements in question are those between France and Spain (1948), France and Italy (1949), France and the U.K. (1950), the U.K. and Switzerland (1952), France and Germany (1955). The last agreement covered both scheduled and non-scheduled air services. In addition to these agreements there was, in the early fifties, a similar provisional agreement between the Netherlands and the U.K. See Wassenbergh, op.cit., at 33.

(40) See 63 Dept. of State Bull. 86 (July 20, 1970).

(41) Ibidem, pp.88-89.

(42) See Rein, Current Policy Problems in International Aviation, 64 Dept. of State Bull. 15 at 17 (Jan. 4, 1971); Browne, The International Angle, 77 The Aeronautical Journal 29 at 33 (1973).

(43) Signed at Belgrade, Sept. 27, 1973, TIAS 7819, as amended (TIAS 8305).

(44) Signed at Ottawa, May 8, 1974, TIAS 7824.

(45) Signed at Amman, Sept. 21, 1974, TIAS 7954.

(46) Interim Agreement, signed at Vienna, Nov. 6, 1973, TIAS 7751, as amended (TIAS 8250).

(47) Signed at Brussels, Oct. 17, 1972, TIAS 7479, as amended (TIAS 8265).

(48) Signed at Washington, May 7, 1973, TIAS 7617, as amended (TIAS 7815), (TIAS 8236).

(49) Signed at Bonn, April 13, 1973, TIAS 7605, as amended (TIAS 7804).

(50) Signed at Washington, June 28/29, 1973, TIAS 7662, as amended (TIAS 8306).

(51) Signed at The Hague, July 11, 1973, TIAS 7771.

(52) Signed at Bern, June 12/July 25, 1974, TIAS 7916.

(53) Signed at Washington, April 2, 1973, TIAS 7594, as amended (TIAS

7832, 8047, 8102, AWST, March 21, 1977, pg. 203).

(54) See *infra*, Ch.VI, para.II.

(55) See, *however*, the slightly modified text in TIAS 8306.

(56) It should, however, be noted that such action would be contrary to the American aviation policy as expressed in the 1970 Statement, *cit. supra*.

(57) Masefield, *The Air Charter Challenge*, Flight International 548 at 551 (1973).

(58) PICAO functioned from June 1945 until April 1947, when ICAO took over.

(59) See, *Records of the Commission on Multilateral Agreement on Commercial Rights in International Civil Air Transport*, ICAO Doc. 5230, A2-EC/10 (1948).

(60) See ICAO Ass., 7th Sess., Resolutions and Indexes to Documentation, ICAO Doc. 7417, A7-P/3, Aug. 27, 1953; Res. A7-15, pp. 27-28. Res. adopted unanimously on July 6, 1953: see ICAO Ass., 7th Sess., Minutes of the Plenary Meetings, ICAO Doc. 7409, A7-P/2, Sept. 1, 1953, at 67.

(61) Literature on PICAO/ICAO attempts at multilateralism: Garnault, *La première Assemblée de l'OACI et le Projet d'Accord Multilatéral sur les libertés commerciales de l'air*, 1 RFDA 231 (1946-1947); Baker, *op.cit.*, *a passim*; Cooper, *The Proposal Multilateral Agreement on Commercial Rights in International Civil Air Transport*, 14 JALC 125 (1947); McClurkin, *The Geneva Commission on a Multilateral Air Transport Agreement*, 15 JALC 39 (1948); OACI, *Rapport final de la Commission chargée d'établir un accord multilatéral sur les droits commerciaux dans le transport aérien civil international*, 2 RFDA 74 (1948); Cribbett, *op.cit.*, at 680 et seq.; Keller, *Der Versuch einer Multilateralen Regelung des Internationalen Luftverkehrs und die Schweizerische Luftverkehrspolitik der Nachkriegszeit*, Ravensburg, 1952; Warner, *How Can a Multilateral Agreement in International Air Transport be Attained?*, Studi in Onore di Antonio Ambrosini, Milano at 587-600 (1957); O'Connor, *op.cit.*, at 49 et seq.

(62) See, O'Connor, *op.cit.*, Table 2 at 129.

(63) See *supra* Para I.

(64) PICAO Doc. 1577, AT/116, April 17, 1946, reissued as PICAO Doc. 1632, EC/2.

(65) *Ibidem*.

(66) *Ibidem*, and O'Connor, *op.cit.*, at 51-54.

(67) Signed at Paris, July 10, 1967, ICAO Doc. 8681.

(68) Articles 5 and 6 of the Agreement.

(69) Article 8 of the Agreement; date of entry into force of the Agreement: May 30, 1968.

(70) Article 2(2): "... tariffs ... shall be established at reasonable levels, due regard being paid to all relevant factors, including cost of operation, reasonable profit, and tariffs of other airlines." Article 2(1) defines "tariff" as: "the prices to be paid for the carriage of passengers, baggage and freight and the conditions under which those prices apply, including prices and conditions for agency and other auxiliary services, but excluding remuneration or conditions for the carriage of mail."

(71) Article 2(6) of the Agreement.

(72) *Ibidem*, Article 2(7) and 3.

(73) *Ibidem*, Article 2(8).

(74) *Ibidem*, Article 1(b).

(75) See ICAO Doc. A21 - WP/60, EC/8, July 30, 1974.

(76) Res. A21 - 27.

(77) See ICAO Doc. AT-WP/1207, Attachment, Summary II.
(78) *Ibidem*.
(79) *Cf.* proposed ratemaking provisions in future bilateral air transport agreements covering both scheduled and non-scheduled air services: see *supra*, para. II.
(80) See *infra*, Chapter VI, para. II.
(81) See ICAO Doc. A21 - WP/21, EC/3, May 27, 1974.
(82) ICAO Circ. 123 - AT/33 (1974).
(83) Res. A21 - 26, para. 1(a). See ICAO Circ. 125 - AT/35 (1975).
(84) IATA Publ., 1st ed. Jan. 1973; 2nd ed. June 1974.
(85) Res. A21-26, para. 1(c).
(86) See ICAO Doc. FRP/1 - Report (1976). See also *infra*, Chapter VIII.
(87) Res. A21-25, para. 3(a). See also *infra*, Chapter VIII.

CHAPTER II: CHARACTER OF IATA

As mentioned in the Introduction, of the world's total international air traffic almost seventy-five percent is carried on scheduled flights. Of those scheduled flights almost ninety-five percent is performed by airlines which are members of IATA. For all those flights, IATA sets the fares and rates, or at least attempts to do so. IATA performs its ratemaking activities in accordance with the applicable provisions in bilateral air transport agreements.

These statistics show the enormous importance of IATA as an organization working in the field of ratemaking in international air transport. In this Chapter an attempt will be made to analyze the character of IATA. Such an analysis of the Association's character will provide an answer to the two following questions: Is IATA a private international or a quasi-public international organization? And: Is IATA an international cartel? The answer to these two questions is not merely of theoretical, but also of practical value. The answer to the first question - whether IATA is a private or quasi-public international organization - has an important impact on the manner in which IATA is to perform its functions. Characterizing IATA as a merely private international organization could easily lead to the conclusion that in performing its functions, the Association would only have to pay attention to the interests of its members, the airline industry. On the other hand, characterizing IATA as a quasi-public international organization would necessarily lead to the conclusion that in performing its functions and especially its ratemaking function, the Association would, like an intergovernmental organization, have to take into account the general interest. It would, therefore, not only have to concern itself with the interests of the airline industry, but also with the interests of the travelling public, the interests of the aviation consumer. The answer to the second question - whether IATA is an international cartel - has an important bearing upon the practical problem if, perhaps, all or certain of IATA's activities are illegal under existing antitrust, anticartel laws (both national and international).

Summarizing the results of the following analysis of IATA's character, it can be said that:

(a) IATA is in principle an international trade association, whose members are the world's (scheduled) international airlines, and as such it is a private international organization;

(b) although IATA is in principle a private international organization, the composition of its member airlines shows a 'public' characteristic in that over fifty percent of them are either entirely or more than one half State-owned. As far as the composition of its member airlines is concerned IATA could thus be called quasi-public. This, in its turn, leads to the conclusion that the Association and its publicly-owned member airlines should, in conducting their business not only take into account their own interests, but also to some extent the general interest, including that of the travelling public;

(c) some of IATA's activities, and in particular, its ratemaking activities, can be labelled quasi-public, as they have been delegated to the Association by Governments in their bilateral air transport agreements. In carrying out these activities IATA and its member airlines should aknowledge this quasi-public character and act accordingly, by taking into account both the airlines' and the consumers' interests;
(d) although IATA is perhaps not an outright cartel, it possesses, especially insofar as its price-fixing activities are concerned, enough characteristics of a cartel to warrant a serious study of the legality of its activities under existing antitrust, anticartel laws. Such a study will show that, at least at the present time, IATA's activities are legal from the antitrust, anticartel point of view.

I. IATA a Private or Quasi-Public International Organization?

The starting point in any discussion of IATA's character must be that IATA is a trade association, an international trade association, and that as such it can be characterized as a private international organization. IATA is the trade association of the world's (scheduled) international airlines. It satisfies the definition of a trade association as a

> "non-profit organization whose members are business firms, usually competitors." (1)

IATA is indeed a non-profit organization. Its members are business firms, that is, airlines, which under certain restrictions, which will later be discussed, compete with each other.

Generally speaking two types of trade associations can be distinguished. The first type, the more common one, is the trade association that confines its activities to representing, before Governmental authorities or otherwise, the views of its members on matters of common interest, and to fostering technical and other cooperation between them. Most of these activities are effected through exchange of information between the trade association members.

The second type of trade association, the less common one, is the association that, besides carrying out the above-mentioned activities, exercises some measure of control over its members. In order to exercise such control frequent use is made of voluntary agreements between association members for controlling, for instance, prices, output and channels of distribution. Such agreements clearly influence the market situation of the particular branch of trade in which the association in question is active. Inasmuch as these agreements restrain free trade, their legality must be tested under antitrust, anticartel laws.(2)

Most trade associations are national associations: their members have the same nationality and their activities do not go beyond national boundaries. Some trade associations are international associations with members of different nationalities and activities which are international in scope.

IATA is a trade association of the second type. It does exercise a certain degree of control over its members, especially in the price-fixing field. Through a system of voluntary agreements between its member airlines, the so-called Traffic Conference Resolutions, IATA, among other things, sets uniform prices, fares and rates, to be applied by all its members for scheduled international air transport. Through these price-fixing activities and also through a number of other activities IATA definitely limits competition between its member airlines. Therefore, the question will have to be studied whether IATA's activities are legal under existing antitrust, anticartel laws.[3]

In this context, it should, however, immediately be remarked that IATA is definitely a free, open trade association. Unlike a number of trade associations of the second type which through a restrictive membership policy, a policy of boycott, try to limit entry into the market - so-called closed trade associations - IATA has always had a very liberal membership policy. Virtually all scheduled international airlines, as long as they satisfy the few IATA membership requirements, are welcome to join the Association.[4] IATA's membership policy does not, therefore, raise any antitrust, anticartel questions.

IATA's member airlines have many different nationalities and the Association's activities cover a thoroughly international field, the field of international civil aviation. Thus, IATA is clearly an international trade association.

Like all trade associations IATA is a private organization. Its members are business firms, airlines. As an international trade association, it is a private international organization. The possibility of international incorporation of private (international) organizations not, or not yet existing, IATA is like other private international organizations incorporated in one particular country. For IATA this country is Canada, the country where it has its (Montreal) head office. The incorporation of IATA was effected by a Special Act of the Canadian Parliament in 1945.[5] Under Canadian law, IATA is thus a corporate body and falls under the legal regime of the Canada Corporations Act.[6] IATA's Act of Incorporation was amended by the Canadian Parliament during the year 1974.[7] This amendment will be dealt with below when discussing IATA's membership provisions.[8]

A rather objectionable characteristic that IATA has in common with many other trade associations and that merits special attention, is the secrecy surrounding its activities and proceedings. IATA's policy of secrecy has come under heavy attack from consumer protection advocates.[9] For the consumer it is important to know, how IATA functions and what it does, so that he can decide whether the Association is working to his benefit or to his detriment.

Most of IATA's activities are carried out behind closed doors,[10] and so far it has always been extremely cautious and superficial in giving information to the general public about what goes on in the Association. For instance, an essential document such as the IATA Manual of Traffic Conference Resolutions, a publication containing all IATA Traffic Conference Resolutions - the voluntary agreements between the IATA member airlines - has only been for sale to the general public since 1968. A subscription to the Manual costs U.S. dollars 500 per year. Furthermore, IATA Traffic Conference Resolution 035 (Unethical Disclosure of Information) prohibits IATA members from disclosing to the outside world knowledge or information obtained as a result of their membership in the Traffic Conferences. An exception is made for information that a member airline has to give to its Government, to courts or to Governmental hearings. Due to all the secrecy surrounding IATA the consumer only has a very vague notion of what IATA is and what it does. This vagueness is still further compounded by the practice of IATA to hide itself behind its member airlines, and the practice of IATA airlines to hide themselves behind the Association. On the one hand IATA overemphasizes the fact that it is nothing more than the airlines which form part of it. On the other, the airlines often explain unpopular IATA rules to the public by saying that they have to adhere to these rules "because IATA forces them to do so". A typical example of this latter practice is the announcement made during flights of IATA airlines that due to "international regulations" the airline "has to" charge the passenger U.S. dollars 2.50 for the use of inflight entertainment equipment (earphones). The "international regulations" are basically nothing more than an IATA Traffic Conference Resolution,(11) a voluntary inter-carrier agreement, providing for such a charge.

Notwithstanding all this, the general public can obtain more detailed information on IATA through the U.S. CAB. Using the above-mentioned exception provided for in Traffic Conference Resolution 035, the CAB, on July 12, 1968, ordered the U.S. air carriers, members of IATA, to submit to it "such documentation and other data as the Board may direct."(12) Subsequently, on July 16, 1968, the Board sent letters to all American carriers setting out which of this documentation and data would be available to the general public and which part thereof would be considered as 'confidential information' not available to the general public.(13) A further move was made by the CAB on August 1, 1972. The Board then sent letters to the U.S. air carriers, members of IATA saying that in the light of, i.a., the Freedom of Information Act(14)

> "the better policy with respect to IATA documentation is not to grant confidential treatment automatically on a blanket basis without particular determinations in particular instances."

Accordingly the Board decided that as of October 1, 1972,

> "all documentation filed with the Board be made publicly available in the absence of compelling reasons to the contrary in particular instances."(15)

As it is now possible for the general public to get detailed information on IATA from the CAB, it would only seem logical that IATA itself should adopt a more open and informative attitude towards the public. A slow development in that direction can indeed be observed in recent years.

In brief, it can be said that IATA is an international trade association, a private international organization, incorporated under the laws of Canada. IATA is furthermore a trade association of the type that exercises a measure of control over its members; in IATA's case particularly in the form of price-fixing agreements between member airlines. IATA is also an open trade association, and has in common with many other trade associations, a policy of secrecy in respect to its activities and procedures.

It would be wrong, however, to categorize IATA as a private international organization without any further qualifications. IATA does have some features of a public international, an intergovernmental organization, and it is, therefore, sometimes called a quasi-public or semi-public or semi-governmental international organization.

From a strictly formal point of view there is a fairly clear-cut distinction between public international and private international organizations. Public international, intergovernmental organizations are created by intergovernmental agreements and their members are States (or State agencies). All other international organizations are usually characterized as private. IATA was neither created by intergovernmental agreement, nor are its members States (or State agencies), and thus, from a formal point of view, it is a private international organization.

From a factual point of view, however, the distinction between private and public international organizations is not so clear. On the one hand, private international organizations sometimes perform functions which would normally be performed by intergovernmental organizations. An organization like the International Committee of the Red Cross (ICRC), for instance, is formally a private organization, but functionally it is almost a public international organization *pur sang*.(16) As shall be seen hereunder, IATA also performs a number of functions of a semi-Governmental nature. On the other hand, public international organizations sometimes perform functions which would normally be performed by private citizens or entities. An example of this is the European Coal and Steel Community (ECSC). The ECSC is formally a public international organization, but is functions are essentially of a "private" nature.(17)

The issue is further complicated by the fact that in some public international organizations one sees, besides member States, private entities participating in the work of the organization at the same level as States or State agencies. This is, for instance, the case with the International Telecommunications Satellite Organization (INTELSAT).(18) In some private international organizations, on the other hand, one encounters members which, although independent legal entities, are wholly or partially owned by States: public corporations and State-owned private companies. Sometimes the members can even be regarded as executive branches of their respective Governments. Besides IATA itself, a good example of this last category is the International Union of Railways, of which almost all the members are State-owned railway companies, many of them having the status of executive Government branches.(19)

Private international organizations which because of the functions that they perform or because of the composition of their membership show characteristics of a public international organization are often called quasi - or semi-Governmental.(20)

From the factual, as opposed to the formal point of view there are two reasons for characterizing IATA as a quasi-public international organization. The first reason lies in the composition of the IATA member airlines and thus relates to the Association as such. The second lies in the character of a number of functions performed by IATA and, therefore, relates to part of the Association's activities.

(a) Ownership of the IATA airlines.

The composition of the IATA member airlines shows a public characteristic in that more than one half of them are either entirely or more than fifty percent State-owned. As can be seen from Appendix A, 88 of IATA's 112 member airlines are active members, and 24 are associate members.

Of IATA's active members,(21) the core of the Association, 39 are entirely State-owned, 24 are fifty or more percent State-owned,(22) four are less than fifty percent State-owned, and 21 are entirely privately-owned. Airlines which are more than fifty percent State-owned can, for practical reasons, be called State-controlled. When acting in IATA they can be regarded as acting in accordance with the will of their Governments, as acting under State supervision and control.

The legal structure of IATA's entirely and for the most part State-owned airlines takes many forms. Most of them are either public corporations, e.g. British Airways, or private companies in which more than fifty percent of the stock is owned by the State, e.g. KLM-Royal Dutch Airlines. Some of those private companies have share capital which is traded on the stock exchange, e.g. again KLM. Others have share capital which is not traded on the stock exchange, and which is often kept by one principal shareholder. This is, for instance, the case, when a big airline holds a minority interest in a smaller airline. The most extreme example is Ariana Afghan Airlines: fifty-one percent of the stock is owned by the State, Afghanistan, whereas the other forty-nine percent of the stock is owned by Pan American World Airways. Some entirely State-owned IATA airlines are neither public corporations nor private companies. The three East European IATA member airlines - CSA of Czechoslovakia, LOT of Poland and JAL of Yugoslavia - can be regarded as subdivisions of their respective Ministries of Transport. Some other airlines, like Air India and South African Airways, also come very close to being part of a branch of the Government. Three IATA airlines are internationally owned: Air Afrique, East African Airways and Scandinavian Airlines System (SAS). East African Airways is entirely State-owned,(23) Air Afrique is sixty percent State-owned,(24) SAS is exactly fifty percent State-owned and is as such a unicum in IATA.(25) Finally, one entirely State-owned IATA member is formally a subsidiary of a public corporation. This airline is Air Canada: it is a subsidiary of the Crown Corporation, Canadian National Railways (CNR).(26)

All the above-mentioned airlines have in common the fact that they are effectively State-owned and State-controlled. In addition to this group of airlines, there are several IATA airlines which are on the one hand entirely privately-owned, but which are, on the other hand, so strictly controlled by their respective Governments that they too can be regarded as acting in accordance with the will of their Governments when acting in IATA. This is especially true for the U.S. IATA member airlines. They are 12 in number, they are all entirely privately-owned and they are all strictly controlled by an independent Government agency, the CAB.(27) It should be noted, however, that the control that a Government can exercise over its entirely or more than fifty percent State-owned airline is different in character from the control that the CAB exercises over its privately-owned American IATA airlines. The first kind of control can be exercised at any time: before, during or after a State-owned airline's actions in IATA. Here the Government is the sole or principal owner of the airline and can as such exercise a decisive control over that airline's management. Whereas the first kind of control can thus be preventive in character, the latter is only repressive. Once the CAB had given U.S. airlines permission to participate in IATA's activities,(28) the only way it could in the future exercise control over their activities in IATA was after their actions in IATA. Here the first initiative rests with the private management of the airlines in question.

The reason why Governments tend to exercise a certain measure of control over international air transport in general and over an Association like IATA in particular will be discussed below in Chapter IV. One of these reasons, however, should be mentioned here, and that is the public utility character of international air transport, calling for a high degree of Government control in order to strike a just balance between airline and consumer interests. Governments can acknowledge the public utility character of international air transport either through a strict external control over privately-owned airlines, as done by the CAB, or through ownership of, and thus internal control over their national airlines.

The fact that the majority of the IATA member airlines falls in the category of entirely or more than fifty percent State-owned airlines means that IATA, as far as the composition of its members is concerned, can be called a quasi-public international organization, or at least a private international organization with very strong public characteristics. Whether more or less independent public corporations or State-owned private companies, or again dependent executive branches of the Government, all these IATA airlines are, or at least can be effectively controlled by their respective Governments. Together with the strict control that some Governments exercise over privately-owned IATA airlines, it can be said that in respect to the great majority of IATA airlines, Government influence on the decision-making process is very big, if not decisive.

What is the influence of all this State-ownership and effective State-control of IATA airlines, plus strict Government control over privately-owned IATA airlines, on the conduct of IATA airlines in the organization and on the conduct of the Association itself? It is submitted that Governments through their external and internal control over IATA airlines and taking into account the public utility character of international air transport should make the IATA airlines' conduct in the Association "quasi-public", "semi-governmental" in the sense that the IATA airlines should not exclusively look at their own financial and other interests in conducting their business, but to a certain extent also at the general interest, including the interest of the aviation consumer. This not only applies to the manner in which IATA airlines conduct their business in the Association, but also to the manner in which the Association itself conducts its business. After all, the Association is nothing more than the conglomerate of its members.

(b) IATA's Quasi-public Functions

IATA's functions can be divided into two groups, its quasi-public functions and its other functions. Those other functions will, as a matter of convenience, be called IATA's trade association functions. It is not always easy to distinguish between IATA's quasi-public and its trade association functions. Generaly speaking, IATA's quasi-public functions are those which have been delegated to the Association in bilateral air transport agreements and in the 1967 International Agreement on the procedure for the establishment of tariffs for scheduled air services.(29) As already pointed out, IATA's most important quasi-public function is wihtout any doubt its ratemaking function. This is, at the same time, the most important function of IATA as a whole. By far the most bilateral air transport agreements, in one way or another, delegate ratemaking in scheduled international air transport to IATA. In addition, the above-mentioned 1967 multilateral agreement does the same. Because of this massive delegation, both bilaterally and multilaterally, of ratemaking power by Governments to IATA, its ratemaking function is definitely quasi-public in character. IATA performs this function, because Governments are unwilling or unable to do so themselves. In accordance, however, with most bilateral air transport agreements, and also with the 1967 multilateral agreement IATA does not perform its ratemaking function independently. IATA agreed rates and fares are in by far the great majority of cases subject to Government approval.

Although international ratemaking is IATA's clearest and most important quasi-public function, it is not the only one. Governments have in some of their bilateral air transport agreements and in the 1967 multilateral agreement delegated more than only international ratemaking to IATA. Some bilateral agreements and also the 1967 agreement delegate to IATA the determination of tariffs for scheduled international air transport. The term tariffs is wider in scope than the term fares and rates: it usually includes, besides the prices to be paid for air transportation, the conditions under which those prices apply, often including prices and conditions for agency and other auxiliary services. Besides delegating international ratemaking to IATA, a small number of bilateral agreements delegates to the Association, again under the condition of Government approval, the determination of agency commissions, currency conversion rates and conditions of carriage. As to the delegation by Governments to IATA of other functions than merely ratemaking, the strange situation occurs that those functions are only partially quasi-public in character. They may be quasi-public according to some bilateral agreements, whereas they fall under IATA's other trade association functions according to other bilateral agreements.(30)

At the end of the preceding sub-paragraph, it was concluded that IATA as a quasi-publicly composed international organization should, in conducting its business, not only take into account its own interests, the interests of its members, the airline industry, but also the general interest. This conclusion applies to all IATA's functions. It applies, however, more strongly to IATA's quasi-public functions than it does to its trade association functions. Whereas it would still be defensible to say that it is only logical that IATA, in performing its trade association functions, would look primarily at its own and its members' interests, this most certainly does not hold true for IATA's quasi-public functions. As IATA's quasi-public functions have been delegated to the Association by Governments, IATA should in performing these functions act in a "Governmental" manner. It should, like Governments, take into account the public utility character of international air transport and accordingly try to strike a just balance between airline and consumer interests. This applies in particular to IATA's clearest, most important quasi-public function, i.e. international ratemaking. Concrete arguments in favour of this last opinion can be found in the bilateral air transport agreements themselves. By far the most bilateral agreements delegating ratemaking to IATA follow literally the Bermuda phraseology that:

> "The rates to be agreed ..... shall be fixed at reasonable levels, due regard being paid to all relevant factors, such as cost of operation, reasonable profit and the rates charged by any other air carriers."

In the same spirit Article 2, paragraph 2 of the 1967 multilateral agreement provides:

> "The tariffs to be charged by the airlines of one Party for the carriage to or from the territory of the other Party shall be established at reasonable levels, due regard being paid to all relevant factors, including cost of operation, reasonable profit, and the tariffs of other airlines."

As noted before, these provisions clearly do not permit IATA and its member airlines to set fares, rates and tariffs at the highest level that the traffic will bear. Rates, fares and tariffs should rather cover the costs of operation, and leave a certain margin for reasonable profits. It is indeed questionable, whether IATA in performing its ratemaking function has adhered to the above principles. This is the reason why it is sometimes defended, especially by aviation consumer advocates, that the present IATA ratemaking system should be replaced by a system of either intergovernmentally agreed scheduled international fares and rates or by a system of scheduled international fares and rates determined on a free enterprise basis, on the basis of demand and supply.

II. IATA an International Cartel?

Under no legal system are trade associations illegal *per se*. When, however, their activities tend in one way or another to restrict trade, to restrict competition, then they may be illegal under antitrust, anticartel laws.(31) With respect to IATA two questions must be answered. The first question is more or less theoretical in nature and reads: can IATA be characterized as an international cartel? The second questions is more practical: are some or all of IATA's activities illegal under existing antitrust, anticartel laws? In the foregoing paragraph it has already been pointed out that especially IATA's rate-making function gives rise to antitrust considerations. Through the system of uniform IATA fares and rates for scheduled international air transport the Association eliminates virtually every form of price competition between its member airlines. As shall be seen hereunder, some of IATA's other functions can also be labelled as competition restricting. It should be remembered, however, that no antitrust allegations can be maintained in respect of IATA's membership policy. IATA is an *open* trade association and has never followed a policy of "boycott". In other words, it has never tried to limit competition by a restrictive membership policy which would make entry into the scheduled airline industry difficult or impossible for newcomers.(32)

A good definition of "cartel" is hard to find. Following is a selection of definitions. The Encyclopaedia Britannica defines "cartel" as

> " an organization of independent firms or individuals for the purpose of exerting some form of restrictive or monopolistic influence on the production or sale of a commodity or group of commodities .... the most common forms of control are created for the regulation of prices or output, or division of marketing areas."

Gazdik, the General Counsel of IATA, adopts the following definition of "international cartel":

> "a combination or association of producers or traders of two or more countries with the purpose of regulating competition by price control, allotment of territory or customers, limitation of output or other measures."(33)

Kronstein developed this definition:

> "The modern cartel ..... may be defined as a co-ordination of the economic behaviour of independent partners, based upon their consent, which results in regulation of one or more markets."(34)

Generally speaking it can be said that cartels are aimed at regulating the economic conditions in one or more markets through a system of limiting or eliminating competition between the participating persons or legal entities. An international cartel, then, is one with participants in two or more countries aimed at the regulation of an international market or markets. Cartels can take very different organizational structures ranging from a mere "gentleman's agreement" via contractual agreements to complete legal entities.(35) If IATA is to be characterized as a cartel, it is one of the last type.

A difference should also be made between private and public cartels, or in other words between privately-created and (inter) Governmentally-created cartels.

Throughout most of its existence IATA has emphatically denied that it would be an international cartel. Only during recent years has the Association begun to admit that it might be a cartel, adding, however, that, if so, its activities are nevertheless legal under existing antitrust laws.(36) The U.S.A. is the only country where IATA is generally considered to be a cartel. Elsewhere in the world, opinions are divided. Literature on the subject is scarce.(37) Occasionally IATA is called a cartel in non-American literature. Rinck, for instance, writes:

> "Die IATA ist ein internationales, von allen Staaten Zugelassenen Kartell .... Die IATA ist wohl das grösste internationale Kartell der ganzen Wirtschaft." (IATA is an international cartel, recognized by all States .... IATA is about the biggest international cartel of the entire economy).(38)

The controversy regarding IATA's character is best illustrated in the testimony of Sir William P. Hildred, former Director General of IATA, before the U.S. "Celler Committee" in 1956.(39) Sir William's arguments against calling IATA a cartel can be summarized as follows:

(a) IATA does not limit membership, nor does it exclude competitors;

(b) IATA does not limit competition: there is competition between IATA airlines amongst themselves, and also competition between IATA airlines as a group and outside international charter airlines as a group;

(c) IATA does not divide the market: the allocation of scheduled international air routes is determined on an intergovernmental basis in bilateral air transport agreements;

(d) IATA does not control output, production: capacity and frequencies are determined in accordance with the applicable provisions in bilateral air transport agreements;

(e) IATA does not fix prices: IATA agreed fares and rates are recommended to Governments for approval.

Arguments (a) and (c) are certainly valid. The situation in respect to the other arguments is somewhat different. To start with the last argument: for all <u>practical</u> purposes it can be said that IATA <u>does</u> fix prices. It is true that in accordance with the provisions of most bilateral air transport agreements IATA agreed fares and rates must be submitted to individual Governments for approval, but this approval is in most cases merely perfunctory, and practically always IATA agreed fares and rates do become the actual fares and rates.(40) Furthermore, a <u>legal</u> argument for indentifying price-recommendation with price-fixing can be found in the American antitrust case law, where suggestions, recommendations, or resolutions concerning prices or pricing practices are seen as price-fixing.(41)

As to argument (d), that IATA does not control output, it should be noted that, although the argument is in principle true, there is a certain interdependence between prices and output. To put it more concretely: the level of IATA fares and rates will to a certain extent influence the demand for air transportation.(42) This demand, in its turn, has its influence on the supply, namely, the capacity and frequencies offered.

The argument that IATA does not limit competition, argument (b), cannot hold true. IATA eliminates virtually all price competition between its member airlines, and through a system of product standardization also a good deal of the service competition. For instance, service standards such as seating density on the aircraft of IATA airlines, meals, beverages and other services to be offered on the flights of IATA airlines, are all standardized. Limiting service competition is a necessary complement to eliminating price competition. The effect of eliminating price competition may be annihilated, if this form of competition is replaced by another form of competition, i.e. service competition.(43) In this context, it should perhaps be noted that the traditional rationale for limiting price and other competition between airlines is said to be the very capital-intensive and oligopolistic[44] character of the airline industry. This character of the industry would make competition in general, and price competition in particular rather hazardous. It would easily lead to destructive tariff wars between airlines. True or not, the argument that IATA would not limit competition cannot hold true, even though IATA airlines may still try to compete with each other as much as possible - legally and often illegally - within the framework of the Association and outside thereof with independent charter airlines.

The above-mentioned "Celler Committee" did not follow Sir William's reasoning, but instead endorsed the CAB's view that IATA is an "all-embracing international cartel".[45] Although it may be too strong to put it that way, IATA does have many features of an international cartel, especially as far as its ratemaking and product standardization activities are concerned. They lead to a very important limitation, if not elimination of competition between IATA member airlines. Therefore, devoid of the bad connotation that the term "cartel" often rightfully or unrightfully entails, the use of that term is certainly not inappropriate with respect to IATA.

One writer[46] argues, that, if IATA is to be characterized as a cartel, it would probably be better to qualify it as a public than as a private international cartel. This opinion is erroneous. IATA inter-carrier agreements on rates, fares, product standards and other matters may be subject to Government approval, but that does not take away their character of basically inter-carrier reached agreements. The agreements are reached, in the first instance, between carriers and not between Governments. A comparison with intergovernmentally created public cartels like the <u>International Sugar Council</u>, the <u>International Tin Council</u> or any other organ created by existing international commodity agreements,[47] or a comparison with a public international cartel like the <u>Organization of Petroleum Exporting Countries</u> (OPEC) would be misleading. These public international cartels have all been created by intergovernmental agreement, whereas IATA was created by an agreement amongst airlines. Further, whereas agreements in IATA are basically concluded on the inter-carrier level, they are concluded on the intergovernmental level in the above-mentioned public international cartels. IATA is thus certainly not a public international cartel. If it is to be a cartel, it is to be characterized a private international cartel, or possibly as a quasi-public international cartel. The reasons, then, for calling IATA a quasi-public international cartel, would fall in the same category as those for calling the Association as such a quasi-public international organization.[48]

The second question to be answered in this paragraph is whether all or certain of IATA's activities are illegal under existing antitrust laws. Gazdik[49] has studied this question under five different headings, corresponding to five different groups of IATA activities: price-fixing, product standardization, common selling agencies, common effort to ensure compliance and industry advisory activities.[50] For all five groups he comes to the conclusion that they are legal under existing antitrust laws.[51] This conclusion is, at least at the present time, correct. Antitrust laws can roughly be divided into two groups: those that contain <u>absolute prohibitions</u> against certain restrictive practices and those that only guard against <u>abuses</u> of restrictive practices.[52] Under neither of the two groups are IATA's activities at the present time illegal, even under the strict U.S. antitrust laws.

Singled out for discussion here are the antitrust legislation of the U.S. and the European Economic Community (EEC). Both are legislations containing absolute prohibitions against certain restrictive practices.

Whereas many of IATA's activities, not only its price-fixing but also its product standardization and common agency selling activities, would to a very large extent be illegal under the Sherman and Clayton Acts,(53) they become legal when approved by the CAB under the provisions of the Federal Aviation Act.(54) Section 412(a) of the Federal Aviation Act(55) requires every air carrier to file with the CAB copies of contracts and agreements

> "between such air carrier and any other air carrier, foreign air carrier, or other carrier for pooling or apportioning earnings, losses, traffic, service, or equipment, or relating to the establishment of transportation rates, fares, charges or classifications, or for ....., or for other cooperative working agreements."

Section 412(b)(56) then empowers the Board to disapprove such contracts and agreements, when it finds them to be

> "adverse to the public interest or in violation of the Act" (i.e., the Federal Aviation Act).

When not adverse to the public interest or in violation of the Act, the contracts and agreements are approved by the Board. Board approval under Section 412 relieves the parties to such contracts and agreements from the operations of the U.S. antitrust laws: Section 414 of the Act.(57) In accordance with the provisions of Section 412 the CAB requires that all IATA Traffic Conference Resolutions be filed with it.(58) The Board then takes action on such IATA Resolutions in accordance with the conditions and procedures set out in, i.a., Order E-11954 (Nov. 13, 1957), Order 68-7-55 (July 12, 1968), Part 261 (Filing of Agreements) of its Economic Regulations(59) and Part 302 (Rules of Procedure in Economic Proceedings) of its Procedural Regulations.(60)

The CAB's authority to grant antitrust immunity under Sections 412 and 414 of the Federal Aviation Act has been challenged in court many times, often in relation to IATA's agency programme.(61) Two antitrust cases involving IATA's price-fixing activities were brought against the CAB by ACAP.

ACAP holds the view that for the benefit of the aviation consumer IATA's ratemaking machinery ought to be replaced by an international ratemaking system which would rely on free competition, on the forces of supply and demand.(62) In ACAP, Pillai and Robertson v. CAB(63) plaintiffs argued that the above-mentioned CAB's 1946 and 1955 approvals of the IATA ratemaking machinery were ultra vires the Federal Aviation Act, because they were adverse to the public interest and they involved errors of fact and law. The Court rejected this argument, not on substantial, but on procedural grounds. The doctrine of primary jurisdiction obliged plaintiffs to pursue and exhaust administrative remedies first. Plaintiffs had failed to do this.(64) Among other things, plaintiffs further contended that, if the Federal Aviation Act did at all permit the CAB to approve the IATA ratemaking machinery, Sections 412(b) and 414 of the Act should be declared unconstitutional

> "as authorizing the imposition of restrictions on the freedom of travel without due process."

This last argument was rejected by the Court on the basis that said Sections of the Federal Aviation Act had withstood previous constitutional attacks.(65)

In Pillai, Goldwyn and ACAP v. CAB,(66) ACAP was more successful in its claims against the CAB. The case will be discussed in Chapter VII. The decision in the case was based on the general rule that the CAB has a rather wide discretion in granting antitrust immunity under Sections 412 and 414 of the Federal Aviation Act, as long as it presents enough factual justification for such action.(67)

The antitrust legislation of the EEC is contained in Articles 85-94 of the 1957 Treaty Establishing the European Economic Community (Treaty of Rome).(68) Regulations pursuant to Articles 85 and 86 of the Treaty were issued by Regulation No.17 of the Council of Ministers of the EEC in 1962.(69) During the same year the Council adopted another Regulation, Regulation No.141, exempting (air) transport from the effects of Articles 85 and 86 of the Treaty and of Council Regulation No.17.(70) Article 1 of Regulation No.141 reads:

> "Regulation No.17 shall not apply to agreements, decisions and concerted practices in the transport sector which have as their object or result the fixing of transport prices or terms, the restriction of control of demand for transport or the distribution of transport markets or dominant positions, within the meaning of Article 86 of the Treaty, on the transport market."

As far as air and sea transportation is concerned, the duration of validity of Regulation No.141 is indefinite.

It should be noted that in issuing Regulation No.141 the Council of Ministers of the EEC did not give an unequivocal answer to the difficult question whether or not, apart from Title IV on Transport (Articles 74-84), the Treaty Provisions apply to the transport sector in general, and to air and sea transport in particular. This question was finally decided in 1974 by the Court of Justice of the European Communities in the case of The Commission of the European Communities v. The French Republic.(71) The Court ruled

> "... si, en vertu de l'article 84, paragraphe 2, les transports maritimes et aériens sont, tant que le Conseil n'en a pas décidé autrement, soustraits aux règles du Titre IV de la deuxième partie du traité, relative à la politique commune des transports, ils en restent, au même titre que les autres modes de transport, soumis aux règles générales du traité."(72)

With regard to IATA it would seem that pursuant to Council Regulation No.141, its activities are legal under the antitrust laws of the EEC.(73)

Before concluding this paragraph it should be noted that inter-carrier agreements within IATA do not constitute the only form of airline cooperation, which may give rise to antitrust considerations. Many such forms of airline cooperation exist outside IATA.(74) Two of them are of particular interest: pooling agreements and capacity reduction agreements.

A pooling agreement can be defined as an agreement between two or more airline companies for the joint exploitation of an air route or air routes, whereby capacity, costs of operation and/or revenues are shared between the participating companies in accordance with a predetermined formula.(75) Pooling agreements are very common on intra-European air routes and also on many intercontinental air routes such as those from Europe to the Far East and Australia and from Canada to Europe and Australia. A number of bilateral air transport agreements contain provisions for the pooling of services between designated air carriers. Sometimes pooling is compulsory under bilateral agreements.(76) No pooling agreements exist on intra-North American air routes or on air routes to and from the U.S.A. American aviation policy has traditionally been against pooling because of the fact that it limits competition between the participating airlines and might result in a lower level of service to the travelling public.(77) Under the above-mentioned Sections 412 and 414 of the Federal Aviation Act the U.S. CAB would have the authority to approve pooling agreements and by doing so to relieve them from the operations of the U.S. antitrust laws. So far the CAB has, in accordance with general American aviation policy, never approved pooling agreements. In relation to the fuel crisis it has, however, approved a number of more limited capacity reduction agreements, both domestically and internationally.(78)

A capacity reduction agreement can be defined as an agreement between two or more airline companies for the reciprocal and proportionate reduction of capacity on an air route or air routes flown by the participating companies. In the U.S.A. the desirability of capacity reduction agreements was reviewed in the Capacity Reduction Agreements Case.(79) The Initial Decision of the Administrative Law Judge, Robert E. Seaver, in the case(80) concluded that capacity reduction agreements are adverse to the public interest and not justified either on economic or on fuel-saving grounds. This decision was reviewed by the CAB, which stayed its effectiveness.(81) The final decision of the Board in the case(82) rejected capacity reduction agreements in U.S. domestic air transport,(83) but did not absolutely exclude them for international air transportation to and from the U.S.A.(84)

(1) Lamb and Shields, Trade Association Law and Practice, Little, Brown & Co., Boston/Toronto at 3 (1971).

(2) See infra, para. II.

(3) Idem.

(4) See also infra, Ch. III, para. I.

(5) Act of Incorporation, 9-10 Geo.VI, Chap.51, Assented to December 18, 1945.

(6) Canada Corporations Act, 13-14 Eliz.II, Chap.52, Assented to April 3rd, 1965, R.S.C. 1970, Ch. C-32.

(7) 23 Eliz.II, Chap.26, Assented to February 27th, 1975.

(8) See infra Ch. III, para. I.

(9) See, i.a., Pillai, op.cit., at 37-38.

(10) See infra, Ch. III, para. I.

(11) IATA Traffic Conference Resolution 100 (Conditions of Service - In-flight Entertainment).

(12) Order 68-7-55, July 12, 1968.

(13) See Part 310 of the Procedural Regulations of the CAB, (14 C.F.R. Part 310).

(14) PL 90-23, June 5, 1967, 81 Stat.54.

(15) See 14 C.F.R. Part 310.

(16) See, e.g., Ruegger, L'Organisation de la Croix Rouge Internationale sous ses Aspects Juridiques/The Juridical Aspects of the Organization of the International Red Cross, 82 Recueil des Cours 377 (1953/1).

(17) See, e.g., Friedmann, Ed., Anti-Trust Laws. A Comparative Symposium, Carswell Co. Ltd., Toronto at 186-187, 512-515, 579-585 (1956); Lasok and Bridge, An Introduction to the Law and Institutions of the European Communities, Butterworths, 1973.

(18) See Agreement Relating to the International Telecommunications Satellite Organization "INTELSAT" and Operating Agreement Relating to the International Telecommunications Satellite Organization "INTELSAT", Washington, August 20, 1971, TIAS 7532.

(19) See Wedgwood, International Rail Transport, Oxford Univ. Press, Oxford, 1946.

(20) On the distinction between private and public international organizations, cf. Chuang, op.cit., at 1-13.

(21) For the distinction between active and associate IATA members see infra, Ch. III, para. I.

(22) Of these airlines only one is exactly fifty percent State-owned. All others are more than fifty percent State-owned.

(23) East African Airlines, created in 1967 as part of the economic union of Kenya, Tanzania and Uganda, is formally a public corporation of Kenya. Financially not only Kenya, but also Tanzania (and Uganda) participate.

(24) Air Afrique was created by the Treaty of Yaoundé in 1961 (Treaty on Air Transport in Africa, ICAO Circ.98 - AT/19, 1970). At present ten ex-French colonies participate in it and each owns six percent of the shares. The remaining share capital is owned by SODETRAF, a subsidiary of Union de Transports Aériens (UTA), a privately-owned French airline. Air Afrique is incorporated

in the Ivory Coast.

(25) Scandinavian Airlines System (SAS) is a consortium of three airlines (ABA of Sweden, DDL of Denmark and DNL of Norway), of which the first owns 3/7th and the two others own 2/7th each. The three constituting airlines are all fifty percent owned by their respective Governments. See Scandinavian Airlines System Consortium Agreement and Related Agreements, ICAO Circ. 99 - AT/20, 1970.

(26) On this subject, see also Chuang, op.cit., at 137, et seq.

(27) See infra, Ch. IV, para. III.

(28) In the form of an approval of IATA's Traffic Conference machinery: see supra, Ch. I, para. II.

(29) ICAO Doc. 8681.

(30) On the delegation of ratemaking and other functions to IATA, see also Chuang, op.cit., at 41-42.

(31) See Gazdik, Antitrust Laws and International Airline Cooperation, 135 Recueil des Cours 481 at 489 (1972/I). The terms antitrust and anticartel laws will be used as being synonymous.

(32) For the antitrust implications of trade associations' membership rules see, Lamb and Shield, op.cit., at 202 et seq.

(33) Gazdik, op.cit., at 487.

(34) Kronstein, The Law of International Cartels, Cornell Univ. Press, Ithaca/London at 41 (1973).

(35) Cf. Friedmann and Verloren van Themaat, International Cartels and Combines, in Friedmann, Ed., op.cit., at 471.

(36) Gazdik, op.cit., at 505.

(37) The major exception is Pillai's Doctoral Dissertation, Yale Univ., Conn: The Air Net, op.cit.

(38) Rinck, Interessengemeinschaften und Kartelle im Luftverkehr, in Festschrift für Otto Riese, Verlag C.F. Müller, Karlsruhe, at 499 (1964).

(39) Hearings on Monopoly Problems in Regulated Industries before the Antitrust Subcomm. of the House Comm. on the Judiciary, U.S. House of Representatives, 84th Cong., 2nd Sess., at 1023 - 1054 (1956), reprinted in part in Lowenfeld, Aviation Law, Matthew Bender, New York, at III-22 to III-29 (1972).

(40) See also infra Ch. IV, para. II.

(41) Cf. Lamb and Shields, op.cit., at 68.

(42) To what extent will depend on the elasticity of demand: for the concept of elasticity of demand, see infra, Ch. V, para. I.

(43) For examples of IATA Traffic Conference Resolutions limiting service competition through product standardization, see infra, Ch. III, para. III.

(44) See infra, Ch. III, para. II.

(45) Report of the Subcomm. (Celler Comm.) of the House Comm. on the Judiciary, U.S. House of Representatives, 85th Cong., 1st Sess., at 276 (1957).

(46) Chuang, op.cit., at 153.

(47) See Kronstein, op.cit., at 10 et seq.

(48) See supra, para. I of this Chapter.

(49) Gazdik, op.cit., at 489-504.

(50) For a survey of IATA activities see infra, Ch. III, para. III.

(51) There is some doubt as to the legality of IATA's activities under the revised Canadian Combines Investigation Act, R.S.C. 1970, Ch. C-23, as amended (see also Gazdik, op.cit., at 493).

(52) For a review of several antitrust laws see: Rinck, op.cit., at 499; Rinck, The International Factors in German Air Transport, 33 JALC 102 at 107 (1967); Review of Cartel and Restraint of Trade Legislation, unpublished IATA study; Chuang, op.cit., at

106-111; Gazdik, op.cit., a passim.

(53) Sherman Act, An Act to protect trade and commerce against unlawful restraints and monopolies, Act of July 2, 1890, 26 Stat. 209 as amended; Clayton Act, An Act to supplement existing laws against unlawful restraints and monopolies, and for other purposes, Act of Oct. 15, 1914, 38 Stat. 730 as amended.

(54) Federal Aviation Act, Act of Aug. 23, 1958, 72 Stat. 731, as amended.

(55) 49 U.S.C. 1382(a).

(56) 49 U.S.C. 1382(b).

(57) 49 U.S.C. 1384.

(58) Order E-9305, June 15, 1955.

(59) 14 C.F.R. Part 261.

(60) 14 C.F.R. Part 302.

(61) For a short description of IATA's agency programme see infra, Ch. III, para. III. Selection of antitrust cases involving IATA's agency programme: John Caceres, d/b/a Caceres Agency, et al. v. IATA, et al., USCA, 2nd Circ., Jan. 13, 1970, 11 AVI 17.408 (previous reference: USDC, SDNY, Jan. 30, 1969, 10 AVI 18.228); Robert Hefler, d/b/a Party Time Tours v. IATA, et al., USDC, SDNY, May 22, 1970, 11 AVI 17.540; E.A. McQuade Tours Inc. v. Consolidated Air Tour Manual Committee, et al., USCA, 5th Circ., Aug. 21, 1972, certiorari denied, 12 AVI 17.549; Thomas P. Noone Travel Agency v. IATA, et al., USDC, D. of Mass., Dec. 11, 1972 (unreported).

(62) See also Pillai, Consumer Protection in Aviation Rate Regulation, 38 JALC 215 (1972).

(63) USDC, D.C. Circ., July 12, 1972, 12 AVI 17.500. See also earlier decisions of the Court of Appeals in NACA, et al. v. CAB, USCA, D.C. Circ., May 28, 1970, 11 AVI 17.571, and in NACA, et al. v. CAB, USCA, D.C. Circ., March 9, 1971, 11 AVI 17.989.

(64) The administrative remedies in casu are Section 1002(a) of the Federal Aviation Act, 49 U.S.C. 1482(a) (Filing of Complaints Authorized), and paragraphs 302.300 - 302.317 of the CAB's Procedural Regulations, 14 C.F.R. Part 302. The doctrine of primary jurisdiction means that, "when a claim originally cognizable in the courts is asserted against a member of a regulatory industry" (i.e., the airline industry) "and raises issues that have been placed by a regulatory scheme" (i.e., the Federal Aviation Act) "within the special competence of an administrative agency" (i.e., the CAB) "the doctrine of primary jurisdiction operates to postpone adjudication of the controversy pending administrative determination of the designated issues." (See: CAB Held to Have Exclusive Jurisdiction to Grant Injunctive Relief Against Acts Allegedly in Violation of Antitrust Laws, 63 Columbia L.R. 932 (1963). On Primary Jurisdiction see also: Coultas, The Doctrine of Primary Jurisdiction: Determination of Express and Implied Immunity from the Antitrust Laws, 39 JALC 559 (1973).

(65) McManus v. CAB, USCA, 2nd Circ., Feb. 6, 1961, 7 AVI 17.260 and USCA, 2nd Circ., Nov. 16, 1962, 8 AVI 17.271.

(66) USCA, D.C. Circ., Aug. 22, 1973, 12 AVI 18.036.

(67) See also American Importers Association v. CAB, USCA, D.C. Circ., Nov. 29, 1972, 12 AVI 17.656.

(68) For the text of Articles 85-94 see Graupner, The Rules of Competition in the European Economic Community. A Study of the Substantive Law on a Comparative Law Basis, Nijhoff, The Hague, at 198 et seq. (1965).

(69) For the text of Council Regulation No. 17, see Graupner, op.cit., at 205 et seq.

(70) For the text of Council Regulation No. 141, see Graupner, op.cit., at 219 et seq.

(71) Case No. 167/73, Recueil 1974, p.359. On the case see: Moussu, L'Application du traité de Rome au transport maritime à propos de l'arrêt de la Cour des Communautés européennes du 4 avril 1974, Annuaire de Droit Maritime et Aérien 149 (1974).

(72) Para. 32 of the decision. On the question of the applicability of the EEC Treaty to the transport sector see, i.a., Graupner, op.cit., at 35; Stabenow, The International Factors in Air Transport under the Treaty Establishing the European Economic Community, 33 JALC 117 at 117-119 (1967); Deringer, The Competition Law of the European Economic Community. A Commentary on the EEC Rules of Competition (Articles 85-90) Including the Implementing Regulations and Directives, CCH, Inc., Chicago, Ill., at 185 et seq. (1968).

(73) See also Gazdik, IATA et la libre concurrence, Journée d'étude 'Problèmes juridiques de la navigation aérienne internationale', 6 Referate gehalten am 6./7. Nov., 1969 an der Universität Basel, ASDA/SVLR Publ. 35 at 37 (1969); Stabenow, op.cit., at 122-125; Gazdik, op.cit., at 497.

(74) See Summary of Materials Collected on Cooperative Agreements and Arrangements, ICAO Circ., 84-AT/14 (1967).

(75) Haanappel, Background of the Dutch - American Aviation Conflict, I Annals of Air and Space Law, 63 at 79-80 (1976).

(76) See British Air Transport in the Seventies, op.cit., at 94 et seq.

(77) See, Statement by President Nixon, June 22, 1970, and Statement of International Air Transportation Policy, op.cit., at 89.

(78) See, i.a., Order 73-11-34, Nov. 8, 1973.

(79) CAB Docket 22908.

(80) Decision served Nov. 8, 1974.

(81) Order 75-1-32, Jan. 8, 1975.

(82) Order 75-7-98, July 21, 1975.

(83) The same decision was reached by the USCA in USA v. CAB, USCA, D.C. Circ., April 23, 1975, 13 AVI 17.702. See also Regulatory Reform: Report of the CAB special staff, CAB Publ., July 1975, at 95.

(84) Order 75-7-98, op.cit., at 15. In this context it should perhaps be noted that one American aviation expert is of the opinion that the present network of bilateral air transport agreements should be replaced by a new network of bilateral agreements, which would deregulate Government control of international ratemaking, but which would replace this control by a strict Governmental control over capacity and frequencies in international air transport. See, Lowenfeld, A New Takeoff for International Air Transport, 54 Foreign Affairs 36 (1975).

CHAPTER III: ORGANIZATION AND ACTIVITIES OF IATA

Within the framework of this book a survey of IATA's organization and activities is indispensable. A survey of IATA's organizational structure is necessary for a good understanding of how IATA performs its ratemaking functions; a survey of its activities, for a good understanding of the Association's place in the overall structure of the international air transport world.

Organizationally IATA can be divided into two parts: the trade association and the Traffic Conferences. The trade association represents the basic organizational structure of IATA. It consists of, i.a., an (Annual) General Meeting, an Executive Committee, Standing Committees, a Secretary General and a Secretariat. The Traffic Conferences represent the real decision making body of IATA. It is, for instance, through the Traffic Conference machinery that IATA performs its ratemaking function. Whereas the various organs of IATA's trade association structure are ultimately responsible to the (Annual) General Meeting as the highest authority in the Association, the Traffic Conferences are primarily responsible to the Governments of the individual IATA airlines. Traffic Conference actions can only become effective with the approval of the interested Governments. The primary reason for this lies in the fact that Governments, in their bilateral air transport agreements, have reserved for themselves the right to approve or disapprove of rates and fares agreed upon in the IATA Traffic Conferences.(1)

The first paragraph of this Chapter is devoted to a study of IATA as a trade association. Paragraph II deals with IATA's Traffic Conference machinery. Finally, Paragraph III will give a short survey of IATA's overall activities.

I. The Trade Association

IATA's "Charter" comprises two documents: the Act of Incorporation and the Articles of Association.(2) IATA's Articles of Association were adopted in the English text by the International Air Transport Operators Conference at Havana, Cuba, April 16 - 19, 1945, at which the Association was founded. The French and Spanish translations were approved by the subsequent first Annual General Meeting of the Association at Montreal, in October, 1945. The Act of Incorporation,(3) by which the Association was incorporated in Canada, was passed by the Canadian Parliament in the fall of 1945, and received Royal Assent on December 18, 1945. The Articles of Association have been amended several times by succeeding Annual General Meetings. The Act of Incorporation was only amended once, in 1974.(4) This amendment consisted of a change in the definition of "air service" and "air transport enterprise" in Article 1 of the Act. The amendment had become necessary by the abortive attempt of the 30th Annual General Meeting of IATA, held at Montreal in September, 1974, to provide for the possibility in principle of charter only airlines joining IATA.(5) Until that time membership in the Association had only been open to scheduled (international) air carriers.

The General Meeting's decision to open the Association up to charter only airlines must be seen in the light of IATA's wish to bring these carriers within its institutional framework so as to limit price competition between IATA members on the one hand and charter only carriers on the other. Charter only carriers have, generally speaking, been able to offer air transportation to the public for considerably lower prices than the scheduled IATA carriers. Consequently the past decade has shown an ever increasing competition between the two classes of carriers. Bringing the charter only airlines within IATA's institutional framework and especially within its uniform ratemaking structure would possibly put an end to this competition. To-date charter only airlines have shown little enthusiasm to join IATA. In fact, no such airline has as yet joined or has made an application to that effect. This holds true even for those charter only carriers which are subsidiaries of IATA airlines.(6) Apparently their parent companies, themselves IATA members, have, under the circumstances, not deemed such action to be appropriate. The charter price structure, based upon the law of supply and demand coupled with the general "charter" principle of attaining an almost one hundred percent load factor,(7) has resulted in a general fare level which is considerably lower than the scheduled IATA fare level. This, in its turn, has given the charter only airlines a great competitive advantage over the scheduled IATA carriers. Even if due to the sharp rise in fuel prices, inflation and economic depression many charter only airlines have recently been encountering financial difficulties, they are hesitant to join IATA and thus run the risk of being forced to adapt to the IATA uniform price structure.(8)

Article 3 of the Act of Incorporation and Article III of the Articles of Association provide, in identical wording, that the aims and objects of IATA shall be:

(1) to promote safe, regular and economical air transport for the benefit of the peoples of the world, to foster air commerce, and to study the problems connected therewith;
(2) to provide means for collaboration among the air transport enterprises engaged directly or indirectly in international air transport services;
(3) to cooperate with the International Civil Aviation Organization and other International Organizations.

The principal organs of the Association are:

- The (Annual) General Meeting, in which the final authority of the Association is vested;
- The Executive Committee, whose members are elected by the General Meeting and are charged with the day-to-day direction of the policy of the Association;
- The four Standing Committees - Financial, Legal, Technical and Traffic - of which the members are appointed by the Executive Committee subject to confirmation by the Annual General Meeting following the appointment. The Standing Committees assist the Executive Committee and work under its direction. The Traffic Committee also assists the Traffic Conferences in a policy advisory capacity;
- The Director General, appointed by the Executive Committee subject to confirmation by the General Meeting, and his Secretariat. They assist the above-mentioned organs;
- The Traffic Conferences, which, though formally an integral part of the Association, have a semi-autonomous status within IATA. They will, as mentioned earlier, be discussed in the following paragraph.(9)

IATA has two classes of membership: active and associate.[10] At the time of IATA's 31st Annual General Meeting in 1975, the Association counted 112 airlines, of which 88 were active and 24 were associate members.[11] Active membership in the Association is open to any air transport enterprise, providing international (and domestic) scheduled air services. Air transport enterprises only providing domestic scheduled air services are eligible for associate membership. After changing Article 1 of the Act of Incorporation (see supra), the 30th Annual General Meeting of 1974 proposed to amend the membership provisions of the Articles of Association as follows. Eligible as active members would be: "(a) any air transport enterprise, as defined in the amended Article 1 of the Act of Incorporation, which is operating a scheduled air service, as defined in the same Article of the Act, between the territories of two or more States as a designated air carrier under an intergovernmental air transport agreement; (b) any other air transport enterprise as defined in the amended Article 1 of the Act, which is operating an air service as defined in the Act between the territories of two or more States.[12]" The active members covered under (a) would correspond with the present class of active members comprising air transport enterprises providing scheduled international (and domestic) air services. The requirement, however, that the air transport enterprise must be a designated air carrier under an intergovernmental air transport agreement, was new. It should be noted that there are very few or no air transport enterprises which perform all their scheduled international air services outside the framework of a bilateral air transport agreement, and would thus fall outside the newly defined class of active IATA members covered under (a). For instance, until the coming into force of the route schedule to the Canada - U.S.A. bilateral air transport agreement, as amended in 1974,[13] the Canadian regional air carrier Nordair could, in the event that it would have wished to join IATA, have been affected by the proposed "designated air carrier" provision. Its only international scheduled air service, Montreal (Quebec) - Hamilton (Ontario) - Pittsburg (Pennsylvania), was not covered in the route schedule to the old, unamended, Canada - U.S.A. bilateral air transport agreement.[14] The active members covered under (b) would include international charter only airlines, should they wish to join IATA, and any scheduled international air carriers affected by the above-mentioned "designated air carrier" requirement. The provisions as to associate IATA members were not proposed to change substantially in 1974: eligible as associate IATA members were and would be air transport enterprises only providing domestic scheduled air services.[15] Associate members have no voting rights in IATA.[16] Whereas the change in Article 1 of IATA's Act of Incorporation has become law,[17] the proposed amendments to the membership provisions of the Articles of Association have not. They did not receive the necessary benediction from the U.S. CAB,[18] with the result that international charter only airlines are now eligible for IATA membership under the Act of Incorporation, but not under the implementing provisions of the Articles of Association. In fact this means that the pre-1974 membership provisions have remained in force.

According to Article 1 of the Act of Incorporation, an airline, in order to be eligible for IATA membership, must fly under the proper authority and under the flag of a State eligible for ICAO membership. Until 1968, this provision was repeated in Article IV of the Articles of Association. In 1968, the General Meeting deleted the provision from Article IV. The Articles of Association now only contain provisions for the termination of IATA membership for airlines flying under the flag of a State which has expressly been excluded from ICAO membership.[19] Article 93 of the Chicago Convention[20] contains rather onerous admission procedures for "former enemy States" wishing to join ICAO. In practice, this Article has been interpreted very liberally with the result that all States have been regarded as eligible for ICAO membership, unless expressly rejected.[21] IATA has followed the same liberal attitude in interpreting its ICAO eligibility requirement, and has, therefore, never encountered any problems in admitting to the Association flag carriers of "former enemy States", such as Alitalia, Lufthansa and Japan Air Lines.

Applications for IATA membership must be made to the Executive Committee, which handles these applications in conformity with the rules laid down in Article IV(5)(6) of the Articles of Association and Article VII of the Rules and Regulations of the Executive Committee. In accordance with Article IV(5)(6), the Executive Committee has so far followed a very liberal membership policy. Every airline satisfying the few above-mentioned eligibility requirements is welcome to join the Association. This policy has led to the characterization of IATA as an open trade association.[22] However, when proposing to amend the Articles of Association so as to allow charter only airlines to become active IATA members, the 30th Annual General Meeting, in 1974, also proposed to amend Article IV(5) of the Articles of Association. With respect to active scheduled IATA members the amended version of Article IV(5) would certainly have led to a continuation of the open membership policy. With regard to other future active (charter) and associate members of IATA the amended version of Article IV(5) would have provided that the Executive Committee shall from time to time set qualification standards for their admission "having regard to such factors as the length of time that the applicant has been established as an air transport enterprise and the extent of its operations."[23] As mentioned before, the proposed 1974 amendments did not become law.

IATA has two budgets: one for the Association, one for the Traffic Conferences. The Association's budget is fixed every year by the Annual General Meeting upon the recommendation of the Executive Committee.[24] The Traffic Conference budget must, after adoption by the Traffic Conferences, be approved by the Executive Committee.[25] Both the membership dues for the Association and the assessments for the Traffic Conferences are, at least as far as the active members are concerned, related to revenue tonne-kilometres performed in international services (hereinafter RTKMS). Associate members pay fixed membership dues, and, if participating in Traffic Conference activities, fixed assessments not related to RTKMS.[26] Membership dues amounted to a total of U.S. dollars 4.598.548 in 1973.[27] Approximately fifty percent of the membership dues are usually accounted for by the dues of the ten or eleven largest IATA airlines in terms of RTKMS.[28] This means that some ten percent of the IATA members pay half the Association's budget. Much the same is true for the Traffic Conference assessments. They amounted to a total of U.S. dollars 2.759.500 in 1973.[29] Besides the revenues derived from dues and assessments IATA also derives substantial revenues from charges for services rendered to its members and from fines imposed upon its members under the compliance provisions of Article XII of the Provisions for the Regulation and Conduct of the IATA Traffic Conferences.[30] In fact, fines imposed by IATA upon its member airlines constitute a major source of income for the Association. In 1973, such fines amounted to a total of U.S. dollars 2.709.127.[31] It should be remembered that membership dues and Traffic Conference assessments only cover the administrative and IATA personnel costs. They do not cover the often very high additional costs that IATA members and their delegates incur in attending IATA meetings and Traffic Conferences.

> Article VII(1) of the Articles of Association provides that "The ultimate authority of the Association is vested in the General Meeting, composed of representatives of the Active Members of the Association."

There is a General Meeting every year. This is the Annual General Meeting.(32) The latest Annual General Meeting was held at Singapore in the fall of 1976. Special General Meetings may be called either by the Executive Committee at any time or at the request, in writing, of one-third of the active members addressed to the Executive Committee.(33) General Meetings are not open to the public.(34) According to Article VIII(1)(c) of the Articles of Association the functions of the General Meeting are the following:

(a) To elect a President of IATA from among the representatives of airlines holding active membership in the Association. The position of President is in principle merely honorary. In practice every General Meeting elects as President the president of (one of) the airline(s) of the country where the next Annual General Meeting is to take place. The President takes office at the conclusion of the Annual General Meeting at which he is elected and presides over the next Annual General Meeting;(35)

(b) To elect the members of the Executive Committee, subject to the nomination procedure approved by the 27th Annual General Meeting, in 1971. The Committee shall be composed of not less than nine and not more than twenty-one persons chosen from among representatives of the active members. At present the Committee has twenty-one members. Members are elected for terms of three years and one-third of the total membership is open for election every year;(36)

(c) To receive and to consider reports of the Executive Committee or other Committees - i.a., the Standing Committees - or officers of the Association;

(d) To pass upon the accounts for the past year;

(e) To designate technical and other committees to be organized by the Executive Committee. The Standing Committees were, among others, created according to this provision;

(f) To transact such other business as may be on the agenda for the meeting or as may be proposed by the Executive Committee.

A majority of the active members present or represented at any General Meeting constitutes a quorum. Each active member has one equal vote(37) and all matters, except amendments to the Articles of Association, are decided by a majority of the votes duly cast.(38)

Each year the Executive Committee, charged with the day-to-day direction of the Association's policy,(39) holds two regular meetings, immediately before and after the Annual General Meeting, and an unspecified number of additional regular and/or special meetings.(40) Executive Committee meetings are closed. Only the Committee members, the Director General and such other officers as may be designated by him are entitled to be present.(41) Seven members of the Committee constitute a quorum at any meeting. Decisions of the Committee, however, are valid when approved by the majority of all the Committee members.(42)

The Director General, with the approval of the Executive Committee, has established a number of Special Committees.(43) The Executive Committee has established a number of Subcommittees of its members.(44)

The four Standing Committees assist the Executive Committee and work under its direction.(45) The Financial, Legal, Technical and Traffic Committees are all governed by the Rules and Regulations of the Standing Committees. Membership in the Financial, Technical and Traffic Committees is limited to persons having a major responsibility within their airlines for policy-making in respectively the financial, technical or commercial field. Membership in the Legal Committee is limited to members of the legal profession, employed by or actively associated with an IATA member airline.(46) Committee members act as representatives of IATA, and not as representatives of a member of IATA.(47) There used to be five Standing Committees. The functions of the fifth Committee, the Medical Committee, are now performed by the Technical Committee.

Both the Executive Committee and the Financial Committee are concerned with the operation of the IATA Clearing House. The Clearing House was set up at London, in January, 1947, in accordance with a Resolution passed at the 2nd IATA Annual General Meeting, held at Cairo, in October, 1946. The operations of the Clearing House are governed by the IATA Clearing House Regulations, promulgated by the Executive Committee. Certain of the Regulations may be amended or deleted only by the Executive Committee. Others may be deleted or amended by the Director General, subject to prior consultation with the Financial Committee.(48) The Clearing House works under the supervision of the Director General, who consults with the Financial Committee as to the management and the progress of the House, and who also appoints its "managers".(49) Membership in the Clearing House is open to IATA members on a voluntary basis. In 1975, 75 of the 112 IATA members were also members of the Clearing House.(50) Since 1973, and under certain conditions, membership in the House has also been open to non-IATA scheduled air carriers, parties to the IATA Multilateral Interline Traffic Agreements.(51) The Clearing House settles monthly accounts for interline revenue transactions between its members. As far as possible these accounts are settled without the actual transfer of funds. For instance, during the period 1947 to 1969, almost ninety percent of the overall total of bills received by the Clearing House was settled without the actual transfer of funds.(52) The Clearing House may certainly be considered as one of IATA's most useful and effective institutions. In May, 1948, an Interclearance Agreement was concluded between the IATA Clearing House and the Airlines Clearing House, Inc., the U.S. domestic Clearing House.

The IATA Secretariat is headed by the Director General. He is the "chief executive and administrative officer of the Association", and is responsible to the Executive Committee by which he is appointed, subject to conformation by the General Meeting.(53) IATA's present Director General is Mr. Knut Hammarskjöld.(54) As "chief executive officer" he appoints the staff of the Secretariat, although in practice he is only directly involved in senior personnel appointments. In certain respects he is limited in his power to appoint senior personnel. The Secretary and the Treasurer, for instance, are elected by the Executive Committee upon the recommendation of the Director General. They work under the latter's supervision and authority.(55) Among other things, they fulfill the administrative duties which IATA has to perform as a Canadian Corporation under the Canada Corporations Act.(56) The Treasurer is formally known within IATA as the Assistant Director General Administration and Finance - Treasurer. Besides being responsible for the budget and general financial affairs of the Association, he is also responsible for the day-to-day direction of the organization in terms of personnel, accommodation, publications, communications, etc. The Secretary handles, i.a., all membership matters and services all Executive Committee and General Meetings. The Breaches Commissioner also stands as an exception to the Director General's general powers. As the Commissioner performs quasi-judicial functions, his tenure and terms of appointment are specially set out in the Provisions for the Regulation and Conduct of the IATA Traffic Conferences. He is appointed by the Director General with prior approval of the Executive Committee(57) and plays a central role in IATA's compliance machinery.(58) There is also a special section of the IATA Secretariat involved in compliance matters. This section is the Compliance Office, headed by the Compliance Director, who is assisted by investigators spread all over the world.(59) Appointment by the Director General of other staff of the rank of Assistant Director General is also subject to the Executive Committee's approval.(60) There are five Assistant Directors General. Mention has already been made of the Assistant Director General Administration and Finance - Treasurer. The other Assistant Director Generals are:

- Assistant Director General Traffic, head of the Traffic Department. This Department has three main divisions: the Traffic Conference Office, which functions as Secretariat for the Traffic Conferences; the Agency Administration, responsible for the operation of IATA's extensive agency programme; Traffic Services and Facilitation, i.a., serving as Secretariat for the Permanent Traffic Conference Committees;
- Assistant Director General Technical, head of the Technical Department and performing a multitude of functions in IATA's extensive technical activities;
- Assistant Director General, General Counsel, head of the Office of the General Counsel. Apart from strictly legal functions, the General Counsel and his Office also work in the fields of security and charges for the use of air navigation facilities;
- Assistant Director General Governmental and Industry Affairs, charged with, i.a., the maintenance of relations with intergovernmental organizations and Governments.

Besides the officers, offices and departments mentioned above, IATA also has a Public Relations Office, headed by the Public Relations Director, an Industry Finance Director, a Chief Economist and a Commissioner Commercial Planning and Coordination.

IATA's Secretarial staff is divided over its head office in Montreal, its other main office in Geneva and a number of regional offices. The importance of the IATA Secretariat, though formally not a decision-making body, should not be underestimated. Due to its great experience and expertise in aviation matters, the Secretariat does in practice exercise a great deal of influence on IATA's decision-making process.

II. The Traffic Conferences(61)

Most of IATA's activities finally find their expression in Resolutions and Recommended Practices adopted by the Traffic Conferences. IATA Traffic Conference Resolutions can be defined as agreements adopted by the unanimous vote of the Traffic Conference members. They become binding on the members when approved by interested Governments. Recommended Practices are not binding on the Traffic Conference members: they do not have the force of agreements, but represent the views of the majority of the Traffic Conference members on subjects which are not, or not yet, fit for inclusion in Traffic Conference Resolutions.

The Traffic Conferences function more or less independently

from the rest of IATA and have a semi-autonomous status within the Association. The reason for this is that the Traffic Conferences are primarily responsible to Governments. Governments have in their bilateral air transport agreements which delegate ratemaking power to IATA, reserved for themselves the right to approve or to disapprove the rates and fares agreed upon in the Traffic Conferences. The relation between Traffic Conferences and Governments is studied in more detail in Chapter IV, paragraph II.

The Traffic Conferences derive their legal existence from Article VIII(5) of the Articles of Association. They are governed by the Provisions for the Regulation and Conduct of the IATA Traffic Conferences, which as mentioned before were initially adopted by IATA's first Annual General Meeting, in 1945. These Provisions may be amended at any time by the Executive Committee.(62) An exception, however, is made for the much debated "unanimity rule", to be discussed later. This rule can only be amended by the Executive Committee after prior approval by the Annual General Meeting.(63) Certain other powers with respect to the Traffic Conferences are given to the Executive Committee in Articles I(2), II(2) and X(2)(3) of the Provisions for the Regulation and Conduct of the IATA Traffic Conferences. A close link exists between the Traffic Committee, one of the Standing Committees of the Association, and the Traffic Conferences. As mentioned earlier, the Traffic Committee functions as a policy advisory committee to the Traffic Conferences. It also acts as a steering committee to the Conferences while in session, and is, i.a., empowered to create such (Traffic Conference) working groups and sub-committees as it deems necessary.

There are three Traffic Conferences - TC 1, TC 2, TC 3 - each encompassing a different geographical area of the world.(64) Each of these Traffic Conferences may have two classes of members: voting and non-voting. Each active IATA member operating a scheduled commercial international air transport service between two or more points within the area of any Traffic Conference shall be a voting member of that Traffic Conference. Each active IATA member operating scheduled commercial international air transport operations between a single point within the area of one Traffic Conference, and one or more points within another Traffic Conference area, shall be qualified for voting membership in both of such Traffic Conferences, and must become a voting member of one. Any IATA member, whether active or associate, may become a non-voting member of a Traffic Conference in which it cannot qualify as a voting member. Membership, voting or non-voting, in a Traffic Conference shall be contemporaneous only with membership in IATA.(65)

The aims, objects and purposes of the Traffic Conferences are the same as those of IATA itself.(66) The Traffic Conferences may consider and act upon all traffic matters of concern to their members in their respective areas and shall concern themselves with all international matters involving passengers, cargo and mail in their respective areas, particularly the following:

(a) Analysis of operating costs;
(b) Fares, rates and charges for passengers and cargo;
(c) Schedules;
(d) Approval of agencies and their administration.(67)

There are individual and joint meetings of Traffic Conferences. Regular individual meetings of each Traffic Conference - TC 1, TC 2, TC 3 - are held not less frequently than once every two years. All other meetings are considered as special meetings.(68) Joint meetings of Traffic Conferences are held for the purpose of determining fares, rates and related matters between points within one Traffic Conference area, and points within one or more other Traffic Conference areas. These meetings are usually held at the same place and time as a regular meeting of one of the Traffic Conferences concerned.(69) The joint meetings of Traffic Conferences are referred to as Joint Traffic Conferences -JT-. Altogether there are, therefore, seven Conferences:

- TC 1 :	dealing with matters affecting TC 1;
- TC 2 :	idem TC 2;
- TC 3 :	idem TC 3;
- TC 12 :	idem TC 1 and TC 2;
- JT 13 :	idem TC 1 and TC 3;
- JT 23 :	idem TC 2 and TC 3; and
- JT 123:	idem TC 1, TC 2 and TC 3.

All Conference meetings are *closed* meetings,(70) surrounded with ample secrecy.(71) This secrecy has at times come under heavy attack. On several occasions, the U.S. CAB has insisted on the presence of some of its officers at Conference meetings. Without that presence, the CAB argued, it would not be sufficiently able to exercise the required control over rates and fares agreed upon in the Traffic Conferences. Consumer groups have argued that the closed character of Conference meetings would be detrimental to the interests of the user of air transportation, who has no way of knowing how the fares and rates which he ultimately is going to pay, have been determined. A request made by the American aviation consumer group ACAP to attend Conference meetings was turned down by IATA. The Association usually limits the disclosure of information concerning Traffic Conference proceedings and results to the issuance of summary press releases. IATA defends its policy of secrecy in this respect on practical grounds: for all commercial enterprises, including airlines, pricing policy is a highly sensitive issue, necessarily surrounded by a large degree of secrecy. Furthermore, as shall be seen below, the "*unanimity rule*" makes reaching agreement in the Conferences necessarily a bargaining process. The presence of outsiders - be it Government representatives, the press, consumer representatives or the general public - would make that bargaining process most embarrassing for the airlines involved. Under the present circumstances it is up to Governments to find reasonable means to control the actions of the IATA Traffic Conferences. Without such control the consumer would be inadequately protected against the concerted pricing actions of the IATA airlines in their Traffic Conferences.

In view of the fact that all IATA fares and rates are *interrelated*, it is the general practice in establishing a new level of worldwide fares and rates for *all* seven Conferences to meet at the same time and the same place, in the form of so-called *Composite Conferences*. In 1964, a division was made between passenger and cargo subjects, and since that time *separate* Conferences have been organized, one for cargo, one for passenger subjects. Under normal circumstances Composite Passenger Conferences would take place in the fall of alternate years, with the object of the new fares and conditions going into effect on the 1st of April following and remaining in force during a period of two years. Composite Cargo Conferences would take place in the spring of the intervening years with the object of the new rates and conditions going into effect on the 1st of October following and also remaining in force for a period of two years. Recent circumstances - among others inflation, charter competition, fuel scarcity and prices, currency fluctuations - have made it impossible to adhere to this schedule and special Conference meetings have been much more frequent than in the past. This refers especially to meetings dealing with fares, rates and related conditions on the key North Atlantic routes. At present meetings of TC 1, TC 2 and JT 12 - dealing with fares and rates on, i.a., the intra-American, intra-European and North Atlantic routes - are generally scheduled before the Composite Conference. Only after the Composite Conference has been held are meetings of TC 3, JT 13 and JT 23 organized.

Only action in the form of a Resolution taken at an individual or joint meeting of Traffic Conference (s) shall be binding on the member airlines thereof.(72) Such action can only be taken upon the unanimous affirmative vote of all members represented at any meeting.(73) Under certain circumstances action by mail vote is possible.(74) The Conferences thus work with the system of a unanimity rule. This rule has been the subject of much debate, and several proposals have been made for its reform.(75) As long as the rule remains in existence, it will necessarily continue to make reaching agreements in the Traffic Conferences an action by compromise, a bargaining process. By virtue of the rule every member airline of a Traffic Conference or Joint Traffic Conference holds an effective veto to protect itself from being forced to act counter to its own beliefs. Even a Traffic Conference member participating in a joint meeting of its Traffic Conference with another Traffic Conference, while not itself providing air services on the inter-Conference air routes concerned, holds such a veto power.(76) The unanimity rule can work both in favour of the large and in favour of the small carriers. On the one hand, a minority of large carriers cannot impose its will upon a majority of small carriers. On the other, a majority of small carriers cannot overrule a minority of large carriers.(77)

Whenever it proves to be impossible to reach agreement in the Conferences on fares and rates in a certain area or on certain routes, or whenever such agreement, reached in the Conferences, is subsequently disapproved by Governments, a so-called open fare or rate situation will arise. In that case fares and rates will have to be determined in accordance with the provisions in the applicable bilateral air transport agreements regulating such situations.(78) Usually, however, it does not go that far. Most open fare or rate situations result in a maintenance of the status quo until a subsequent Traffic Conference is able to reach a new agreement, acceptable to both the Traffic Conference members and to the Governments concerned.

Each Traffic Conference has four officers: a Chairman, a First Vice-Chairman, a Second Vice-Chairman and a Secretary. The Chairman of the Composite Conferences and the Secretary and staff for each Traffic Conference is provided by the Director General. The Chairman of the Composite Conferences shall not be an employee of one of the IATA member airlines. The Secretary and staff are IATA employees. The Secretary of the different Traffic Conferences is in fact the head of the Secretariat's Traffic Conference Office. All other above-mentioned officers are elected by a majority vote - exception to the unanimity rule - of the members of the Traffic Conference, represented at a regular meeting of such a Conference. They take office from the close of such a regular Conference meeting, and hold office until the close of the next subsequent regular Conference meeting.(79)

The Composite Conference has a number of permanent Committees which are responsible to the Composite Conference as a whole.(80) These Permanent Conference Committees are the following:
(a) The Passenger Agency Committee;
(b) The Cargo Agency Committee;

(c) The Passenger Traffic Procedures Committee;
(d) The Cargo Traffic Procedures Committee;
(e) The Reservations Committee; and
(f) The Cost Committee.

Permanent Conference Committees, other than the Cost Committee, may take action in the form of Resolutions on matters on the agenda for the meeting and within the terms of reference of the Committee. If unanimously agreed by the Committee and by all members attending the meeting and entitled to vote, such action shall have the same force as a Conference Resolution, provided it has been circulated to all members of the Traffic Conference concerned and has not been protested within 45 days after the date of such circulation by one-fourth or more of the members entitled to vote on such Resolution which members were not represented at the meeting. The Cost Committee has the important task of making periodical analyses of costs for use as one of the bases on which fare and rate levels may be developed. The information gathered by the Cost Committee is derived from detailed questionnaires(81) sent to the IATA member airlines.

All Permanent Conference Committees are governed by the Rules and Procedures for the Permanent Committees of the Traffic Conferences. In addition hereto there are separate Rules of Procedure for the Cost Committee.(82)

There are also a number of more specialized Traffic Conference Subcommittees and Working Groups.(83) They are governed by the General Rules and Procedures for Traffic Subcommittees and Working Groups.(84)

The present Traffic Conference structure only provides a machinery for the determination of scheduled international air fares and rates. The Traffic Conferences have never set international charter air tariffs, neither for the charter flights performed by their own scheduled IATA members, nor, evidently, for the charter flights performed by charter only airlines. In some ways, however, the Traffic Conferences have somewhat restricted the right of their member airlines to perform charter flights. This was done with a view to restricting a too rapid growth of charter flights to the detriment of the scheduled flights.(85) If one day IATA succeeds in incorporating international charter only airlines into its structure, it will be necessary either to create a separate Charter Traffic Conference or to allow for the participation of charter only airlines in the already existing Traffic Conferences, whose competence would then have to be enlarged so as to include not only the determination of scheduled international, but also of international charter tariffs. IATA's 29th Annual General Meeting held at Auckland (New Zealand) in 1973, was already advised of amendments made by the Executive Committee to the Provisions for the Regulation and Conduct of the IATA Traffic Conferences. These amendments provided for the establishment of a separate Charter Traffic Conference. However, they did not receive the necessary Governmental approval.(86)

In the meantime, when deciding to open up the Association to charter only airlines, IATA's 30th Annual General Meeting in 1974, passed the following Resolution.(87) Participation by charter only airlines in the Traffic Conferences

> "shall be limited to joint meetings of Traffic Conferences 1 and 2 held for the purpose of determining charter prices and/or fares and rates on charter flights and/or conditions of sales and service applicable to charter flights between any point in Traffic Conference 1 and any point in Europe over the Atlantic. This limited participation ... shall

not be extended beyond this area, nor shall this provision be amended or rescinded without approval of a General Meeting of the membership by a 4/5 vote of the active members present in person or by proxy and voting."

Not only would this Resolution have limited the possible participation by charter only airlines in the Traffic Conferences to the determination of trans-atlantic charter tariffs, but it would also have implied that future charter only Association members would just be able to vote on charter tariffs, whereas scheduled IATA members would be able to vote on both scheduled and charter tariffs. This imbalance in the voting power of scheduled and charter only airlines was without any doubt one of the major reasons for the charter only airlines' reluctance to join IATA. In this context, it should be remembered that the 1974 amendments to the Articles of Association did not receive the necessary approval of the U.S. CAB.(88) Such approval must be obtained before IATA can make any definite arrangements for participation of charter only airlines in the Traffic Conference machinery.

Reference to IATA's compliance machinery was already made in mentioning the Secretariat's Compliance Office and the function of the Breaches Commissioner.(89) IATA's compliance machinery works in accordance with the rules laid down in Article XII of the Provisions for the Regulation and Conduct of the IATA Traffic Conferences.(90) The compliance machinery is a necessary complement to the system of binding Traffic Conference Resolutions. It tries to ensure that Traffic Conference members adhere to the Resolutions which they themselves have adopted at the Traffic Conferences. This is especially important in relation to those Traffic Conference Resolutions which set uniform rates and fares and uniform service standards for scheduled international flights of IATA airlines. These competition limiting Resolutions are generally considered to be necessary in the airline industry because of its oligopolistic character. The oligopolistic character of the airline industry comprises two elements. In the first place, the airline industry is highly capital-intensive and entry into the industry is thus difficult and limited. In other words, there are relatively few "producers", few airlines in the industry. In the second place, the airline industry lacks product differentiation. All airlines basically offer the same "product": rapid point-to-point transportation by efficient, modern aircraft. Under these circumstances price, and to a lesser extent service competition are considered hazardous for the industry. Such competition would easily lead to destructive tariff wars between airlines. This is the rationale why in principle airlines will be willing to agree on uniform fares, rates and service trandards through the IATA Traffic Conferences. Often, however, airlines will still want to compete with each other to a certain extent. They may do so, for instance, through experiments with capacity and frequencies, if allowed under bilateral agreements (*supra* Ch. I, Para. II) and if not precluded by pooling or capacity reduction agreements (*supra* Ch. II, Para. II). All airlines wish to have as large as possible a part of the air transport market. To that end they will compete with each other, not only to the extent allowed by the IATA Traffic Conference Resolutions, but also beyond that. It is this latter form of competition which the IATA compliance machinery tries to combat. In particular, it tries to prevent IATA airlines from giving illegal discounts on the fares and rates agreed upon through the IATA Traffic Conferences. It also tries to prevent IATA airlines from giving excessive commissions to travel agents.(91) Airlines will often give such excessive commissions in order to induce travel agents to attract more passengers and cargo for their flights.(92)

Technically the compliance machinery works as follows. Complaints that an IATA member airline has violated one or more Traffic Conference Resolutions may be filed with the Director General by the Compliance Director or by any IATA member. Complaints filed by one IATA member against another are relatively rare. Most complaints stem from action taken by the Compliance Office. Usually complaints are first investigated by the Compliance Office. To facilitate its work, IATA members are obliged to maintain accounts, books and records in accordance with generally accepted accounting principles. Upon request, they are obliged to make these documents available to the Compliance Office. Failure to do so is regarded as a Traffic Conference action breach.(93) After investigation of a complaint by the Compliance Office, the Director General may either "dismiss the claim and so advise the Member concerned, or refer the complaint ... to a Commission for hearing and decision."(94) The Commission, a quasi-judicial body, consists of a single Commissioner, the above-mentioned Breaches Commissionner. After hearing on the complaint in question, the Commission which to a very great extent sets its own rules of procedure, decides the case and may impose upon the member complained against the following penalties:

(a) notification to all the Conference members on the findings of the Commission;

(b) reprimand;

(c) a fine for each breach of a Traffic Conference Resolution not in excess of U.S. dollars 50.000;

(d) expulsion from IATA.(95)

For complaints of minor importance the Provisions for the Regulation and Conduct of the IATA Traffic Conferences provide a summary procedure. In this case the maximum fine to be imposed is U.S. dollars 5000.(96) Hearings of the Commission are held behind closed doors and reports of the decisions are not made public. Those reports are sent to the Director General, who forwards them to all members.(97) On the basis of "new evidence", an imposed fine of more than U.S. dollars 25.000 or combined fines of more than U.S. dollars 100.000, a convicted member may apply to the Appeals Board for leave to appeal.(98) The Appeals Board consists of the Breaches Commissioner and two other members nominated for each appeal by the Director General from a panel of retired senior airline personnel.(99) If the Board approves the application for leave to appeal, it shall conduct a hearing(100) and thereafter confirm, overrule or alter the decision of the Commission. The Board's decision is final.(101) At the present time, fines imposed under IATA's compliance machinery total almost 3.000.000 dollars per year.(102) IATA, essentially a private organization, cannot always legally force its members to pay the fines imposed upon them. Under such circumstances expulsion of the member refusing to pay its fines is the ultimate remedy under Article V(2)(a)(ii) of the Articles of Association. In conclusion, it should be noted that many Governments have their own machinery for adherence to the Traffic Conference Resolutions approved by them and applicable to IATA airlines flying to, from or via their territories.(103) Stricter Governmental action in this field can be expected after a request to that effect made by the special ICAO Air Transport Conference of April 1977.

III. Activities of IATA

In view of the fact that most of IATA's activities finally find their expression in Resolutions and Recommended Practices adopted by the Traffic Conferences, a survey of these Resolutions and Practices would give a good general impression of the Association's overall activities.(104) In comparison with the existing number of Traffic Conference Resolutions, the number of Recommended Practices is extremely small. The following survey of IATA's activities will, with one exception, be limited to a review of IATA Traffic Conference Resolutions. These Resolutions have all been published in the IATA Manual of Traffic Conference Resolutions. The Manual is constantly being kept up to date. Blocks of numbers have been assigned to the different groups of subjects covered by the Resolutions. In the following review the earlier made distinction between IATA's trade association and quasi-public functions should be kept in mind.(105)

Resolutions 001-009 deal with so-called Administrative matters. They include provisions as to the period of validity of Resolutions, revalidation of Resolutions and Governmental approval of Resolutions. Some of the Administrative Resolutions will be studied in more detail in Chapter IV, paragraph II, dealing with Government control of IATA.

Resolutions 010-049 concern General Tariff Subjects. These Resolutions deal with matters which have to be taken into account before an actual rate or fare can be constructed. Among other things they determine the general rules to be followed in constructing fares and rates. They deal with the currency in which these fares and rates have to be paid, and with such matters as "unethical disclosure of information",(106) and certain advertising practices. The controversial Resolution 045, giving conditions under which IATA members may perform international charter flights, is also contained under the heading General Tariff Subjects.(107) A number of Resolutions falling under this heading will be studied in Chapter V.

Resolutions 050-099 contain the actual IATA fares and the conditions pertaining to such fares.(108) Of special significance are Resolutions 050 and 060 dealing respectively with First and Economy Class Conditions of Service. As pointed out earlier, elimination of service competition is a necessary complement to the elimination of price competition. The system of uniform IATA fares is aimed exactly at that elimination of price competition between IATA airlines and is in accordance with the generally accepted principle that price competition is regarded harmful in an oligopolistic industry such as the airline industry. If unlimited service competition were to replace price competition, the purpose of the uniform IATA tariff system would be defeated. The tariffs would still be nominally identical, but their intrinsic value would be different, since every airline would be able to offer its passengers an entirely different standard of service. Price competition having been eliminated by IATA's uniform tariff structure, service competition has become extremely popular amongst IATA airlines. This is evidenced by the advertising policy of the IATA airlines. Not the product as such - point to point transportation - is so much advertised. It is rather the service surrounding the product that is being advertised: the efficiency and the friendliness of the airline's personnel, its food, its give-aways, the tourist attractions of its home country, its airport facilities, etc. Service competition provides the IATA airlines, via a back door, with the possibility of competing directly with each other. Through service competition IATA airlines try to artificially differentiate their basically undifferentiated product: point to point transportation. The aim of service competition is, of course, to attract as many passengers as possible. While service competition may, at a first glance, be beneficial to the air traveller, it should be borne in mind that it is the air traveller himself who, eventually, pays for this service. The better, the more luxurious the service that an airline offers, the higher the eventual fare to be paid by the passenger. At times service competition has given rise to strong controversies amongst IATA airlines. One such controversy, for instance, was caused by the introduction of inflight entertainment on the flights of certain IATA airlines in the sixties. The problem was that some IATA airlines had equipped their aircraft with inflight entertainment facilities, whereas others had not, and did, at the time, not intend to do so. These latter airlines were afraid to lose passengers to the airlines which had already installed inflight entertainment facilities on their aircraft and intended to offer this entertainment to their passengers free of charge. The compromise reached consisted of the adoption of the still valid Resolution 100, effective April 1, 1967, which obliges IATA airlines to charge their passengers $2,50 for the use of inflight entertainment equipment (earphones).(109)

The purpose of Resolutions 050 and 060 is to put a certain limit to the service competition between IATA airlines. The Resolutions determine such things as (minimum) seating density on aircraft, whether or not lounge accommodation and alcoholic beverages may be offered, what kinds of meals may be served, what items may be given to the passengers free of charge (e.g., newspapers, magazines, brochures, beverages, candies) and what items may be sold to the passengers on board the aircraft (e.g., spirits, cigarettes, perfume).

Resolutions 100-499 cover a wide range of so-called Passenger Traffic Subjects: fare related matters and conditions of service(110) not dealt with under Resolutions 050-099. Amongst these Resolutions one is of very special interest to air lawyers. The Resolution in question is Resolution 275B. It promulgates the IATA Conditions of Contract for Passengers and Baggage. There are also IATA Conditions of Contract for Cargo. These latter Conditions are contained in Resolution 600B.(111) In short, the IATA Conditions of Contract, printed on all uniform IATA Passenger Tickets and Baggage Checks(112) and on all uniform IATA Air Waybills(113) form the abstract of the more general IATA Conditions of Carriage. At present, there are only IATA General Conditions of Carriage for Passengers and Baggage. They are contained in a Recommended Practice, No. 1013, and are thus not binding upon IATA member airlines. No IATA General Conditions of Carriage for Cargo exist at the present time.(114)

The drawing up of conditions of contract and carriage is one of IATA's oldest and best known trade association functions.(115) The first IATA Conditions of Carriage, the so-called Vienna Conditions, were developed as early as 1927 by the Association's predecessor, the International Air Traffic Association. The present IATA Conditions of Contract and Carriage for Passengers and Baggage and the Conditions of Contract for Cargo have a very wide application. Formally their use is only compulsory for "interline international carriage", i.e., international carriage in which more than one IATA carrier takes part. In practice, however, the IATA members use the uniform IATA conditions as much as possible: when allowed by the national authorities concerned, they use them for "on-line international carriage", i.e., international carriage in which only one IATA carrier takes part, and also for purely domestic carriage. Furthermore, the use of the IATA conditions is not limited to IATA carriers alone. There are also non-IATA scheduled (international) carriers which use the IATA conditions of contract, and the same is true for a number of charter air carriers. In addition hereto many carriers still use, as their own, conditions such as the now no longer valid 1949 IATA General Conditions of Carriage for Cargo (Bermuda Conditions). In general, the IATA Conditions of Contract and Carriage stay within the liability regime as created by the Warsaw Convention,(116) the Hague Protocol,(117) the Montreal Agreement(118) and the Guatemala City Protocol.(119)

Resolutions 500-649 deal with Cargo Traffic Subjects. They are subdivided as follows:

500-529 General Provisions;
530-549 Bulk Unitization;
550-569 Basic Cargo Rates;
570-589 Discounts;
590-599 Commodity Rates and Class Rates;
600-649 Forms.

The subject of cargo rates will be studied in more detail in Chapter V, paragraph II.

Resolutions 650-699 deal with air mail matters. The transportation of air mail has played a major role in the development of scheduled (international) air services, especially in the period before World War II. The transportation of mail continues to form a major, though decreasing source of revenues for airlines. IATA does not set rates for the transportation of air mail. This task is left, at least in part, to an intergovernmental organization, the Universal Postal Union (UPU). Approximately every five years the UPU's Universal Postal Congresses determine the maximum level of so-called foreign origin air mail conveyance rates. The level of national origin air mail conveyance rates is not determined by the UPU, but by contracts between airlines and national postal authorities. These latter air mail conveyance rates are indirectly influences by the UPU set foreign origin air mail conveyance rates and, therefore, show a tendency to conform to them. The presently valid UPU air mail conveyance rates were adopted by the Union's 1974 Lausanne Universal Postal Congress. They will remain in force until 1981. The distances used for the calculation of air mail conveyance payments are based upon a formula agreed upon between the UPU and IATA. The actual rates are determined in Gold Francs. Close cooperation between IATA and the UPU exists in the form of a joint UPU/IATA Working Group, falling under the supervision of the UPU Executive Council. The determination of foreign origin air mail conveyance rates forms an interesting example of direct intergovernmental involvement in international ratemaking.(120)

Resolutions 700-719 (Schedules and Timetables), 720-799 (Reservations) and 800-899 (Agency) contain many multilateral interline traffic agreements. The development of these interline agreements is a typical trade association function of IATA and is aimed at the free interchange of traffic amongst participating carriers. The Agreements provide for the mutual acceptance of traffic documents, i.a., the IATA Passenger Ticket and Baggage Check and the IATA Air Waybill, and for uniform procedures for reservations and for handling, transfer, rerouting of all interline passengers, baggage and cargo between participating carriers.(121) Not only an IATA member airline, but any airline operating scheduled air transport services is eligible to become a party to the IATA multilateral interline traffic agreements. In September 1974, 137 non-IATA carriers were participating in the multilateral interline traffic agreements.(122)

Resolutions 800-899 are concerned with IATA's extensive agency programme.(123) The agency programme is applied through the Traffic Conferences' Agency Administration Boards for Passenger Agents and Cargo Registration and Review Boards for Cargo Agents. The Boards are assisted by the Secretariat's Agency Administration. The essence of the IATA agency programme is that IATA member airlines may only pay commission to so-called IATA Approved Agents. IATA Passenger Agents are all required to sign the IATA Passenger Sales Agency Agreement,(124) which sets out the conditions of their appointment. Resolutions adopted by the individual Traffic Conferences establish the maximum rates of commission which may be paid to Approved Agents for sales of IATA air transportation. The system of maximum commission rates is an essential complement to the uniform IATA fares and rates system. Without such a system the agency network could be used as a means to undermine the uniform fares and rates structure. Excessive commission payments by IATA airlines to individual travel agents would in fact be tantamount to a fare or rate reduction and would induce travel agents to sell transportation only on the airlines offering the highest rate of commission. For the same reason, to prevent the agency programme from becoming a means to undermine the uniform IATA tariff structure, the splitting of commission between agents and customers is forbidden. Among the standards applied in the appointment of new IATA Approved Agents is the need for the existence of such new agents. One of the purposes of the agency programme is, namely, to keep the number of IATA Agents at a reasonable, but not excessive level. This standard of "need" is, however, not applied in the appointment of IATA Approved Agents in the U.S.A., where the use of such a standard would be contrary to the existing anti-trust laws.

The IATA agency programme has been in serious peril since Pan Am's decision to withdraw from the IATA Passenger Agency Resolutions on April 9, 1975.(125) In withdrawing from the Agency Resolutions Pan Am pointed out that in recent years the Resolutions had been violated by IATA member airlines to such an extent that, in adhering to them, the company would lose a very considerable part of its travel market. Since the denunciation by an IATA member of a Traffic Conference Resolution is usually enough to make the Resolution invalid vis-à-vis all participating carriers,(126) the Pan Am action invalidated almost the whole of IATA's passenger agency programme with serious repercussions not only on the agency programme itself, but also on the whole IATA uniform fares and rates structure. Whereas the overall commission rate in force before Pan Am's action was a flat seven percent, the airline soon began to offer an additional three percent commission on all business in excess of ninety percent of that booked on Pan Am in the prior year. Pan Am's action, of course praised by a powerful trade association such as the American Society of Travel Agents (ASTA), was matched by numerous other IATA airlines. It was, however, successfully challenged in court by the British Department of Trade, which wished to see Pan Am adhere to the old seven percent commission rate. In overruling a previous Queen's Bench Division decision, the Court of Appeal decided that the British Secretary of State did indeed, under Articles 60 and 79 of the 1974 Air Navigation Order, have the power to order Pan Am to adhere to the seven percent commission rate.(127)

After several rounds of negotiations IATA member airlines, including Pan Am, succeeded in saving their Passenger Agency Resolutions by raising the basic commission level to eight percent and by introducing an additional three percent commission on the sales of inclusive tour charters. An incentive commission system would furthermore be introduced in 1978, but in the meantime, in the fall of 1976, another agency commission war broke out on the North Atlantic with no immediate solution in sight.(128)

Finally, Resolutions 900-999 deal with facilitation matters. IATA's facilitation activities are aimed at the standardization, simplification and sometimes elimination of Governmental documentation and procedures required in international air transport. IATA has a special Facilitation Advisory Committee, one of the above-mentioned Special Committees created by the Director General, with the approval of the Executive Committee. In facilitation matters there is close cooperation between IATA and ICAO. Annex 9 to the Chicago Convention, developed by ICAO, contains standards and recommended practices for States in the facilitation field. It was recently announced that IATA is planning to develop a computerized passport card to replace the presently existing passport booklets. These passport cards could be fed into computers to be installed at international airports. These computers would contain customs, immigration and security information on the passport holder. The purpose of this computerized passport system is, of course, to speed up customs, immigration and security procedures at the world's international airports.

In concluding this paragraph, it should be stressed that the above survey of IATA's activities is far from being exhaustive. It is aimed at giving an overall idea of IATA's activities and, at certain points, at explaining the interdependence between IATA's ratemaking and other activities.

(1) See _supra_, Ch. I, para. II, _a passim_.
(2) For the text of the _Act of Incorporation_ and the _Articles of Association_ see: _Act of Incorporation, Articles of Association, Rules and Regulations_, IATA Publ., 14th Ed., Sept. 1974.
(3) 9-10 Geo. VI, Chap. 51 (1945).
(4) 23 Eliz. II, Chap. 26 (1974).
(5) See IATA Doc. AGM 30/24. E, _infra_, Appendix C.
(6) See _supra_, Introduction: ACCA members (footnote 8).
(7) By "load factor" is meant the percentage obtained by dividing the number of seats sold on aircraft by the number of seats available on aircraft. See also _infra_, Ch. VI, para. II.
(8) See also _infra_, Ch. VI, para. II and Ch. VIII, para. III.
(9) For a description of IATA's organizational structure see also, Chuang, _op.cit._, at 43 et seq. For an _Organization Chart_ of IATA see _infra_, Appendix B.
(10) Article IV(1) Arts. of Assoc.
(11) See, _infra_, Appendix A.
(12) Article IV(2), Arts. of Assoc. See _infra_, Appendix C.
(13) _Agreement between the U.S.A. and Canada, Amending the Agreement of January 16, 1966_, Effected by Exchange of Notes, Signed at Ottawa, May 8, 1974, TIAS 7824.
(14) _Air Transport Agreement between the Government of the U.S.A. and the Government of Canada_, Signed at Ottawa, January 17, 1966.
(15) Article IV(3), Arts. of Assoc.
(16) Article VIII(4), Arts. of Assoc.
(17) See _supra_, footnote 4.
(18) See AWST, Sept. 27, 1976, at 27. See also _infra_, para. II.
(19) Article V(2)(b), Arts. of Assoc.
(20) _Convention on International Civil Aviation_, signed at Chicago, Dec. 7, 1944, ICAO Doc. 2187.
(21) See, Buergenthal, _op.cit._, at 18 et seq.
(22) See, _supra_, Ch. II, para. I.
(23) See _infra_, Appendix C.
(24) Art. VI(1)(2) Arts. of Assoc. and Art. IX(1) Rules and Regulations of the Executive Committee (R. & R. of the ExC.).
(25) Art. X Provs. for the Regulation and Conduct of the IATA TCs, Art. IX(2) R. & R. of the ExC.
(26) For an explanation, see _Statement of Hammarskjöld_, Director General of IATA, before the Subcomm. on Aviation of the Comm. on Commerce, U.S. Senate, 92nd Cong., 1st Sess., on S. 2423, Serial No.92-40, at 143, 144, 146 (1971).
(27) IATA 1973 Financial Statement.
(28) In alphabetical order: Air Canada, Air France, Alitalia, British Airways, Japan Air Lines, KLM Royal Dutch Airlines, Lufthansa, Pan American World Airways, Quantas, Scandinavian Airlines System, Trans World Airlines.
(29) IATA 1973 Financial Statement.
(30) See, _infra_, para. II.
(31) IATA 1973 Financial Statement.
(32) Art. VIII(1)(a), Arts. of Assoc.

(33) Art. VIII(2). Arts. of Assoc.

(34) Rule 17 of the Rules of Procedure of General Meetings.

(35) Art. IX(1), Arts. of Assoc., and Rule 9 of the Rules of Procedure of General Meetings.

(36) Art. IX(2)(a)(b), Arts. of Assoc., and Art. III R. & R. of the ExC.

(37) Art. VIII(3), Arts. of Assoc.

(38) Rule 36 of the Rules of Procedure of General Meetings. For amendments to the Articles of Association, a four-fifth majority is required: Art. XII, Arts. of Assoc.

(39) Art. XI(3), Arts. of Assoc., and Art. II, R. & R. of the ExC.

(40) Art. IX(7), Arts. of Assoc., and Art. IV(1)(2), R. & R. of the ExC.

(41) Art. IV(3), R. & R. of the ExC.

(42) Art. IX(2)(c), Arts. of Assoc., and Art. IV(1)(2), R. & R. of the ExC.

(43) Art. IX(6), Arts. of Assoc., and Art. VI(5)(6)(7)(8), R. & R. of the ExC.

(44) Art. IX(2)(d), Arts. of Assoc., and Art. VI(12), R. & R. of the ExC.

(45) Art. IX(6), Arts. of Assoc., and Art. VI(1)(2), R. & R. of the ExC.

(46) Art. I(4)(5) Rules and Regulations of the Standing Committees.

(47) Ibidem, Art. I(2).

(48) Art. VI(13), R. & R. of the ExC., and Art. 35 IATA Clearing House Regulations.

(49) Arts. 4 and 5, IATA Clearing House Regulations.

(50) See, infra, Appendix A.

(51) Art. 3, IATA Clearing House Regulations. For a discussion of the IATA Multilateral Interline Traffic Agreements, see infra, para. III.

(52) See Aspects of World Airline Cooperation, Clearing House, IATA Publ., 1969.

(53) Art. IX(5)(a), Arts. of Assoc., and Art. V(2), R. & R. of the ExC.

(54) Mr. Hammarskjöld's appointment was confirmed by a Resolution adopted at IATA's 20th Annual General Meeting at Bogota, Colombia, Sept., 1964. (32 IATA Bull. 18, 1964). Mr. Hammarskjöld assumed office in April, 1966.

(55) Art. IX(5)(b), Arts. of Assoc., and Art. V(3)(4), R. & R. of the ExC.

(56) 13-14 Eliz. II, Chap. 52, Assented to April 3rd, 1965, R.S.C. 1970, Ch. C-32.

(57) Art. XII(12) Provs. for the Regulation and Conduct of the IATA TCs and Art. V(2) R. & R. of the ExC.

(58) See infra, para. II.

(59) See infra, para. II.

(60) Art. V(2)(iv) R. & R. of the ExC.

(61) See also: Gazdik, Ratemaking and the IATA Traffic Conferences, 16 JALC 312 (1949); Gazdik, Traffic Conference Machinery, 15 IATA Bull. 63 (June 1952); Sheehan, IATA Traffic Conference Machinery, 17 IATA Bull. 45 (Mid-Year 1953); Cohen, Crisis in the Conferences: A Case History in International Air Fares and Rates Negotiation, 27 JALC 150 (1960); Wood, The IATA Traffic Conferences: An Airline Man's View, Paper presented to the Second Air Transport Conference of N.Y.U. held at N.Y. on May 24, 1962; McCook Bond, A Critical Comparison of the IATA Traffic Conferences and the Maritime Shipping Conferences, unpublished term-paper, McGill Univ., Montreal, (1964); Cohen, Confessions of a Former IATA Man, 34 JALC 610 (1968); Pillai, op.cit., at 35-52; Chuang, op.cit., at 64-75; Agreeing Fares and Rates, IATA Publ., 2nd ed., June, 1974, at 11 et seq.

(62) Art. XIII Provs. for the Regulation and Conduct of the IATA TCs

(Hereinafter Provs. R. & C. IATA TCs).

(63) See Rules and Regulations of the Standing Committees under Traffic Committee and Art. XI(9) Provs. R. & C. IATA TCs.

(64) Article I Provs. R. & C. IATA TCs:
- TC 1: encompassing North and South America and the islands adjacent thereto; Greenland, Bermuda, the West Indies and islands of the Caribbean Sea; the Hawaiian Islands (including Midway and Palmyra);
- TC 2: encompassing Europe (including the part of the USSR in Europe) and the islands adjacent thereto; Iceland, the Azores, Africa and the islands adjacent thereto; Ascension Island; that part of Asia lying West and including Iran;
- TC 3: encompassing Asia and the islands adjacent thereto except that portion included in TC 2; the East Indies, Australia, New Zealand and the islands adjacent thereto; the islands of the Pacific Ocean except those included in TC 1.

Until 1947 there were nine different Traffic Conferences.

(65) Art. III Provs. R. & C. IATA TCs.

(66) Art. II(1) Provs. R. & C. IATA TCs.

(67) Art. IV(1) Provs. R. & C. IATA TCs.

(68) Art. V(1)(3) Provs. R. & C. IATA TCs.

(69) Art. VI(1)(4) Provs. R. & C. IATA TCs.

(70) Agreeing Fares and Rates, op.cit., at 33.

(71) See IATA T.C. Res. 035, discussed supra, Ch. II, para. I.

(72) Art. II(4) Provs. R. & C. IATA TCs.

(73) Ibidem, Art. VII(1).

(74) Ibidem, Art. VIII.

(75) See infra, Ch. VIII, para. III.

(76) For instance, in the past TC 2 member British European Airways (BEA), which did not operate transatlantic air services, sometimes threatened to veto JT 12 (North Atlantic) fares.

(77) On the unanimity rule see also Pillai, op.cit., at 68-83.

(78) See supra, Ch. I, para. II.

(79) Art. IX Provs. R. & C. IATA TCs.

(80) Art. XI(1) to (8) Provs. R. & C. IATA TCs.

(81) See Agreeing Fares and Rates, op.cit., Appendix T at 234-237.

(82) Ibidem, Appendix B at 174-178 and Appendix S at 233.

(83) Art. XI(9)(10) Provs. R. & C. IATA TCs. For an organization chart of all IATA Traffic Conference Committees see Agreeing Fares and Rates, op.cit., Appendix D at 181.

(84) Agreeing Fares and Rates, op.cit., Appendix C at 179-180.

(85) See infra, Ch. VI, para. II.

(86) Report of Executive Committee, 30th AGM, Montreal, Sept., 1974, at 2; See also CAB Docket 26713.

(87) IATA Doc. AGM 30/24.E, infra, Appendix C.

(88) See supra footnote 18 and CAB Docket 27756: comments against the approval of the amendments to the Articles of Association were filed on May 23, 1975, by the CAB's OCA, the member carriers of NACA and the Antitrust Division of the U.S. Department of Justice. The main thrust of the three comments was that CAB approval of the amendments to the Articles of Association would have a severe anti-competitive impact on the existing international air tariff structure. The CAB agreed with these comments and consequently rejected the approval of the proposed amendments.

(89) See supra, para. I.

(90) See also Tauber, Enforcement of IATA Agreements, 10 Harvard Int. L.J. 1 (1969); Chuang, op.cit., at 94 et seq; Agreeing Fares and Rates, op.cit., at 63 et seq.

(91) Some insight into the extent of illegal discounts and excessive commission payments can be found in a 1973-75 U.S. Federal Grand Jury Investigation before the USDC, EDNY. Nineteen out of the twenty-three airlines involved admitted the giving of illegal discounts to travel agents and passengers on transatlantic flights. See Montreal Star Feb. 11, 1975.

(92) For IATA's agency programme, see infra, para. III.

(93) Art. XII(6) Provs. R. & C. IATA TCs.

(94) Ibidem, Art. XII(7).

(95) Art. XII(13)(14) Provs. R. & C. IATA TCs; Res. II, 27th AGM of IATA and Decision, 74th ExC of IATA.

(96) Ibidem, Art. XII(20).

(97) Ibidem, Art. XII(15).

(98) Ibidem, Art. XII(16)(a).

(99) Ibidem, Art. XII(16)(d).

(100) Ibidem, Art. XII(16)(k).

(101) Art. XII(16)(1) Provs. R. & C. IATA TCs.

(102) See supra, Ch. III, para. I. In order to induce IATA members to adhere more strictly to IATA rules and Traffic Conference Resolutions, the Association's 31st AGM, in 1975, decided that members should, in a Multilateral Agreement between them and the Association, reconfirm their membership obligations and determination to adhere to Traffic Conference Resolutions and the Provs. R. & C. IATA TCs. See Larose-Aubry, Annual General Meeting of IATA, 1 Air Law 135 et seq. (1976).

(103) See, e.g., Section 902 (d) of the U.S. Federal Aviation Act, 72 Stat. 731 as amended, 49 U.S.C. 1471.

(104) See also, "The Aims and Activities of IATA", Appendix to U.S. Congressional Statement of Hammarskjöld, op.cit.; Chuang, op.cit., at 76 et seq. Brancker, IATA and what it does, Sijthoff, Leyden, 1977.

(105) See supra, Ch. II, para. I.

(106) TC Res. 035, cit. supra, Ch. II, para. I.

(107) See infra, Ch. VI, para. II.

(108) Res. 050-059 First Class Fares; 060-069 Economy Class Fares; 070-099 Special Fares (e.g. excursion, inclusive tour, group, student, family, emigrant, etc.)

(109) See for more details infra, Chapter VII, para. II.

(110) e.g., Resolution 100, cit. supra.

(111) Res. 600 B falls within the group of IATA Traffic Conference Resolutions dealing with Cargo Traffic Subjects.

(112) Res. 275.

(113) Res. 600.

(114) On the IATA Conditions of Contract and Carriage see the following article and book, and the literature cited there: Haanappel, The IATA Conditions of Contract and Carriage for Passengers and Baggage, IX European Transport Law 650 (1974), and Wolfgang, Die IATA, Eine Organisation des grenzüberschreitenden Luftlinienverkehrs und ihre Allgemeinen Beförderungsbedingungen, Lang, Bern/Frankfurt, 1973.

(115) A very limited number of bilateral air transport agreements delegates to IATA the task of drawing up conditions of contract and carriage. In general, however, the developing of conditions of contract and carriage is to be regarded as a typical trade association function. See also supra, Ch. II, para. I.

(116) Convention for the Unification of Certain Rules Relating to International Carriage by Air, Signed at Warsaw on October 12, 1929, T.S. 876.

(117) *Protocol to Amend the Convention for the Unification of Certain Rules Relating to International Carriage by Air Signed at Warsaw on October 12, 1929*, Signed at The Hague on September 28, 1955, ICAO Doc. 7632.

(118) *Agreement Relating to Liability Limitations of the Warsaw Convention and The Hague Protocol*, effective May 16, 1966, Agreement CAB 18990, approved by CAB Order E-23680, May 13, 1966.

(119) *Protocol to Amend the Convention for the Unification of Certain Rules Relating to International Carriage by Air Signed at Warsaw on October 12, 1929, as Amended by the Protocol done at The Hague on September 28, 1955*, Signed at Guatemala City on March 8, 1971, ICAO Doc. 8932.

(120) See the following literature: *Air Mail Study*, ICAO Doc. 8240 - AT/716 (1962); revising the *Air Mail Study* of ICAO Doc. 5348 - AT/654 (1948); Codding, *The Universal Postal Union. Coordinator of the International Mails*, NYU Press, New York, 1964; Dirlewanger, *Die Preisdifferenzierung im Internationalen Luftverkehr*, Verlag Herbert Lang & Cie. A.G., Bern at 192 et seq. (1969).

(121) See, *Agreeing Fares and Rates*, *op.cit.*, at 44 et seq. and 54.

(122) *Report of Traffic Committee, 30th AGM*, Montreal, Sept. 1974, at 6.

(123) See Brunner, *Die Rechtsstellung der IATA Agenten*, Journées d'étude "Problèmes juridiques de la navigation aérienne internationale", 6 Referate gehalten am 6/7 Nov., 1969 an der Universität Basel, ASDA/SVLR Publ. 1969 at 16; Lester, *Sales Agency Contracts in the Field of Air Transport*, 135 Recueil des Cours 433 (1972/I); *Agreeing Fares and Rates*, *op.cit.*, at 57 et seq.

(124) Res. 820 A.

(125) See Pan Am letter to IATA, reprinted in *Aviation Daily*, April 14, 1975, at backs of pp. 242-244.

(126) See *infra*, Ch. IV, para. II.

(127) Leave to appeal to the House of Lords was refused. See *Pan American World Airways* v. *Department of Trade*, Court of Appeal, July 28,29, 1975, I Lloyd's L.R. 257 (1976). It is interesting to note Lord Denning's (M.R.) statement, that the Bermuda Agreement forms no part of the municipal law of Britain (pg. 260).

(128) AWST, Dec. 22, 1975 at 38; AWST, Feb. 14, 1977 at 24.

CHAPTER IV: GOVERNMENT CONTROL OF INTERNATIONAL RATEMAKING

Ratemaking in international air transport is, as already noted in the Introduction to this book, a matter of vital importance for airlines, consumers and Governments. For airlines the level of international air fares and rates forms one of the cornerstones of their economic viability. For airline users the level of international air fares and rates forms the yardstick by which to measure their financial capability to make use of international air transport. Governments, as the guardians of the public interest, have the difficult task of striking a just balance between the often opposed financial and other interests of airlines on the one hand and consumers on the other.

In controlling international ratemaking, Governments pay attention to both scheduled and charter fares and rates. In practice, however, Government involvement in scheduled international ratemaking is considerably more active than in international charter ratemaking.

This Chapter will, in the first, place, examine the reason why Governments tend to regulate international air transport in general, and international air tariffs in particular. It will also study how Governments control IATA agreed rates and fares. Finally, a study will be made of how the U.S. CAB deals with the regulation of international air fares and rates. The reason for singling out the CAB lies in the fact that without any doubt the U.S.A. is civil air power number one in the world, and that the ratemaking policy of its CAB is one of great expertise and of substantial impact on the overall international tariff structure.

I. Rationale for Government Control

The answer to the question "Why do Governments regulate, c.q., control international air fares and rates?" depends on the answer to the more general question "Why do Governments regulate (international) air transport as such?" In a socialist economy the answer to the last question is not hard to give. In such an economic system the State is involved in the regulation of every aspect of economic life, and hence also in the regulation of the economic sector of (international) air transport. The rationale for Government control and regulation of (international) air transport is, however, more complicated in a capitalistic, free enterprise economy. It should first be remarked that, granted that in the industrialized Western world there are very few or no purely capitalistic economic systems left, it remains a fact that also in our modern, "mixed" economies one of the central economic laws can still be said to be that of demand and supply. Applying the law of demand and supply to the determination of (international) air fares and rates would lead to the fixing of those fares and rates at the level, where the supply of air transportation by carriers would meet the demand for such transportation by users. It should immediately be remembered, however, that no pure and simple application of the law of demand and supply is possible in the case of (international) air transport. The air transport industry is, as explained earlier, oligopolistic in character. Inter alia due to the fact that the industry is highly capital intensive, entry into it is far from being free and unlimited. Consequently there are a limited number of suppliers in the industry which, in its turn, distorts the classical application of the law of demand and supply. In order to avoid tariff wars the industry, therefore, heavily relies on an inter-carrier agreed uniform price structure, reached through the IATA ratemaking machinery. Nevertheless, the application of the law of demand and supply plays a considerably more important role in the determination of international charter air tariffs.

In a free enterprise or "mixed" economy, the answer to the question, why Governments regulate (international) air transport, lies not so much in the oligopolistic character of the airline industry as such, but rather in its public utility character.

As all other modes of public or common transportation, air transport is a public utility. Pillai(1) correctly calls international air transport a "world public utility".(2) The term "public utilities" is used for a branch of industries legally affected with a public interest and, therefore, conducted under Government regulation.(3) They occupy an intermediate position between State services and services offered by private enterprises. The main services performed by public utilities include public transportation - be it by rail, road, water or air - communications - radio, television, telegraph, telephone - gas, water and electricity services, and finally such community services as sanitation and irrigation. Public utilities fall under the obligation to render reasonably adequate and stable service to all who apply. They fall within the class of industries whose services form a "common necessity" for the public. Public utility services are usually best performed by either a monopoly - one supplier, e.g., one telephone company in one country, Province or State - or an oligopoly - few suppliers, e.g., in the transportation field. On the one hand, Government authorities allow public utilities to be performed by a monopoly or oligopoly. On the other hand, in order to prevent public utilities from abusing their monopolistic, c.q., oligopolistic position and to assure adequate and stable service to the public, Governments regulate those public utilities. One of the most important forms of public utility regulation then, is the regulation of prices charged by utilities for their services to the public.

Government regulation of public utilities generally takes one of two forms: public utilities are either performed by State-owned or partially State-owned enterprises, or they are performed by private enterprises which are strictly controlled by a Government agency, Ministry or Department. The first form of regulation could be called the Western European public utility concept, whereas the latter could be called the American concept. Railways and telephone companies, for instance, are generally speaking State-owned in Western Europe, whereas in the U.S.A. they are privately-owned, but regulated by independent regulatory agencies.(4) In the Western European concept Governmental ownership of public utilities gives the competent State authorities the power to regulate those utilities directly from within. In the American concept public utilities are basically autonomous private enterprises, controlled and regulated from the outside by competent State authorities.

Public utility regulation of international air transport in Western Europe is generally exercised through complete or partial State-ownership of international airline companies. In the U.S.A., on the other hand, all (international) airline companies are entirely privately-owned, but at the same time strictly regulated and controlled by the CAB, an independent regulatory agency, created by Congress.(5) Two countries in the Western world have a sort of "mixed" system: Canada and Great Britain. Of Canada's two major international airlines Air Canada is entirely State-owned, whereas Canadian Pacific Airlines is entirely privately-owned. In the U.K. British Airways is entirely State-owned. Britain's second most important international airline, on the other hand, British Caledonian Airways, is entirely privately-owned. Both Canada and Great Britain have a semi-autonomous regulatory aviation authority. In Canada, this authority is the Canadian Transport Commission (CTC)(6) and in Great Britain it is the Civil Aviation Authority (CAA).(7)

Most States have given their appropriate regulatory authorities at least two powers with respect to the economic regulation of (international) civil aviation. In the first place, through a system of licensing, they have given them the power to control entry into the airline industry.(8) In the second, they have given their regulatory authorities the power to control air fares and rates.(9) The extent of these and other powers differs from country to country. In general, however, it must be said that most States have the power to determine air fares and rates for international air transportation to, from or via their respective territories. In practice, the tariff control exercised by most States is rather perfunctory. IATA agreed scheduled international air fares and rates are seldom disapproved by Governments.(10) Furthermore, the determination of international charter air fares and rates is mostly left to the free forces of the market place.(11) At this point it should be recalled that most bilateral air transport agreements, in delegating ratemaking power to designated air carriers or to IATA, reserve to State authorities the power to disapprove of rates and fares determined by those designated air carriers or by IATA.(12)

It is often said that, in practice, Government control of international ratemaking has been weak or almost non-existent, and that this has been to the detriment of the aviation consumer, who has seen himself faced with ever and unnecessarily rising air fares and rates. To a certain extent this criticism is certainly valid. In many instances regulatory aviation authorities have been more concerned about the financial well being of their flag carriers than of that of their travelling public. In other words, regulatory authorities have often lost sight of the public utility character of international air transport, and have paid more attention to other factors involved in its regulation. Such other factors include foreign policy, national defence, national prestige and national economy considerations.(13) For national defence, economy and prestige considerations it is important for a State to have a large and financially strong national airline. A strong and big national flag carrier forms a valuable military air transport reserve for times of war. A financially sound airline forms an important foreign currency earning source for the country of which that airline is a national. Finally, having a large national airline enhances the prestige of a given country. This last consideration is especially applicable to developing nations.

It is submitted that Governments should not give too much consideration to the above-mentioned "secondary" factors involved in Government regulation of international air transport, but rather should look primarily at the public utility character of international air transport so as to strike a just balance between the financial interests of the airline industry on the one hand and those of the consumers on the other. Governmental control of air fares and rates is of utmost significance to the travelling public. In an ideal situation

Governments should instruct their national air carriers and through them IATA, to charge the public international air fares and rates, which would allow the carriers to make a rate of return on investments which is sufficient to attract new capital for the airline industry, but which is not so high that carriers would start making excessive profits at the expense of the public. In doing so, Governments would recognize the public utility character of international air transport. Furthermore, in allowing carriers a reasonable rate of return on investments, they would prevent the necessity of direct subsidization. In principle the practice of direct subsidization of international air transport should be rejected.[14] Although such subsidization might bring the level of international air fares and rates down and would thus allow a larger section of the public to make use of international air transport, it would be unjust to pass the costs of such direct subsidization on to the taxpayer. After all, only a rather small percentage of the population, even of Western countries, is financially able to travel by air internationally.[15]

II. Government Control of IATA[16]

Governments derive their authority to control IATA agreed fares and rates from two sources. The first source is international, the second national in character. The international source consists of the standard clause found in the majority of bilateral air transport agreements and providing that international fares and rates agreed upon by designated air carriers and/or by IATA shall be subject to Government approval.[17] The second source, the national one, consists of the different national legislative provisions giving competent regulatory authorities the power to control, c.q. determine international air fares and rates.[18]

The importance of Governmental control of IATA fares and rates is evident, when one takes into account the fact that over two-thirds of the total international air traffic is carried on scheduled international flights and that IATA sets the fares and rates for almost all these flights through its ratemaking machinery.

IATA has always recognized the fact that Governments possess the power to control the fares and rates which are determined through its ratemaking machinery. The Association also recognizes that Governments can go further than that and control the IATA ratemaking machinery as such. One Government indeed, that of the U.S.A., reserves the right to disapprove changes in IATA's Articles of Association and Provisions for the Regulation and Conduct of the IATA Traffic Conferences.[19]

IATA's internal rules for Government control are, with one exception which will be discussed later, contained in the so-called Administrative Traffic Conference Resolutions, Resolutions 001-009.[20] These Resolutions apply to the control of fares and rates as well as of other Traffic Conference Resolutions. Of the Administrative Resolutions, Resolution 001, the Permanent Effectiveness Resolution, is definitely the most important one.

Paragraph 1 of Resolution 001 provides that each Traffic Conference Resolution shall contain a filing period, an effectiveness date and an expiry date.[21] The filing period is meant to give interested Governments the time to decide whether they are going to approve a Traffic Conference Resolution or not. Paragraph 2 of Resolution 001 obliges each Traffic Conference member to notify the Secretary of the Traffic Conference as to whether its Government wishes to approve all or certain Traffic Conference Resolutions, and if so that member must file those Resolutions with its Government prior to the commencement of the filing period. The filing period then represents the time during which Governments can decide on the approval or disapproval of a particular Traffic Conference Resolution. Sometimes it happens that Governments delay in taking action on filed Resolutions and in those cases the filing period must be extended(22) and the effectiveness date adjusted.(23) After commencement of the filing period and until such time as all necessary Government approvals have been received, IATA member airlines may only advertise and sell air transportation against the rates and fares agreed upon in the Resolution(s) under Governmental consideration, if they do so under the qualification "subject to Government approval".(24) Following the filing period or any Government extension thereof, the Secretary of the Traffic Conferences informs all Conference members specifying the effective date of the Resolution in question.(25) When not disapproved by Governments, the Resolution comes into effect on that date. It is the responsibility of each Traffic Conference member to notify the Secretary of the Traffic Conferences which Resolution(s) need to be approved by its Government. In the event that the Secretary has not received such notification by the end of the filing period or any extension thereof, Resolution 006 provides that the Government in question is deemed not to object to the promulgation by the Secretary of the effective date(s) of the Resolution(s).

The IATA filing period, described above, should not be confused with <u>national</u> filing regulations obliging carriers to file their tariffs with the appropriate Governmental aviation authorities.(26) These national filing regulations generally apply to all fares and rates, whether determined through the IATA ratemaking machinery or otherwise.

Governments have the right to approve IATA Traffic Conference Resolutions in whole or in part, to disapprove them, or to approve them subject to reservations and conditions. The effect of such Governmental action depends on the type of IATA Resolution. The IATA Resolutions have been divided into four Types: A, AA, B and Condition C.(27) More than one of these Types may appear in a single Resolution. This is the case, when, for instance, one paragraph of a Resolution is designated Type A, while other paragraphs are designated Type B or Condition C. The general rule is that one or more Government disapprovals of an entire Resolution make that Resolution void. The situation as to Governmental disapproval(s) of a part or parts of a Resolution is governed by the Type of Resolution. Government disapproval of a portion or portions of a Type A Resolution is considered as rendering that entire Resolution void. On the other hand, Government disapproval of a portion or portions of a Type B Resolution is considered as only rendering the disapproved portion or portions void. The remainder of the Resolution remains in force, unless one or more Type A paragraphs included in a Type B Resolution are disapproved. In such a case the whole Type B Resolution is considered as being void.

When a Resolution is "tied-in" with another Resolution or Resolutions, as is the case with many fares and rates Resolutions, then Government disapproval of such a Resolution or part thereof, as the case may be, also renders the other Resolution(s) void.(28)

In the event of a disapproval of a Type AA Resolution or part of a Resolution designated AA, the pre-existing Resolution or part thereof to be replaced by the Type AA Resolution or provision shall become effective at a later date, or until 180 days after the next meeting of the Traffic Conferences, whichever may be earlier.

As the effect of a Governmental disapproval of only a part of a Resolution may thus be to render that entire Resolution, and sometimes also other "tied-in" Resolutions void, Governments have more often resorted to giving conditional approvals than to giving disapprovals of Traffic Conference Resolutions. Generally speaking conditionally approved Traffic Conference Resolutions are considered as being qualified by the Governmental conditions under which they have been approved. The Resolutions themselves together with their conditions are published in the IATA Manual of Traffic Conference Resolutions. An exception to the above described general rule occurs in case of a Condition C Resolution or in case of a portion of a Resolution designated under Condition C. In these cases conditional Governmental approval is considered to be a disapproval of such a Resolution or portion thereof.

Whenever a Government conditions its approval of a Type A, AA or B Resolution, then every Traffic Conference member may, within thirty days after notification by the Secretary of the Traffic Conferences of such a Government reservation, notify the Secretary that the Resolution in question shall not come into force with respect to that member.(29) In practice this procedure is not followed very often. As described above, in the great majority of cases in which Government approval has been given subject to certain conditions, the terms of the Resolution are considered to be qualified by those conditions.

Difficult as the distinction may sometimes be, conditionally approved IATA fares and rates Resolutions should not be confused with Government ordered fares and rates.(30) Whereas conditionally approved IATA fares and rates remain IATA fares and rates, Government ordered fares and rates fall outside the category of IATA fares and rates. One Administrative Traffic Conference Resolution provision, however, applies to both conditionally approved and to Government ordered fares and rates. Resolution 001(8) provides that, if by means of a Government condition or reservation, or by means of a Government order to its national airline(s), a Government actually alters the level of fares and rates contained in a Resolution, such alteration is deemed to be a Government disapproval of such fares and rates.

It was stated before that there is one exception to the system that the IATA internal rules for Government control are contained in its Administrative Traffic Conference Resolutions. This exception is Article II(3) of the Provisions for the Regulation and Conduct of the IATA Traffic Conferences. The paragraph in question reads:

> "... any action taken at a meeting or joint meeting of Traffic Conference (s) shall become binding at such time and such manner as may be prescribed by the Conference(s), provided further that where a member certifies in writing to the Secretary, Traffic Conferences ... that such action would require it to contravene an applicable law of regulation or official policy of the State of which such member is a national, the member shall not be bound thereby, and each other member, upon receiving notice from the Secretary, shall have the right to indicate to the Secretary whether it will continue to be bound thereby."

Thus, not only have Governments the right to disapprove or to condition Traffic Conference Resolutions, but also Traffic Conference members themselves have the right to say that under certain conditions they will not be bound by the Resolutions which they previously adopted at a Traffic Conference. It should be noted that the above-quoted grounds on which Traffic Conference members can take this action are very wide.

Government conditions and reservations can be divided into

three main groups:(31)

a) conditions ensuring that the provisions of Resolutions are not contrary to national legislations or rules made under such legislations. An example of this group are the numerous conditions relating to filing requirements under national regulations;

b) conditions aimed at protecting the aviation consumer. The conditions falling into this group are not very numerous;

c) conditions aimed at protecting the competitive position of national carriers being weakened. A standard example of this last group is the following reservation attached to many Resolutions:

> "Reservations and conditions which may be imposed by other Governments shall not affect the contents of this Resolution insofar as transportation to or from ... (the State making the condition) provided by ... (the national airline) is concerned."

In order to assist Governments in taking action on filed Traffic Conference Resolutions, paragraph 5 of the already mentioned Resolution 035 (Unethical Disclosure of Information) provides that, whereas in general it is not allowed to Traffic Conference members to disclose information or knowledge obtained as a result of their Traffic Conference membership, this rule does not prohibit members from disclosing such information to their Governments.

It has already been stated that in the past Government control of international ratemaking was weak or almost non-existent. As far as IATA fares and rates are concerned the control exercised by most Governments has been merely perfunctory. In addition hereto, most Government disapprovals or conditions to fares and rates Resolutions have been more inspired by the wish of Governments to protect the financial and other interests of their national flag carriers than those of their aviation consumers. These factors have resulted in a system of Government control of IATA fares and rates which has been of little or no avail to the aviation consumer.

In those instances where Governments have indeed controlled the level of IATA fares and rates, they have not only resorted to the use of Government disapprovals and conditions, a form of repressive control, but also to the system of pre-Conference briefings, a form of preventive control. In pre-Conference briefings Governmental aviation authorities instruct their national carrier(s) as to the level of fares and rates which they would like to see as the end result of a particular IATA Traffic Conference, or Conferences. Whether national carriers, members of IATA, are bound by such Governmental instructions during Traffic Conference negotiations, depends on the legal relationship between such carriers and their respective Governments. Generally speaking it can be said that whenever a particular IATA airline is more than fifty percent Government-owned, the Government's say in the internal business of that airline is big enough to consider the airline bound by the instructions of its Government. It should be noted that, in practice, strict and inflexible Governmental pre-Conference instructions tend to make the Traffic Conference negotiating process, after all a bargaining process working with a unanimity rule, most difficult.

III. The U.S. Civil Aeronautics Board

There are several reasons which warrant a thorough discussion of the control that the U.S.A., through its Civil Aeronautics Board, exercises over international ratemaking. In the opening sentences of this Chapter it was already mentioned that undoubtedly the U.S.A. is civil air power number one in the world. U.S. airlines perform some twenty-five percent of overall international air traffic.[32] It is, therefore, logical that the CAB's policy with respect to international air fares and rates has an important impact on the international tariff structure as such. The U.S. CAB also possesses a great deal of expertise in the regulation of international air fares and rates. This expertise was acquired in the regulation of U.S. domestic air fares and rates, and was later applied to the field of international fares and rates. Another important factor leading to a discussion of the CAB's tariff policy is that, of the world's regulatory aviation authorities, the CAB has probably been the most consumer oriented. In the words of Secor D. Browne, former CAB Chairman:

> "... our primary responsibility is the public's convenience and necessity for air transport of their persons and their goods. Our philosophy is that you need a healthy air transport industry to do that, but the public is first, the industry is second."[33]

Furthermore, the CAB has always been the sharpest critic of IATA.[34] Finally, in the field of international charter tariffs, the CAB has for a very long time favoured the development of cheap international air charter transportation.

In this paragraph the emphasis will be on CAB control of IATA agreed international air fares and rates. Until recently, the determination of other international air fares and rates, charter or non-IATA scheduled, was left by the CAB to the free forces of the market place. This was, as shall be seen hereunder, mainly due to a lack of CAB power over non-IATA international air fares and rates.

At the time of the conclusion of the 1946 Bermuda Agreement U.S. tariff regulation was exercised in accordance with the _Civil Aeronautics Act_ of 1938.[35] The tariff provisions of this _Act_ were _without change_ reenacted in the _Federal Aviation Act_ of 1958.[36] The first and only change in the tariff provisions of the Act did not take place until March 1972. Both under the pre- and post- 1972 version of the Act the power of the CAB over domestic air tariffs is stronger than over international air tariffs.

The situation which prevailed until March 1972 can be described as follows. Section 403(a) of the _Federal Aviation Act_[37] requires _all_ air carriers, whether American or foreign, whether domestic or international, to file their tariffs[38] with the CAB, and to print and keep open for public inspection all of such currently effective tariffs. Apart from the power which the CAB has under the same Section 403(a) of the Act to reject filed tariffs on procedural grounds, Section 1002(d) of the Act[39] empowers the Board to reject tariffs for _domestic_ air transportation, when it finds these tariffs to be "unjust or unreasonable, or unduly discriminatory, or unduly preferential, or unduly prejudicial". The Board then has the power "to prescribe lawful tariffs instead".[40] With respect to tariffs for _foreign_ air transportation, however, Section 1002(f) of the _Federal Aviation Act_[41] limits the Board's power to the removal of _discriminatory_ tariffs. This power over tariffs for foreign air transportation was not enlarged until 1972 when Subsection (j) was added to Section 1002. From 1946 to 1972 the CAB was thus faced with a very limited _direct_ power over international air fares and rates. The power embodied in Section 1002(f) can indeed be regarded as being so limited that in practice it is almost tantamount to a non-existing power.[42]

The reasons, why Congress in 1938 gave the CAB full power over domestic, but only very limited power over foreign air tariffs, are not very clear. One writer(43) seeks to answer this problem through a comparison with foreign shipping regulation:

> "Perhaps it /the reason/ lies in the historical development of our waterborne commerce, since rate regulation over shipping to foreign points has never been exercised by the Federal Government."

He then continues to say:

> "... it is possible that the Congress in adopting the Act /i.e., the Civil Aeronautics Act/ did not envisage the function presently performed by IATA in the fixing of common rates between international points."

The CAB itself remarks on the subject:(44)

> "The legislative history ... indicates that Congress was concerned about the complexity of international rate regulations and was not certain of the exact nature of statutory authority to grant in the area."

So much is sure that lack of CAB power over foreign air tariffs was in conformity with American international tariff policy at the time of the 1944 Chicago Conference. Although perhaps not directly opposed to a system of inter-carrier agreed international fares and rates, the Americans were at the time opposed to a system of international tariff control through an International Air Authority or otherwise.(45) It will, however, be recalled that in concluding the Bermuda Agreement, which would serve as an example for the majority of bilateral air transport agreements concluded by the U.S.A., the Americans gave up their opposition against international tariff control.(46) In fact, the Bermuda Agreement itself provides:

> "The Executive Branch of the Government of the United States agrees to use its best efforts to secure legislation empowering the aeronautical authorities of the United States to fix fair and economic rates for the transport of persons and property by air on international services and to suspend proposed rates in a manner comparable to that in which the Civil Aeronautics Board at present is empowered to act with respect to such rates for the transport of persons and property by air within the United States."(47)

It would not be until 1972, that the CAB was given this power, and then only in a somewhat weaker form.

To say that from 1946 until 1972 the CAB was powerless with regard to international air fares and rates would be incorrect. The CAB has always been able to control the bulk of international air fares and rates, namely, those agreed upon through the IATA ratemaking machinery. For that purpose the CAB has used and continues to use the provisions of Sections 412 and 414 of the Federal Aviation Act, described above.(48) Under these Sections all inter-carrier agreements, including those reached through IATA for the purpose of determining international fares and rates, are subject to CAB approval. Once approved by the Board, they are exempt from the operation of the U.S. antitrust laws. Whereas Section 1002(f) of the Federal Aviation Act gives the CAB only a very limited power over tariffs individually filed by air carriers for foreign air transportation, Section 412 gives the Board a much broader power over tariffs collectively files for foreign air transportation by IATA carriers, namely, the power to disapprove them. The extent of this power should nevertheless not be overestimated. Once the CAB has disapproved an IATA agreed tariff, IATA carriers are free to file new individual tariffs with the CAB, over which the Board has, under Section 1002(f), only a very limited say.(49) These individual tariffs may not be immune from the operation of the U.S. antitrust laws, but the decision to bring an antitrust action rests not with the CAB, but with the Justice Department.(50) It is, therefore, understandable that, at least until 1972, the CAB preferred the practice of conditionally approving IATA agreed rates and fares to a practice of disapproving them. With the limited power which the Board had until then, it is only logical that disapprovals of IATA fares and rates would, at the very best, result in a mere maintenance of the status quo. Conditional approvals on the other hand afforded the CAB continuing control possibility over the IATA ratemaking machinery, while at the same time they gave the Board the possibility to qualify IATA fares and rates Resolutions by its conditions and reservations.

The limited power of the CAB over international tariffs is now history. In March 1972, the "promise" contained in paragraph (j) of Annex II to the Bermuda Agreement was, at least partially, fulfilled. Public Law 92-259(51) added a new Subsection (j) to Section 1002 of the Federal Aviation Act.

The new Subsection is entitled: "Suspension and Rejection of Rates in Foreign Air Transportation". It empowers the CAB to suspend and reject tariffs for foreign air transportation and thereby places the Board in a much stronger position than the one it was in in the international field before March 1972, when it was only empowered to remove discriminatory tariffs for foreign air transportation. It should be noted that the new legislation does not give the CAB the power to prescribe tariffs for foreign air transportation, i.e., the power that the CAB has over tariffs for domestic air transportation.

Legislation similar to that now contained in Section 1002(j) had been proposed by the CAB several times.(52) What finally caused Congress to pass this legislation was an impending open-fare situation on the North Atlantic for 1972 and objections to the filing by Lufthansa of low excursion fares from the U.S.A. to Germany.(53)

The aim of the new legislation was described as:

> "... to enable the Board to protect travellers, shippers and U.S. air carriers. This new authority would be a discretionary power for the Board, and, when exercised, would be subject to disapproval by the President.(54) Air carriers and foreign air carriers engaged in foreign air transportation would have the duty to establish just and reasonable rates and practices.(55) The objective of the air transportation policy of the U.S. is to provide a system of reasonable rates. Both the interests of consumers and the carriers must be taken into account to achieve this goal. The bill would allow the continuation of the present mechanism for establishing international air transportation fares through the International Air Transport Association (IATA). Under this bill, the Board would be able to suspend and reject fares, rates and practices which are either too high or too low from the standpoint of carrier economic viability. Through the legislation the CAB will have authority more closely equal to that presently held by other nations as to control over international air fares."(56)

Subsection (j) of Section 1002 of the FAA is divided into five paragraphs:

Paragraph 1 empowers the Board to order hearings, with notice, concerning the lawfulness of the rate, fare of classification. Pending the outcome of the hearing, the Board is authorized to suspend and defer the use of such rate, fare or classification for a maximum period of 365 days beyond the effective date. If after hearing, the CAB finds such rate or fare to be "unjust or unreasonable, or unjustly discriminatory, or unduly preferential, or unduly prejudicial" it may reject the tariff and thus, the use of the rate, fare or classification. During the period following suspension or rejection, the affected carrier must operate under the tariff in effect immediately prior to the filing of the new tariff.

Paragraph 2 empowers the Board with similar suspension and rejection authority over existing rates and fares.

Paragraph 3 contains retaliatory provisions for dealing with cases in which a foreign Government has refused to permit an air carrier to charge rates and fares contained in a tariff properly filed with the CAB. Without a hearing, the CAB may suspend the tariff of that country's carrier for up to 365 days, and order such carrier to operate at rates contained in a properly filed tariff of another air carrier. In addition, the foreign carrier's right to operate in the U.S. is conditional upon the right of the U.S. carriers to operate in such foreign country at the CAB's designated tariffs.

Paragraph 4 provides that compliance with the provisions of Subsection (j) and any Board Order issued pursuant thereto is an express condition to the continuance of a permit of any air carrier or foreign air carrier.

Paragraph 5 finally lists factors that the CAB must consider in the exercise of its newly granted authority. These factors are a compilation of Administration and CAB views on tariff policy, including the need for low cost, efficient transportation, at tariffs neither predatory nor monopolistic.(57)

It should be borne in mind that Subsection (j) of Section 1002 not only gives the CAB an enlarged power over IATA fares and rates, but also and above all that it gives the Board, and this for the first time, an effective control over non-IATA international air fares and rates. Soon after the promulgation of Section 1002(j) a conflict arose over the exact extent of the power conferred upon the CAB under the new Subsection. The conflict was related to the Board's plan to issue guidelines for minimum North Atlantic charter fares. Were these intended guidelines tantamount to prescribing fares, a power not given to the Board in Subsection (j)? This question will be further discussed in Chapter VI, paragraph II.

After the above discussion of U.S. legislation regarding international air tariffs, one should now examine, how the 1972 legislation, laid down in Section 1002(j) of the Federal Aviation Act, influences the so-called alternate rate clauses of the Bermuda Agreement(58) and of the majority of other bilateral air transport agreements concluded by the U.S.A. These alternate rate clauses are applicable in cases, where there is no IATA ratemaking machinery available, where the Traffic Conferences are unable to agree on rates and fares, or where Governments disapprove IATA rates and fares or fail to renew their approval of the IATA ratemaking machinery. The relevant bilateral air transport agreements contain two alternate procedures which may be followed in these cases. The first procedure, the type (e) procedure is to be followed

> "in the event that power is conferred by law upon the aeronautical authorities of the U.S. to fix fair and

economic rates for the transport of persons and property by air on international services and to suspend proposed rates in a manner comparable to that in which the CAB at present is empowered to act with respect to such rates for the transport of persons and property by air within the U.S."(59)

The second procedure, the type (f) procedure, is to be followed

"prior to the time when such power may be conferred by law upon the aeronautical authorities of the U.S."(60)

The main difference between the two procedures is that in the event of Governments disagreeing on the rates and fares to be charged by their designated air carriers on the routes specified in the bilateral agreement, the former allows the disputed rates and fares to go into effect provisionally pending the settlement of any dispute in accordance with the arbitration clause contained in the bilateral agreement,(61) whereas the latter allows the Government raising the objection to the rate or fare to take such steps as it may consider necessary to prevent the inauguration or continuation of the service in question at the rate or fare complained of. The type (e) procedure is more favourable for a Government that wants to put into effect <u>lower</u> tariffs than the ones previously effective, whereas the type (f) procedure is more favourable for a Government that wants to put into effect <u>higher</u> tariffs than the ones previously effective. This is because the type (f) procedure allows suspension of the disputed tariffs whereas the type (e) procedure does not allow this. When a proposed low tariff cannot be suspended - type (e) procedure - this gives a clear competitive advantage to the carrier that puts the low tariff into effect. Other carriers will almost automatically be forced to match this competitive advantage, so that the low tariff is likely to become the ultimate one. When a proposed low tariff <u>can</u> be suspended - type (f) procedure - such a competitive advantage <u>will</u> not occur. When a proposed high tariff cannot be suspended - type (e) procedure - then the carrier that introduces the high fare will be at a competitive disadvantage in relation to the carrier that continues to use the old, low tariff. Finally, when a proposed high tariff <u>can</u> be suspended - type (f) procedure - then again such a competitive disadvantage will not occur.

At Bermuda the U.S.A. was in favour of the type (e) procedure, while the U.K. was in favour of the type (f) procedure. The result was the compromise above.(62) At the time that the Bermuda Agreement was concluded, the U.S.A. favoured lower and Great Britain higher tariffs.

Section 1002 (j) of the FAA gives the CAB the power to suspend and reject tariffs for foreign air transportation, but not the full power to prescribe c.q. fix them. Therefore, just as before the introduction of Subsection (j), the type (f) procedure must be deemed to remain in force in the Bermuda type bilateral air transport agreements between the U.S.A. and other countries.

A number of bilateral air transport agreements concluded by the U.S.A. in later years <u>only</u> contain the type (f) procedure.(63) This procedure can thus be regarded as being the generally applicable provision in force under the bilateral air transport agreements concluded by the U.S.A. It should be remarked that, although the type (f) procedure allows a Governmental aviation authority "to take such steps as it may consider necessary to prevent the inauguration or continuation of the service in question at the rate complained of ", it was held in the U.S.A. that this internationally conferred power was not enough to give the CAB the power to suspend and reject international air fares and rates, as long as such power had not been conferred upon the Board through U.S. domestic aviation legislation.(64) As discussed above, such power was finally conferred upon the CAB in March 1972 in Public Law 92-259. Why Confress did not go further in 1972 and did not give the Board real rate-fixing power, is explained in a CAB Order of October, 1973:(65)

> "... For the agency was still denied the ultimate regulatory tool - the power to prescribe rates - because Congress believed that in a political and diplomatic sense it would be very difficult if not impossible for the U.S. to directly impose prescribed rates and fares on foreign nations and their carriers (S. Rept. No. 92-593, 92nd Cong., 2nd Sess., p. 8). And the Congress specifically envisaged maintaining the present mechanisms for establishing international air transportation rates through IATA (id. at 5)."

In concluding this paragraph, a few words should be said about the U.S. philosophy of Government regulation of civil aviation. All U.S. airlines, whether domestic or international, are privately-owned(66) and live under a system of "regulated competition". On the one hand, all U.S. airlines are economically regulated by an independent Government agency, the CAB. On the other hand, this agency

> "In the exercise of its powers and duties ..."

shall allow

> "... competition to the extent necessary to assure the sound development of an air transportation system properly adapted to the needs of the foreign and domestic commerce of the United States, of the Postal Service, and of the national defence ..."(67)

It seems that during recent years, more emphasis is being laid on the importance of competition than on that of regulation in U.S. air transportation policy. In a Report, published in July 1975,(68) a special CAB study group proposed to "deregulate" the U.S. domestic airline industry in favour of more competition between U.S. domestic airlines. Amongst the specific proposals put forward in the Report was a gradual abolition of entry and price control in U.S. domestic air transportation regulation.(69) The proposals were preceded by Hearings (<u>Oversight of CAB Practices and Procedures</u>) before the Subcommittee on Administrative Practice and Procedure of the U.S. Senate Judiciary Committee.(70) They were followed by draft legislation sent to Congress by President Ford on October 8, 1975.(71) The proposed legislation took over many of the CAB's special staff proposals but limited itself, like the special staff Report, to the regulation of U.S. domestic air transportation.(72) New legislative deregulation proposals were sent to Congress by Senators Cannon and Kennedy in January 1977.

In the international air transportation field a study by the U.S. Departments of State and Transportation has culminated in a new <u>U.S. Statement on International Air Transportation Policy</u>, approved by President Ford on September 8, 1976 and replacing the Nixon policy Statement of 1970.(73) Although somewhat reluctantly, the Statement endorses the present system of international ratemaking through IATA and otherwise. Even if the U.S.A. is the biggest aviation power in the world, it could not easily abandon its support of IATA's ratemaking machinery, when the Governments of other nations do not want to follow suit. Indeed, at the present time most nations of the world still seem to be committed to a continuing use of IATA for international ratemaking purposes.(74)

(1) Pillai, *op.cit.*, at 2.

(2) See also, Hammarskjöld, *The Challenging Years Ahead for the World Air Transport Industry*, Address before the American Institute of Aeronautics and Astronautics, Commercial Aircraft Design and Operations Meeting, Los Angeles, June 13, 1967; Lissitzyn, in *Freedom of the Air*, ed. by McWhinney and Bradley, Sijthoff, Leiden/Oceana Publications, Dobbs Ferry, N.Y. at 98 (1968).

(3) On public utilities generally, see *Encyclopaedia Britannica*, Vol. 18 (1968).

(4) In the USA for railways the *Interstate Commerce Commission* (ICC) and for telephone companies the *Federal Communications Commission* (FCC).

(5) On the CAB see *infra*, para. III.

(6) In particular its *Air Transport Committee* (ATC).

(7) On Government ownership of IATA airlines in general, see *supra*, Ch. II, para. I.

(8) For the USA, see Sections 401, 402 and 801 of the *Federal Aviation Act*, 72 Stat. 731, as amended, 49 U.S.C. 1371, 1372, 1461.

(9) For the USA, see *infra*, para. III. For a survey of powers of other Governments with respect to international air fares and rates, see *Hearings before the Subcomm. on Aviation of the Comm. on Commerce*, US Senate, 92nd Cong., 1st Sess., on S.2423, Serial No. 92-40 (1971) at 37-39, and *Hearings before the Subcomm. on Transportation and Aeronautics of the Comm. on Interstate and Foreign Commerce*, US House of Representatives, 92nd Cong., 1st Sess., on H.R. 11416 and H.R. 11825, Serial No. 92-52 (1971) at 83-84.

(10) See *infra*, para. II.

(11) See *infra*, Ch. VI, para. II.

(12) See *supra*, Ch. I, para. II.

(13) Cf. Thornton, *Governments and Airlines*, 25 International Organizations 541 (1971).

(14) Direct and indirect subsidization of international air transport should be distinguished. The latter form of subsidization is generally accepted and consists of the subsidization of the infrastructure of international air transport, e.g., the subsidization of airport and air traffic control facilities. Financial Governmental guarantees to international airlines can be seen as a borderline case between direct and indirect subsidization.

(15) On public utility pricing see Bonbright, *Principles of Public Utility Rates*, Columbia Univ. Press, New York, 1961; Trebing, *Essays on Public Utility Pricing and Regulation*, Institute of Public Utilities, Graduate School of Business Administration, Michigan State Univ., 1971; See also: *CAB General Passenger Fare Investigation*, Order E-16068, Nov. 25, 1960 and *CAB Domestic Passenger Fare Investigation*, Docket 21866, especially Phase 8 (Rate of Return, Order 71-4-58, April 9, 1971,) and Phase 9 (Fare Structure, Order 74-3-82, March 18, 1974, and Order 74-12-109, Dec. 27, 1974). On the Domestic Passenger Fare Investigation, see also, Keyes, *Policy Innovations in the Domestic Passenger Fare Investigation*, 41 JALC 75 (1975).

(16) See generally, Agreeing Fares and Rates, op.cit., at 73 et seq.
(17) See supra, Ch. I, para. II.
(18) See supra, para. I (U.S. House and Senate Hearings 1971, op.cit.).
(19) See supra, Ch. III, para. II, with respect to US CAB approval of changes in IATA's Arts. of Assoc. (1974) and Provs. R. & C. IATA TCs (1973).
(20) See supra, Ch. III, para. III.
(21) The expiry date can be definite or indefinite.
(22) Res. 001(3).
(23) Res. 008.
(24) Res. 001(10)(11).
(25) Res. 001(4).
(26) For U.S. filing regulations see Section 403 of the Federal Aviation Act, 72 Stat. 731, as amended, 49 U.S.C. 1373.
(27) Res. 001(6).
(28) Res. 001(B).
(29) Res. 001(7).
(30) See infra, Ch. VI, para. IV.
(31) Cf. Agreeing Fares and Rates, op.cit., at 74 et seq.
(32) See, A Review of the Economic Situation of Air Transport (1963-1973), op.cit., at 15 et seq.
(33) House Hearings 1971, op.cit., at 34.
(34) A good general, although somewhat outdated analysis of CAB-IATA relations is contained in Bebchick, The International Air Transport Association and the Civil Aeronautics Board, 25 JALC 5 (1958); for a list of CAB disapprovals of IATA Traffic Conference Resolutions see Senate Hearings, 1971, op.cit., at 23-24; on the CAB itself see Burkhardt, CAB - The Civil Aeronautics Board, The Greenhills Publishing Co., Dulles Int. Airport, Va., 1974.
(35) Act of June 23, 1938, 52 Stat. 973.
(36) Act of August 23, 1958, 72 Stat. 731.
(37) 49 U.S.C. 1373.
(38) "Rates tariffs" and "rules tariffs" containing rates, fares and charges for air transportation and also classifications, rules, regulations, practices and services in relation to such air transportation.
(39) 49 U.S.C. 1482.
(40) See generally, Garsek, Summary Power of the Civil Aeronautics Board to Suspend Proposed Airlines Rates, 39 JALC 267 (1973).
(41) 49 U.S.C. 1482.
(42) On one occasion, CAB Chairman Browne announced the Board's intention to use its Section 1002(f) authority with respect to the alleged discriminatory character of, i.a., youth and student fares. See Senate Hearings 1971, op.cit., at 25.
(43) Rentzel, U.S. Regulation and the CAB. The Position of the Civil Aeronautics Board in American Government Tradition and Structure, 13 IATA Bull. 21 at 30 (June 1951).
(44) See Order 71-10-72, Oct. 18, 1971, at 4, nt. 7.
(45) See supra, Ch. I, para. I.
(46) See supra, Ch. I, para. II.
(47) Paragraph (j) of Annex II to the Bermuda Agreement, TIAS 1507.
(48) See supra, Ch. II, para. II.
(49) The extent of CAB power over disapproved IATA fares, both under the Bermuda Agreement and the Federal Aviation Act, was examined in detail in the so-called Chandler Fare Controversy of 1962/1963. See infra, Ch. VII, para. II.
(50) CAB Regulation of International Aviation, 75 Harvard L.R. 580 (1961/1962).

(51) 92nd Cong., H.R. 854, March 1, 1972, 86 Stat. 95. For the legislative history, purpose and background of the Act see: House and Senate Hearings 1971, op.cit.; US Code Congressional and Administrative News, April 20, 1972, No. 3, pp. 806-810 and 968-975; The Ins and Outs of IATA: Improving the Role of the United States in the Regulation of International Air Fares, 81 Yale L.J. 1102 (1971/1972); Public Law 92-259: New CAB Authority Over International Air Fares, 5 N.Y.U. Journal of International Law and Politics 281 (1973).

(52) For a summary of efforts of the CAB to obtain legislation authorizing it to regulate rates, fares and practices in foreign air transportation see House Hearings 1971, op.cit., at 23-24.

(53) See U.S. Code Congressional and Administrative News, at 969, and infra, Ch. VII, para. III.

(54) See Section 2 of Public Law 92-259 adding a new Subsection (b) to Section 801 of the Federal Aviation Act, 49, U.S.C. 1461. This new Subsection provides that any Order of the CAB suspending or rejecting a rate, fare or charge for foreign air transportation must be submitted to the President, before publication. The President is empowered to disapprove such Order, not later than ten days following submission by the Board of any such Order to the President, for reasons of the national defence or the foreign policy of the United States.

(55) See Section 1 of Public Law 92-259 amending Section 404(a) of the Federal Aviation Act, 49 U.S.C. 1374.

(56) House Report (Interstate and Foreign Commerce Comm.) No. 92-854, Feb. 24, 1972 (To accompany H.R. 11416); See U.S. Code Congressional and Administrative News, op.cit., at 968-969.

(57) Cf. Public Law 92-259: New CAB Authority Over International Air Fares, op.cit., at 289-299.

(58) See supra, Ch. I, para. II, and also US House and Senate Hearings 1971, op.cit., at, i.a., 22-23, 88 et seq. (House Hearings) and at 20 et seq., 200-201 (Senate Hearings).

(59) Paragraph (e) of Annex II to the Bermuda Agreement, TIAS 1507.

(60) Paragraph (f) of Annex II to the Bermuda Agreement, TIAS 1507.

(61) Paragraph (g) of Annex II to the Bermuda Agreement, TIAS 1507.

(62) See Statement of Tipton, President of the Air Transport Association of America (ATA), in Senate Hearings 1971, op.cit., at 200.

(63) See, e.g., Handbook on Administrative Clauses in Bilateral Air Transport Agreements, op.cit.; Non-scheduled Air Service Agreements concluded by the U.S.A., supra, Ch. I, para. II; Tariff Clauses in Bilateral Agreements, ICAO Doc. AT-WP/1207, Attachment (1975).

(64) See the discussion of the Chandler Fare Controversy, infra, Ch. VII, para. II.

(65) Order 73-10-55, Oct. 15, 1973, at 13-14.

(66) See infra, Appendix A.

(67) Section 102(d) Federal Aviation Act, 72 Stat. 731, as amended, 49 U.S.C. 1302.

(68) Regulatory Reform, Report of the CAB special staff, op.cit.

(69) Ibidem, at 246 et seq. See also Papers presented to the Symposium on "The Effect of Federal Regulation on Air Transportation", The Univ. of Akron, Nov. 13-14, 1975; reprinted in 9 Akron Law Review 629-671 (1976).

(70) The so-called "Kennedy Hearings", Hearings before the Subcomm. on Administrative Practice and Procedure, Comm. on the Judiciary, U.S. Senate, 93rd Cong., 2nd Sess., Feb. 6, 14, 18, 19, 25 and 26, March 4 and 21, 1975 (3 Vols. and 4 Vols. Appendices). See also Report of the Subcomm., U.S. Senate, 94th Cong., 1st Sess., 1976.

(71) Aviation Act of 1975; see S. 2551, 94th Cong., 1st Sess., and DOT News 83-75, Oct. 8, 1975; see also H.R. 1026, 94th Cong., 1st Sess.

(72) S. 2551 would, for instance, amend section 412 of the Federal Aviation Act (49 U.S.C. 1382) so as to make CAB approval of inter-carrier agreements in US domestic air transportation more difficult (proposed Subsections (c) and (d) of the new Section 412). The CAB's power to approve inter-carrier agreements in international air transportation would, however, not be amended (proposed Sub-section (e) of the new Section 412).

(73) US Statement on International Air Transportation Policy, approved by President Ford on September 8, 1976.

(74) On the possible impact of US deregulation proposals on international civil aviation see Haanappel, Deregulation of the United States System of Government Regulation of Domestic Civil Aviation in Light of the Overall Structure of International Civil Aviation, 9 Akron Law Review 651 (1976).

CHAPTER V: THE MAKING OF IATA FARES AND RATES

Having discussed the organizational structure of the Traffic Conferences,[1] IATA's ratemaking machinery, attention will now be focussed on how, according to which principles and practices, IATA actually determines international air fares and rates.

Many of these principles and practices can be found in Traffic Conference Resolutions 010-049.[2] In dealing with passenger fares, the subject of paragraph I of this Chapter, special attention will be paid to the question, whether IATA in its ratemaking practices has given enough consideration to the economic phenomenon of demand elasticity. What will be said about elasticity of demand in relation to passenger fares, can *mutatis mutandis* be applied to the sector of cargo rates, the subject of paragraph II. In a third paragraph the problem of IATA currency questions will be dealt with separately. Such a special place for currency matters is justified, if one considers that the whole IATA tariff structure has traditionally been based upon the fixed values of the U.S. Dollar and the British Pound Sterling. Now that the era of fixed currency conversion rates seems to be history, IATA will have to find a new, stable monetary standard for the fixing of its international air tariffs.

At the outset it should be mentioned that *formally* all IATA agreed fares and rates are *minimum* fares and rates.[3] In principle, IATA carriers are free to charge higher fares and rates than the ones agreed upon through the IATA Traffic Conference machinery and approved by Governments. For two reasons, however, IATA carriers will seldom or never do so in practice. The first reason is economic in nature, and the second relates to the regulatory aviation systems of many countries. Economically, IATA carriers cannot afford to charge higher tariffs than the minimum tariffs agreed upon in the Traffic Conferences. All IATA carriers basically offer the same *undifferentiated* product, i.e., rapid point-to-point transportation. When an IATA carrier begins charging a higher price for that product than do its fellow member airlines, it would automatically put itself into an impossible competitive position. Passengers and shippers would simply ignore this carrier and prefer the others. In addition hereto, once IATA airlines have had their IATA agreed tariffs approved by the various interested Governments, these tariffs become, in the regulatory aviation systems of many nations, the *actual*, Governmentally sanctioned tariffs. Therefore, one can say that the *minimum* IATA fares and rates in practice always become the actual, *uniform* fares and rates.

Before continuing, this would perhaps be the appropriate place to make a short comparison between the IATA ratemaking machinery and the maritime Shipping Conferences.[4] Whereas the IATA Traffic Conferences constitute the only available machinery in the world for the determination of international air tariffs, there is a multitude of Shipping Conferences for the determination of maritime shipping tariffs. In 1972, there were about 360 different Conferences operating on the various shipping markets of the world.(5) The first such Conference was created in 1875 shortly after the inauguration of regular steamship lines, for the maritime trade between the U.K. and Calcutta (India). Shipping Conferences can be defined as groups of liners operating on routes with basic agreements to charge uniform rates.(6) Each Shipping Conference has its own charter, rules and regulations. A common element in all Conferences is that they fix rates for maritime carriage between certain points. Sometimes these rates are uniform, sometimes they are minimum rates. Some Conferences work with a unanimity rule, others with a majority voting rule. Many Conferences go further than the determination of rates alone, and also provide for a pooling of cargo or revenue.(7) Furthermore, many Shipping Conferences have rather restrictive provisions as to the admission of new member liners, and can as such be qualified as <u>closed</u> trade associations. IATA, as noted earlier,(8) is an <u>open</u> trade association. Inasmuch as Shipping Conferences go further than the determination of rates alone and/or have restrictive membership policies, they are even more competition restricting than IATA. On the other hand, it should be remembered that in ocean shipping there is a considerable amount of competition between different Shipping Conferences amongst themselves. Such competition is absent in the case of international air transport, where there is only one worldwide Conference machinery, the IATA Traffic Conference machinery. Genuine outside competition, however, is both present in ocean shipping and in international air transport. IATA is only concerned with <u>scheduled</u> international air fares and rates. International <u>charter</u> air fares and rates are <u>grosso modo</u> determined by the free forces of the market place. They compete directly with the scheduled international IATA air fares and rates. In ocean shipping the Shipping Conferences are only concerned with rates for maritime carriage by <u>liners</u>. Rates charged by so-called <u>tramps</u>, the maritime equivalent of charters, are not regulated through Shipping Conferences, and compete with inter-liner agreed Conference rates.

Whereas there are thus both parallels and differences between the IATA Traffic Conferences and the Maritime Shipping Conferences, one should be careful in putting the two systems on an equal footing. Although both systems deal with the determination of prices for international transportation, they do not exactly cover the transportation of the same commodities. Until approximately 1950, liners transported the bulk of both intercontinental cargo and passenger traffic. Since 1950, however, the carriage of most intercontinental passenger traffic has gradually been taken over by the airlines. At the present time, liners almost exclusively transport cargo. Consequently the Shipping Conferences are primarily concerned with the determination of <u>cargo rates</u>. Notwithstanding the fact that the carriage of air cargo is becoming increasingly important for the airlines, the bulk of international air traffic still consists of passengers.(9) Consequently the IATA Traffic Conferences are primarily concerned with the determination of <u>passenger fares</u>.

Another important reason why the IATA Traffic Conferences and the maritime Shipping Conferences cannot be put on an equal footing, is that the two systems function in an entirely different institutional framework. International air transport functions within the rather rigid framework of bilateral air transport agreements.(10) Ocean shipping is by and large free from Government regulation and intervention. Most States maintain an "open port" policy. This policy has almost become a rule of customary international shipping law. In a number of instances this "open port" policy has been laid down in international agreements between states.(11) Very few Governments exercise effective economic control over international shipping. Furthermore, unlike the scheduled international IATA airlines, the majority of liners is entirely privately-owned.(12) The only nation, which through an independent regulatory authority, the Federal Maritime Commission (FMC), exercises some form of comprehensive control over international shipping, is the U.S.A.(13)

In conclusion, it can be said that the Maritime Shipping Conferences, which have now been in existence for just over a century, may have served as a model for the IATA Traffic Conferences and that there exist certain organizational and functional parallels between the two systems of Conferences. No true comparison, however, is possible between the two systems of Conferences, since they deal basically with different commodities and live under a different institutional framework.

I. Passenger Fares(14)

IATA passenger fares fall into two groups: normal fares and special fares. Special fares are lower in price than normal fares. Both groups include for each passenger a certain free allowance for baggage accompanying him.(15) Normal fares are of two types: first class(16) and economy class.(17) There is no fixed percentage differential between first and economy class fares. The differential varies from market to market. Normal first and economy class fares are either specifically determined by the appropriate Traffic Conference or Joint Traffic Conference meeting, or they are calculated by the IATA carriers themselves in accordance with the passenger fare construction rules of Resolution 014A.(18) The former fares are called specified fares and the latter additional fares. Since it would be impracticable for the Traffic Conferences to determine explicitly the fares between every single point on the globe served by an IATA airline, the system has been adopted, whereby the Traffic Conferences determine only a certain number of specified fares for travel between certain points, usually key points, and leave the determination of fares between other points to the IATA carriers themselves. In calculating these additional fares, which are basically a combination of specified fares, the IATA airlines then have to follow the construction rules of above-mentioned Resolution 014A.(19) Most normal fares are valid throughout the year. One important exception is the North Atlantic market, where there are seasonal variations in normal fares. On the North Atlantic air routes there are low, shoulder and peak season fares.

A new variety of IATA normal fares has recently been introduced. This class of fares is a first class fare applicable to all travel on the supersonic Concorde. For travel by Concorde IATA airlines' passengers will have to pay a twenty percent surcharge on normal first class fares. An agreement to that effect was reached at a special IATA Traffic Conference held at Cannes on October 2, 1975.(20) The twenty percent surcharge should be seen as a compromise between the "haves" and the "have nots", or in other words as a compromise basically between Air France and British Airways on the one hand, and the remaining IATA airlines on the other. Air France and British Airways wanted the Concorde surcharge to be as low as possible in order to attract as many passengers as they could for their supersonic air services. On the contrary, the majority of IATA airlines which do not possess Concordes, wanted that surcharge to be as high as possible in order to avoid too large a diversion of first class passengers from regular subsonic flights to supersonic flights. Since regular first class fares only come within the financial capability of a very small segment of the travelling public, the same holds *a fortiori* true for Concorde passengers. Apart from certain business travellers and high Governmental officials the Concorde may be used by members of the so-called "Jet set", but certainly not by the average pleasure traveller. It remains to be seen, whether, especially on the North Atlantic market, the Air France and British Airways Concorde services will divert so much first class travel from regular subsonic flights to supersonic Concorde flights that Air France and British Airways themselves, and possibly other North Atlantic air carriers will do away with first class service on regular subsonic flights.

British Airways inaugurated Concorde flights from London to Bahrain on January 21, 1976. On the same date Air France opened its Paris - Rio de Janeiro Concorde line. Concorde services by Air France and British Airways from Paris and London to both New York (John F. Kennedy Airport) and Washington, D.C. (Dulles Airport) were due to begin by the end of May, 1976. Over strong anti-noise and anti-pollution objections, U.S. Secretary of Transportation, William Coleman, gave the go-ahead for two daily Concorde flights to Dulles Airport and four daily Concorde flights to John F. Kennedy Airport on February 4, 1976. This permission was valid for a sixteen months trial period.(21) Inaugural flights into Dulles Airport were performed on May 24, 1976. Concorde flights to John F. Kennedy Airport have been postponed indefinitely due to pending judicial and administrative procedures over the noise and environmental impact of Concorde services to New York. A pro-Concorde decision of the U.S.D.C., S.D.N.Y., is presently in appeal.

During recent years more and more <u>special fares</u>(22) have been introduced by IATA. In order to be eligible for a special fare a passenger must satisfy certain eligibility requirements. He must either belong to a certain class of people -e.g., student, youth, pilgrim, family, senior citizen, teacher, military, ships' crew, group, affinity group fares- , or his trip must be of a certain duration (excursion fares). In order to be eligible for individual or group inclusive tour fares the passenger must buy a certain number of land arrangements together with his air travel. Some special fares are limited to certain times of the day or week: night fares and a certain number of excursion fares. Some excursion fares are valid all year round, others only during specific seasons, during mid-week or the weekend. The very popular North Atlantic excursion fares are, like the normal North Atlantic fares, seasonal in nature. Prices differ from low to shoulder and peak seasons. A surcharge is applicable, when North Atlantic excursion fares are used during weekends. The latest special fare, the Advance Purchase Excursion Fare (APEX) is an excursion fare combined with an advance booking and payment requirement. The APEX fare is clearly meant as the "scheduled" answer to the "non-scheduled" Advance Booking (ABC) or Travel Group Charter (TGC).(23) This then leads to the general observation that undoubtedly many special fares have been introduced by IATA specifically to combat charter competition. Another reason for IATA to introduce special fares is simply to fill up empty aircraft seats, especially in times of serious overcapacity. Group, affinity group, inclusive tour and APEX fares must definitely be regarded as combatting charter.(24)

Most special fares are agreed upon in specified amounts. Some are in the form of percentage reductions from normal fares. Special fares are more readily available in some areas of the world than in others.(25) Their percentage relationship to normal economy fares also differs from area to area.(26) The area in the world, where special fares are most widely available and where their differential with normal economy fares is extremely high (45 to 50 percent) is the North Atlantic.[27] The North Atlantic market is precisely the market, where inter-carrier IATA competition plus charter competition is at its keenest. In that market the availability of special fares is so great that, in 1973, only 23 percent of the North Atlantic IATA airlines' passengers were travelling on normal fares.[28] On the North Atlantic market and possibly elsewhere the point has been reached, where the normal fare paying passenger - generally the business traveller, unable to comply with the eligibility requirements attached to special fares - is as it were, subsidizing the special fare paying passenger - generally, the pleasure traveller, able and willing to comply with the eligibility requirements. Such a fare system may be beneficial to the pleasure traveller, but in fact discriminates against the business traveller. Granted that special fares are a useful means to fill up empty seats, they should not undermine the basic fare structure.[29] It is submitted that such a basic fare structure should in principle be based on a uniform rate per passenger kilometre plus a standard percentage discount for distance taper. IATA alleges that this principle is indeed being used in determining fares,[30] but exceptions to the rule have become so numerous that they have really undermined it. An ideal fare structure should indeed consist of normal fares based on a standard rate per kilometre flown, together with a standard reduction for distance taper. A rational and limited system of special fares should then be found giving a standard reduction from normal fares. The standard rate per kilometre flown and the standard reduction for special fares may, however, differ from area to area, depending on marketing, competitive and geographical conditions.[31] Once a formula for the calculation of a standard rate per kilometre and a standard reduction for special fares have been found for a certain area, this would also make it considerably easier for Governments to control IATA fares. They could simply check the actual IATA fares against the adopted standard rate per kilometre and the standard reduction for special fares. Governments could, together with the IATA airlines, even play a role in the determination of those standard rates and reductions.[32]

The determination of a normal or special IATA fare or of a standard rate per kilometre flown should always be based upon three factors: costs of operation, competition and demand elasticity in the relevant market.[33] Present IATA ratemaking practices certainly take into account the first two factors: costs of operation and competition. The IATA Cost Committee[34] makes detailed studies of the operation costs of the IATA airlines. The costs statistics gathered by the Committee are used by the Traffic Conferences in trying to reach unanimous inter-carrier agreement on tariffs. A survey of IATA fares and rates[35] adequately shows that the question of competition is also given ample consideration in determining IATA tariffs. Competition may be of two sorts: competition by other modes of transportation - rail, road, bus, ship, private car - or competition by charter air transportation. In general it can be said that the stronger outside competition is, the lower IATA tariffs will tend to be. One finds relatively low IATA tariffs especially in markets, where air charter competition is strong. The prime example is the North Atlantic market. Nowhere in the world is charter competition so strong as there. Nowhere in the world are fare and rate levels so low.[36]

Demand elasticity is the factor which is not sufficiently considered by IATA in determining air tariffs. It may be true that demand elasticity is hard to quantify and, therefore, hard to use as a ratemaking factor. On the other hand, however, it remains an important factor, certainly in times of rising air tariffs. In recent years, IATA tariffs have indeed been on the rise. Whereas for many years, air tariffs have actually been falling, mainly due to the introduction of larger and more efficient aircraft, the situation began to change in the early seventies.(37) Since that time, air tariffs have been rising, although still at a slower pace than the general consumer index. Amongst other things, general inflation, the introduction of wide-bodies jets - Boeing 747, DC 10 and L 1011 - depression, a smaller growth in air traffic than anticipated, and above all, sharply risen fuel prices(38) have been responsible for this tariff increase. Inflation and higher fuel prices have led to a direct increase in the airlines' operating costs. The world depression or recession, in its turn, led to a slower increase in air traffic than anticipated, with serious consequences for the airlines' load factors, and still further aggravated by a large increase in capacity resulting from the introduction of wide-bodies jets. All this then indirectly led to higher operating costs. IATA's answer to all these rising operating costs has been tariff increases. These increases, however, might lead to an even slower growth in air traffic, a more serious overcapacity problem, lower load factors, rising operating costs and finally again to higher tariffs. Whether this vicious circle is indeed in conformity with economic reality, depends precisely on the question, whether demand for air transportation is elastic or inelastic. Demand elasticity can be described as the reaction of a percentage change in demand to a percentage change in price. When a change in price leads to a proportionally greater change in demand, demand is considered to be elastic. When a change in price leads to a proportionally equal or smaller change in demand, demand is considered to be inelastic. Mathematically expressed:

$$E = \frac{\Delta d}{\Delta p} \cdot \frac{p}{d}$$

whereby E = elasticity coefficient
Δ = change
d = demand
p = price

An example of an elastic demand:

$$E = \frac{+15}{-\$20} \cdot \frac{\$100}{50} = -1\tfrac{1}{2}$$

An example of an inelastic demand:

$$E = \frac{+5}{-\$20} \cdot \frac{\$100}{50} = -\tfrac{1}{2}$$

In mathematical terms demand is elastic, when, in absolute terms,(39) E is greater than 1.

Should the general demand for air transportation prove to be elastic, then a tariff increase will lead to a proportionally larger decrease in demand. Similarly, a tariff decrease will then lead to a proportionally larger increase in demand. This larger demand for air transportation might in its turn lead to better load factors for the airlines and in the end to a better financial situation for them. Lowering air tariffs or keeping them at a constant level might, in this hypothesis, be a solution to the present overcapacity problem faced by the airlines. It could also put an end to the above-described vicious circle. Above all, it would be to the benefit of the airline user.

Very few studies have been made of demand ealsticity in (international) air transport.(40) As early as 1965, however, an ICAO study(41) concluded that the demand elasticity coefficient for both domestic and international air transport is as high as -2. This figure, of course, is an overall one, and it is probably justified to say that the actual coefficient will vary from market to market. The coefficient is likely to be higher in pleasure travel than in business travel markets. Businessmen can be expected to be willing to pay the "highest fares that the market will bear". For them, time - the speed of air travel - is more important than money. Pleasure travellers, on the other hand, will tend to balance the speed and comfort of air travel against the costs of it. When air travel proves to be far more expensive than surface travel, many pleasure travellers will choose the latter form of transportation, be it by public - rail, bus, ship - or private transport - the family car. Furthermore, pleasure travel is usually paid out of discretionary income, i.e., income not destined for the satisfaction of the primary needs of life. Potential pleasure travellers will balance travel as such, the actual journey plus accommodation and other service, against other uses which may be made of discretionary income. This "overall travel picture", including both travel, accommodation and other services, makes the computation of demand elasticity difficult in air transport. Might the whole or part of the air transport market prove to be elastic, experiements in lowering air fares and rates seem to be warranted, not only to the benefit of the airline user, but also to that of the airlines themselves. In this respect it will be interesting to follow U.S. domestic experiments in lowering air fares, presently taking place.(42)

II. Cargo Rates(43)

Transportation of air cargo has until recently been merely a by-product of (international) air transport. Whereas in the pre-war development period of (international) air transport the carriage of air mail played a predominant role, the post-war period has been characterized by a heavy emphasis on the transportation of passengers. Gradually, however, the transportation of air cargo has become more important and voluminous. For many years air cargo was almost exclusively carried, as a true by-product, in the "belly" of passenger aircraft. Later years saw the appearance of aircraft which can be used for both the carriage of passengers and of cargo.(44) The time of large all-cargo aircraft arrived in the sixties.(45) A further growth of air cargo traffic can certainly be expected. In 1963, 72 percent of the world's scheduled international air traffic consisted of passengers, 22 percent of cargo, and 6 percent of mail. In 1973, these percentages were 65, 31 and 4 respectively.(46)

With respect to the transportation of air cargo, two different rate systems can be adopted: the flat rate and the differential rate system. A flat rate system implies a standard rate per kilometre flown for a certain quantity of goods, regardless of the distance over which the goods travel and regardless of the type of goods. A differential rate system implies a varying rate per kilometre, depending on the type of goods, distance over which the goods travel and the market in question. IATA has opted for the differential rate system. In view of the fact that air cargo space is limited and that certain goods by their very nature are more appropriate to be carried by air than others, the option for the differential rate system seems to be the logical one.

IATA cargo rates not only include transportation from airport to airport, but also certain cargo handling facilities, such as loading, unloading and storage. IATA cargo rates are further of three different types: general cargo,(47) class,(48) and specific commodity(49) rates.

General cargo rates are determined by the Traffic Conferences for all different air cargo routes in the IATA network. These rates are either based on the weight of the goods shipped, the general rule, or on the volume of the goods shipped, the exception used for those goods which are bulky in relation to their weight (i.e., goods of low density). The general cargo rate structure further includes minimum freight charges for small shipments up to a certain weight. Such minimum freight charges are warranted, when one considers that each shipment, small or large, needs certain handling facilities, such as loading and unloading. The general cargo rate structure also includes discounts for large shipments. There is a first 25 percent discount at the low minimum breakpoint of 45 kilogrammes. Higher additional breakpoints are available on selected routes. For shipments approaching breakpoint weights, shippers may avail themselves of the advantage of the reduced rate at the breakpoint, provided they pay for the minimum weight at that breakpoint. For a shipment of 40 kilogrammes, for instance, the shipper may avail himself of the rate at the breakpoint weight of 45 kilogrammes. This rate includes a 25 percent discount and will thus be cheaper than the rate for 40 kilogrammes at the under 45 kilogrammes rate scale.

Class rates apply to the carriage of certain commodities which require either less or more handling than the average shipment. For commodities requiring less than average handling the class rates give a standard reduction from the under 45 kilogrammes general cargo rates. A reduction of 50 percent applies, for instance, to the transportation of newspapers, magazines, periodicals, catalogues and books. For commodities requiring more than average handling the class rates give a standard surcharge on the under 45 kilogrammes general cargo rates. Such is the case for high value goods as gold, bank notes, securities, etc. The surcharge here is between 50 and 100 percent, depending on the area.

The role played by special fares in the IATA fare structure, is played by specific commodity rates in the IATA rate structure. Specific commodity rates are promotional in nature and thus lower than general cargo rates. They only apply to precisely defined commodities on certain specifically determined routes. Sometimes they apply only in one direction, sometimes in both directions. Each Traffic Conference or Joint Traffic Conference has a Specific Commodity Rates Board entitled to initiate a specific commodity rate upon the unanimous vote of the members of the Board in question. An airline which wants to propose and initiate a specific commodity rate may also do so through a mail or cable procedure. When not contested by other airlines, the specific commodity rate may go into effect provisionally, subject to confirmation by the next meeting of the Specific Commodity Rates Board in question.

What has been said in paragraph I concerning costs, competition and demand elasticity, applies *mutatis mutandis* to the field of cargo rates.[(50)] With respect to demand elasticity it should be remarked that the elasticity coefficient may prove to be lower for the demand for cargo transportation than for the demand for passenger transportation. There are more pleasure travellers than there are "pleasure shippers". Most shippers will be businessmen rather than private citizens. Businessmen, as noted before, are more likely to be willing to pay the "highest rates that the market will bear" than are private citizens.

III. Currency Matters[51]

All IATA fares and rates are agreed upon in either of the two IATA basic currencies: the U.S. Dollar[52] or the British Pound Sterling.[53] IATA regulations[54] further stipulate that fares and rates shall only be published in the local currency of the country from which the air transporatoin is to commence, and/or in one or both basic currencies. The IATA Traffic Conferences also determine their own exchange rates for conversion of the Dollar and Pound into local currencies.[55] In principle passengers and shippers are required to pay IATA fares and rates in the currency of the country in which transportation commences. The IATA exchange rates[56] are then used to determine the exact fare or rate in the local currency. Whenever passengers and shippers are allowed to pay in another than the local selling currency, the IATA exchange rates must again be used to calculate the fare or rate in that other currency. The main purpose of the IATA currency rates is to prevent exchange rates from being used in order to rebate the IATA agreed tariff structure.

The above-described fixed IATA currency system has been heavily undermined by the breaking down of the Bretton Woods fixed currency exchange system. The devaluation, first of the U.S. Dollar, later of the British Pound, and the system of fluctuating exchange rates between major currencies, have made the continuing application of the old fixed IATA currency conversion system extremely difficult. A return to the international fixed currency exchange system seems, especially after the 1975 Rambouillet economic summit meeting, extremely unlikely.

As a temporary solution to its currency problems, IATA initiated a system of surcharges and discounts on local selling currencies, designed to compensate for currency changes which have taken place after the introduction of IATA fares and rates. As a more permanent solution, IATA intends to replace its two former basic currencies by one new basic currency: the International Unit of Value (I.U.V.), based upon the Special Drawing Rights (S.D.R.s) of the International Monetary Fund (IMF). The agreement in principle to do so was reached as early as August, 1973, at a special IATA Currency Conference, held at Paris. After the working out of details the new fixed I.U.V. system was due to go into effect on April 1, 1977. S.D.R. conversion rates would in the future be used for conversion of I.U.V. fares and rates into local selling currencies.[57] The implementation of the I.U.V. system has been delayed due to the opposition of a number of carriers. As a temporary solution the U.S. Dollar may be introduced as the only IATA basic currency.[58]

[1] See *supra*, Ch. III, para. II.
[2] *Ibidem*, para. III.
[3] TC Res. 048.
[4] See McCook Bond, *op.cit.*; Chayes, Ehrlich and Lowenfeld, *op.cit.*, at 384-488; Pillai, *op.cit.*, at 113-121; UNCTAD Report TD/B/C.4/62/Rev. 1, *op.cit.*; *The regulation of liner conferences* (a code of conduct for the liner conference system), UNCTAD Report, UN Doc. TD/104/Rev. 1, 1972.
[5] UNCTAD Report TD/B/C.4/62/Rev. 1, *op.cit.*, at 3.
[6] *Ibidem*.
[7] For pooling in international air transport see *supra*, Ch. II, para. II.
[8] See *supra*, Ch. II, para. I and Ch. III, para. I.
[9] See *infra*, para. II.
[10] See *supra*, Ch. I, para. II.
[11] McCook Bond, *op.cit.*, at 28-29 and literature cited there.
[12] The major exception to this rule are the liners sailing under the flags of socialist countries.
[13] See (U.S.) *Shipping Act*, Act of September 7, 1916, as amended, 40 Stat. 903, 46 U.S.C 801-842; see also TD/104/Rev. 1, *op.cit.*, at 11 et seq.
[14] Cf. Agreeing Fares and Rates, *op.cit.*, at 81-89, 110-147.
[15] Excess baggage must be paid for by the passenger at the rate of 1 percent per kilogramme of the one-way first class fare for the route in question.
[16] TC Res. 050-059.
[17] TC Res. 060-069.
[18] Cf. *Agreeing Fares and Rates*, *op.cit.*, at 84 et seq. and App. K, p. 198, et seq.
[19] *Ibidem*.
[20] Approved by the US CAB for a six months period: Order 76-4-75, April 30, 1976.
[21] See, *Montreal Star*, Feb. 5, 1976; for the influence of technology, i.a., the introduction of supersonic aircraft, on IATA ratemaking, see, *Impact of Technology on IATA Ratemaking: Problems, Prognostications, Proposals*, 39 Geo. Wash. L.R. 1167 (1970/1).
[22] TC Res. 070-099.
[23] See *infra*, Ch. VI, para. II.
[24] For a complete list of special fares see, *Agreeing Fares and Rates*, *op.cit.*, App. L, p. 217 et seq.
[25] *Survey of International Air Transport Fares and Rates*, *op.cit.*, at 17.
[26] *Ibidem*.
[27] *Ibidem*.
[28] *Agreeing Fares and Rates*, *op.cit.*, App. V, p. 239.
[29] As long as special fares cover marginal operation costs (i.e. the costs for the transportation of one additional passenger), they may go below average operation costs (i.e., the overall transportation costs of passengers), and will then still tend to bring those average costs down and revenues up. Perhaps IATA should, with respect to special fares, follow the CAB principle applicable to US domestic

discount fares. According to the CAB's Domestic Passenger Fare Investigation (see also supra, Ch. IV, para. I) a discount (i.e., a special) fare must be able to generate "sufficient additional traffic to more than offset (i) the diversion of full-fare traffic, and (ii) the added non-capacity costs associated with the generated traffic, less any savings in cost attributable to the nature of the services provided to the discount traffic." See Phase 5, Discount Fares, of the Domestic Passenger Fare Investigation, CAB Orders 72-12-18, Dec. 5, 1972; 73-5-2, May 1, 1973 and 73-8-55, August 10, 1973; see also Keyes, Policy Innovations in the Domestic Passenger Fare Investigation, op.cit., at 85.

(30) Agreeing Fares and Rates, op.cit., at 83.

(31) Traditionally sixteen different route groups are distinguished by IATA for ratemaking purposes. The proposed standard rate per kilometre could indeed, if marketing, competitive and geographical conditions so warrant, be different from route group to route group. The route groups in question are: North Atlantic, Mid-Atlantic, South Atlantic, North America - South America, North America - Central America, Local South America, Local Europe, Europe - North Africa, Europe - Southern Africa, Local Africa, Europe - Middle East, Europe - Far East/Australasia, Local Far East/Australasia, North and Mid-Pacific, South Pacific, Africa - Far East/Australasia. See, Agreeing Fares and Rates, op.cit., at 103 et seq., and Survey of International Air Transport Fares and Rates, op.cit., a passim.

(32) See infra, Ch. VIII, para. II.

(33) For guidelines concerning an "ideal" tariff structure, see supra, Ch. IV, para. I.

(34) See supra, Ch. III, para. II, and Agreeing Fares and Rates, op.cit., at 99-102.

(35) Survey of International Air Transport Fares and Rates, op.cit., a passim, and Agreeing Fares and Rates, op.cit., at 99-102.

(36) Agreeing Fares and Rates, op.cit., at 114 and 150.

(37) Ibidem, App. Q, p. 231.

(38) Cf. Agreeing Fares and Rates, op.cit., at 95.

(39) The actual E coefficient will usually be negative, as a decrease in price will usually lead to an increase in demand, and as an increase in price will usually lead to a decrease in demand.

(40) See Dirlewanger, Die Preisdifferenzierung im internationalen Luftverkehr, op.cit., at 254 et seq.

(41) A Review of the Economic Situation of Air Transport, ICAO Circ., 73-AT/10 at 39 and 45 (1965).

(42) Ever lower priced "no frills" services and special excursion fares are presently being introduced in U.S. domestic air transport.

(43) Cf. Agreeing Fares and Rates, op.cit., at 90-94, 148-161; for air mail rates see, supra, Ch. III, para. III.

(44) E.g., the McDonnell Douglas Rapid Change Versions and the Boeing Quick Change Versions.

(45) There is even an all-cargo version of the Boeing 747, at the present time the largest existing civil aircraft.

(46) See, A Review of the Economic Situation of Air Transport (1963-1973), op.cit., at 16; see also, Magdelénat, Le fret aérien, Aspects juridiques, Dissertation, Aix-en-Provence, at 9 (1975).

(47) TC Res. 501, 551, 558-570.

(48) TC Res. 521, 595-598.

(49) TC Res. 590.

(50) For a survey of actual cargo rates, see Agreeing Fares and Rates, op.cit., at 150 et seq., and Survey of International Air Transport

Fares and Rates, op.cit., a passim.

(51) Cf. Agreeing Fares and Rates, op.cit., at 39-42.

(52) In Traffic Conference 1 and in Joint Traffic Conferences 1-2, 1-3.

(53) In Traffic Conferences 2 and 3, and in Joint Traffic Conference 2-3.

(54) TC Res. 021.

(55) TC Res. 021 B.

(56) Ibidem.

(57) See Report of Traffic Conferences, 29th AGM, Auckland, Sept. 1973 at 9-11; Annual Report of Director General of IATA, 30th AGM, Montreal, Sept. 1974, at 5, 11; Report of Financial Committee, 30th AGM, Montreal, Sept. 1974 at 2; Annual Report of Director General of IATA, 31st AGM, Oslo, Sept. 1975, at 15-16; Cf. similar developments with respect to the replacement of the Franc Poincaré (Goldfranc) in international air law conventions by S.D.R.s: International Conference on Air Law, Montreal, Sept. 3 - 25, 1975, 1 Air Law 114 (1976).

(58) See AWST, Nov. 22, 1976 at 24.

CHAPTER VI: NON-IATA INTERNATIONAL AIR TARIFFS

In Chapters I and IV of this book both scheduled and non-scheduled, both IATA and non-IATA tariffs have been studied. In Chapters II, III and V, IATA and its scheduled international air tariffs have been the focal point. This sixth Chapter deals with all those international air tariffs, which are not determined through the IATA ratemaking machinery. It should be recalled that of all existing international air tariffs by far the great majority are scheduled IATA tariffs. In fact, almost all scheduled international air tariffs are IATA tariffs. The most important group of non-IATA international air tariffs consists of non-scheduled or charter international air tariffs.(1) These tariffs are the subject of paragraph II of this Chapter.(2) Before that, in paragraph I, attention will be paid to the limited number of existing scheduled international air tariffs of non-IATA airlines. Another group of non-IATA international air tariffs is formed by so-called Government ordered international air tariffs. These Government ordered tariffs can relate to both scheduled and non-scheduled international flights. They are the subject of paragraph IV of this Chapter.

During recent years, several attempts have been made to bring IATA airlines and charter only international airlines closer together in the international tariff field. IATA's abortive attempt to open up the Association to charter only international airlines is an example hereof.(3) Another example, which will be discussed in detail in paragraph III of this Chapter, are the negotiations which have been taking place, during recent years, between IATA airlines and charter only international airlines for the purpose of reaching agreements on uniform minimum international charter tariffs. These negotiations have, however, not yet yielded any tangible results.

International passenger charter flights are considerably more numerous than international cargo charter flights.(4) Consequently there are far more international charter fares than there are international charter rates, and, therefore, the emphasis in this Chapter will be more on charter fares than on charter rates.

The main difference, of course, between IATA tariffs on the one hand and most non-IATA international tariffs on the other, is that the former are uniform tariffs, determined on an inter-carrier basis through the IATA ratemaking machinery, whereas the latter are individual tariffs, basically determined by each individual airline in accordance with the proverbial forces of the marketplace, the law of supply and demand. It should be noted, however, that both kinds of tariffs are under Governmental control. IATA tariffs, however, have probably been under heavier Governmental scrutiny than non-IATA tariffs. One sort of non-IATA international tariffs, the international charter tariffs, have during recent years attracted more and more Government interest, and consequently, as shall be seen hereunder, Government control. This increased Government interest in, and control of international charter tariffs goes hand in hand with the tremendous growth, which international charter transportation has undergone during the past fifteen years.(5)

I. Scheduled International Air Tariffs of Non-IATA Airlines

Only some six percent of the total number of tonne-kilometres performed in scheduled international air services are performed by international airlines which are not members of IATA.(6) *Grosso modo* there are two reasons, why certain scheduled international airlines have stayed outside IATA. The first reason is more or less political in nature. The second is economic.

Many socialist countries have kept their flag carriers outside IATA for what can be called a political reason, namely, their overt or implied reluctance against a capitalistic trade association of profit-minded international airlines. In other countries, a number of airlines, and sometimes their Governments have thought it to be economically desirable to stay outside IATA. By not joining the Association, these airlines can try to undercut the inter-carrier agreed IATA tariffs and service standards, and thus gain a competitive advantage over their IATA counterparts.

Aeroflot, the flag carrier of the USSR, is the largest non-IATA airline in the world. Although its number of international air services is rather limited, Aeroflot is definitely the big "absentee" in IATA.(7) Its example to remain outside IATA was followed by Balkan Bulgarian Transport of Bulgaria, Interflug of the German Democratic Republic, Malev of Hungary and Tarom of Romania. Three other East European airlines, however, have joined IATA. They are CSA of Czechoslovakia, JAT of Yugoslavia and LOT of Poland. CAAC,(8) the flag carrier of the People's Republic of China, is not an IATA member either. Whether the decision of the above-mentioned socialist countries' airlines not to join IATA was entirely politically motivated or not, it remains a fact that they do not compete with IATA tariffs. In general, they charge IATA or IATA inspired tariffs on their scheduled international air services.(9)

The tariffs of these non-IATA airlines of socialist countries are of little concern to IATA. The Association is much more worried about airlines which have stayed outside IATA for economic competitive reasons. The ability of such airlines to undercut the IATA agreed tariff structure will largely depend on the willingness of Governments to cooperate. Whenever the flag carrier or carriers of a particular country are IATA members, their Government will usually not allow a non-IATA airline of another country to fly to that first country at tariffs which are lower than those agreed upon in IATA. Such a permission would definitely put its own IATA flag carrier or carriers at a competitive disadvantage both on direct and on through services.(10) At this point it should be recalled that the bilateral air transport agreements of countries, whose national air carriers are not IATA members, usually do not refer to the IATA ratemaking machinery. Instead they mostly provide that tariffs shall be determined by the designated air carriers of the two countries concerned, under Governmental approval.(11)

Classical examples of non-IATA scheduled tariff competition are the fares and rates offered by the scheduled non-IATA airlines Loftleidir of Iceland,(12) Air Bahama, a Loftleidir subsidiary, and Luxavia of Luxembourg.

Loftleidir maintains scheduled air services from New York and Chicago to Reykjavik, and through services from there to Great Britain, Luxembourg and Scandinavia. Upon the insistence of the British and

Scandinavian Governments, it charges IATA tariffs from the U.S.A. to Great Britain and Scandinavia. On the New York/Chicago to Luxembourg via Iceland routes, however, Loftleidir tariffs are lower than IATA tariffs. In fact these tariffs give a standard reduction from IATA tariffs.[13] The U.S. CAB has never objected to these low Loftleidir tariffs.[14] Luxembourg, at the other end of the inexpensive North Atlantic Loftleidir air routes, which over the years have been beneficial to a large number of air travellers, has always followed a non-IATA policy. It has done so more for economic than for idealistic reasons. By allowing non-IATA airlines to fly to Luxembourg at lower than IATA tariffs, the Luxembourg Government has succeeded in attracting additional traffic to the country. Luxembourg's own flag carrier, Luxair, is not an IATA member, and only performs intra-European air services. On these services, however, it adheres to IATA tariffs.[15]

A Loftleidir subsidiary, Air Bahama, performs low-cost scheduled air services between Luxembourg and Nassau (Bahamas). The combined non-IATA Luxembourg - Nassau and the IATA Nassau - Miami (Florida) fare is lower than the comparable direct IATA fare from Western Europe to Miami. Air Bahama fares from Luxembourg to Nassau can be combined with Loftleidir fares from New York or Chicago to Luxembourg, and *vice versa*.

There is a third non-IATA airline performing low-cost scheduled international air services out of Luxembourg. This airline is Luxavia, and it performs scheduled air services from Luxembourg to Johannesburg (South Africa). The company is Luxembourg based. Until a few years ago, it used to perform its air services under the name Trek Air, a South African based airline. For political reasons, the overflying of black African territory, the company's name was changed, and its base transferred from South Africa to Luxembourg.

In the Far East non-IATA competition does not so much take the form of undercutting IATA tariffs, but rather that of service competition. Non-IATA airlines in the area[16] generally adhere to IATA tariffs, but offer the travelling public service standards which are definitely superior to those of IATA airlines. The superiority of these service standards is widely advertised by the airlines concerned. IATA is becoming increasingly concerned about these non-IATA service standards in the Far East. The recent decision of the IATA Executive Committee to give Director General Hammarskjöld the authority "to suspend enforcement of IATA Traffic Resolutions in particular geographic areas as well as on specific routes" was, amongst other things, inspired by this Far East service competition question.[17]

A number of IATA Traffic Conference Resolutions[18] are specifically aimed at non-IATA competition. Most of them provide:

> "Where a member considers an agreed Resolution relating to fares, rates or traffic practices materially damages its interests by preventing it from meeting a fare, rate or practice of a non-IATA air carrier, such Member may reduce the IATA specific fare or rate or modify or suspend a Conference traffic practice by rescinding to the extent necessary the appropriate Conference Resolution."

When an IATA carrier thus reduces an IATA fare or rate, or modifies or suspends an IATA practice, it may only do so under certain conditions. It will have to notify the Secretary of the Traffic Conferences of such action, and it will be limited in its right to advertise the action.

II. <u>Non-Scheduled International Air Tariffs</u>.

Since international charter, or non-scheduled air transportation has rapidly grown in importance during the past fifteen years, and now constitutes some 25 percent of the total international air transport market, a thorough study of the fares and rates applicable to such transportation seems to be appropriate. It has already been pointed out several times that, apart from a certain amount of Government intervention, to be discussed below, international charter fares and rates are determined by individual carriers through the mechanism of the law of supply and demand, through the free forces of the marketplace. There is a very simple economic reason, why charter air tariffs are necessarily lower than scheduled tariffs. The essence of a scheduled air service is that it gives direct, regular, dependable and easily accessible service to the general public. In order to accomplish that purpose scheduled airlines must plan their services in such a fashion that they will satisfy the demand for air services, both in "peak" seasons, when demand for air transportation is high, and in "low" seasons, when such demand is small. It is estimated, that scheduled international air services, in order to maintain their service standards to the public can never operate with load factors exceeding 65 to 70 percent.(19) Scheduled international air services will thus necessarily be operated with a minimum average of 30 to 35 percent of empty seats and cargo space. Users of scheduled international air services will have to pay for those empty seats and cargo space. International charter air services, on the other hand, operate in principle with a 100 percent load factor. The whole capacity of the aircraft is chartered by one or more middlemen for the purpose of reselling that capacity to the public. This is called the planeload principle. Thus, since basically every seat on a charter aircraft is filled, bringing the average load factor to close to 100 percent, tariffs on international air charter services can be lower than those on scheduled international air services, where the maximum attainable load factor ranges between 65 and 70 percent.(20) In fact, average load factors on scheduled international air services have consistently been lower than 65 percent. From 1963 to 1972 they hovered around fifty percent,(21) but nevertheless, during that period, remained above the break-even load factor, the load factor required to cover operating expenses.(22) Since 1972, load factors on scheduled international air services have been rising.(23) Due to inflation, the fuel crisis and overcapacity airlines have seen themselves forced to restrain capacity voluntarily or through capacity reduction agreements.(24) Due to sharply increased operating costs the break-even load factors have, however, also been on the increase since 1972, bringing many scheduled international airlines into the red. At the same time that scheduled international load factors have been increasing, load factors on international charter air services have been going down somewhat.(25) On the whole, however, average load factors on international charter air services have remained well above those on scheduled international air services, and consequently international charter air tariffs are still well below scheduled international air tariffs.

A disputed point has always been, whether international charter air services divert traffic from scheduled international air services, or in other words, whether they impair the development of such scheduled air services. It is submitted that this is not the case. Adhering to the earlier made distinction between business and pleasure travellers,(26) it must be said that international air charter transportation, with its low tariffs, has opened up new horizons for pleasure travellers.

Had such charter air transportation not existed, many of them would probably never have travelled by air. It is true that there is only one air travel market,[27] but this market comprises both a pleasure travel and a business travel segment. The business traveller will usually travel on scheduled services. The pleasure traveller can travel both on scheduled and charter services, and will choose that form of service, which is the most convenient to him. Price considerations will be amongst his primary concerns. He will probably choose between a charter flight or one of the many special fares available on IATA flights.[28] In this context, it should be noted that the special IATA fares have mainly been adopted to combat charter competition. For instance, affinity group fares were IATA's answer to affinity group charters. Individual or group inclusive tour fares were IATA's answer to inclusive tour charters (ITCs). APEX fares were its answer to ABCs and TGCs.[29] Without charter competition IATA would perhaps never have adopted some of these special fares. Charter competition has definitely been to the benefit of the aviation consumer. It has made air travel accessible to people, who would otherwise never have travelled by air. It had the by-effect of IATA introducing low special fares.[30] Instead of impairing the development of scheduled international air services, the development of international charter air transportation has simply enlarged the overall air travel market. In the words of the U.S. Court of Appeals:

> "The consistent lamentations and predictions of doom by diversion raised by the scheduled air carriers in the past have proved, to our way of thinking, to be considerably overstated."[31]

A discussion of international air charter tariffs should necessarily be preceded by a summary discussion of the regulatory framework, within which non-scheduled international air services function. A short enumeration of the types of international air charter services, available to the public, is also indispensable.

The basic international provisions governing both scheduled and non-scheduled international air services are contained in Articles 5 and 6 of the Chicago Convention.[32] Whereas scheduled international air services can, according to Article 6 of the Convention, only be operated with prior Governmental permission,[33] commercial rights for non-scheduled air services are exchanged on a multilateral basis in paragraph 2 of Article 5 of the Convention, subject, however,

> "to the right of any State ..... to impose such regulations, conditions or limitations as it may consider desirable."

Shortly after the conclusion of the Convention in 1944, there were two warnings from ICAO to member States not to interpret this provision too restrictively. In 1949, the ICAO Secretariat issued the opinion that member States were not entitled to require prior permission for non-scheduled air services.[34] In much weaker terms the ICAO Council, in 1952, urged States not

> "to render the operation of this important form of air transport /i.e. non-scheduled air transport/ impossible or non-effective."[35]

States have, nevertheless, given a very restrictive interpretation to Article 5(2), with the result that, in practice, prior Governmental approval is required for almost all international charter flights. This approval can be in the form of an individual approval for every single charter flight, an approval for certain series or kinds of charter flights, for certain charter operators, or a combination thereof.[36] Until recently, one State, Israel, even banned charter flights altogether.

Not only did the ICAO Council, in 1952, warn States not to interpret Article 5(2) too restrictively, it also, on the same occasion, attempted to define the concept "scheduled international air service".[37] Every international air service which would not fit into the Council's definition, would automatically be a non-scheduled international air service. According to the Council's definition, the most important characteristics of a scheduled international air service are that it is "open to use by members of the public", and that it is operated in accordance with a "published timetable, or with flights so regular or frequent that they constitute a recognizable systematic series." It should be kept in mind that the Council's definition was given long before the proliferation of international charter air services. In 1952, non-scheduled international air services were mostly limited to so-called own use or single entity charters - charters, whereby one person charters the whole aircraft for his own use, or that of his personnel or merchandise -, planeload cargo or military charters, and special passenger charters for the carriage of, for instance, pilgrims and immigrants. The present situation is entirely different. Most charters are performed on such a regular basis, and are planned so long ahead, that it can indeed be said that they are performed in accordance with a published timetable. This is especially true for such "programme charters" as ABCs and TGCs. For these charter types, and also for affinity group and inclusive tour charters, it has sometimes been argued that, for all practical purposes, they can be brought under the 1952 ICAO Council definition of a scheduled international air service.[38] As far as ITCs are concerned, this argument was rejected by ICAO in 1962.[39] The ICAO Council, however, has again recently taken up the question of determining, whether "programme charters" should be characterized as scheduled or non-scheduled. It is not impossible that the 1962 position may be reversed. It is submitted that as long as international charter flights are not sold directly to the public by the airlines, but rather through intermediaries - group or tour organizers - they do not come under the 1952 ICAO characterization of being "open to use by members of the public." As long as, in U.S. regulatory terms, passengers are not "individually ticketed"[40] by the airlines, but rather as "groups" through intermediaries,[41] the air services which they use, cannot be brought under the 1952 ICAO definition. It is granted, however, that the terms "open to use by members of the public" and "individually ticketed" are, in this fashion, given a very narrow interpretation. Unlike affinity group charters, only open to certain segments of the public, members of recognized affinity groups, ABCs, TGCs and ITCs can indeed be used by the general public at large, although not directly, but rather indirectly through intermediaries. In U.S. Courts it was specifically upheld that both ITCs and TGCs are not to be considered as "individually ticketed" services.[42]

Whatever one may think about the ICAO definition of a scheduled international air service, or the American distinction between "group" and "individually ticketed" travel, they are still today's reality. Thought should, however, be given to new distinctions and definitions. The British Edwards Report, for instance, uses the criterion of "collective nature" of the demand.[43] Collective demand air services, or in the present terminology, scheduled air services, cater to the traveller's demand for continuously available air service. They are performed according to published timetables, and are open to any traveller at any time. Besides these collective demand air services, there may be other air services, whether or not performed in accordance with published timetables, catering to the special demand of certain groups of travellers, whose main concern it is to secure the cheapest form of air transportation. To reach that aim, these travellers will be willing to comply with certain requirements: membership of an association for affinity group charters, prior booking and payment for ABCs/TGCs, the purchase of ground arrangements for ITCs. The latter form of air services are called "bulk air transportation" in the 1970 US Statement of International Air Transportation Policy.(44) Under such "bulk air transportation" would also certainly fall the Sky Train concept, introduced by Laker Airways of Great Britain, in 1972. Laker, a charter company, proposed to begin very low cost, daily, non-reservation air services from London to New York, and vice versa. The services would be on a "first come, first served" basis. The U.S. supplemental airline, Trans International Airlines (TIA), followed Laker's example and applied to the CAB for permission to perform similar low-cost air services between New York and London. To date no CAB approval was obtained for these two new air services. It seems, however, that CAB approval for one of the two services, that of Laker Airways, is now forthcoming. The British CAA originally approved Laker's proposal on September 26, 1972. More than three years later, in mid-February, 1976, the CAA withdrew its approval for Laker's Sky Train. The withdrawal was part of a revision by the British Labour Government of the policy of inter-carrier competition by British air carriers. Trade Minister Store remarked that Sky Train would cause severe competition for British Airways' North Atlantic scheduled air services, that Sky Train would add to the existing overcapacity problem on the North Atlantic, that it would generate little additional traffic, and finally, that it would "confer no really worthwhile benefits to the consumer". (45) As far as this last argument is concerned, it is submitted that the Sky Train concept would certainly have the same advantage for the consumer as existing international air charter services: low-cost air transportation, this time not under prior booking and payment conditions, as applicable to ABCs, but on the condition that no advance bookings can be made, and that the air services are thus performed on "first come, first served" basis. Shortly after February 1976, Laker took the Department of Trade to court and won its case. On 30 July, the Queen's Bench Division ruled that the Department had exceeded its powers under The Civil Aviation Act of 1971 in revoking Laker's Sky Train licence. The Department's subsequent appeal was dismissed.(46) Together with the forthcoming CAB approval Sky Train should thus soon become reality. It should be noted that Sky Train does not fit into the present definition of a non-scheduled international air service. There will be no middlemen between Laker and the travelling public. Passengers will be "individually ticketed" by the carrier. Sky Train does, in fact, mean the entrance of a charter only airline, Laker into the scheduled international market.

Government regulation of non-scheduled international air transportation takes three forms: unilateral, bilateral and multilateral regulation.(47) A true mixture of unilateral charter regulations imposed by individual States, has resulted from the "regulations, conditions or limitations" clause of Article 5(2) of the Chicago Convention. The only common element in these unilateral regulations is that, very often, at least in the past, they either literally or in a modified version copied the provisions of the IATA agreed charter rules, contained in Traffic Conference Resolution 045.

Resolution 045 will be discussed hereunder. Since the unilateral charter regulations of one country may be different from those of another, the question must be answered: which set of charter regulations governs charter flights between two countries? The regulations of the country, where the charter flights commence, i.e., the country of origin rule? Or the regulations of the country, for which the charter flights are destined, i.e., the country of destination rule? In the past, it has often been held that the more restrictive of the two sets of rules should apply. A more modern approach, laid down in the Memoranda of Understanding on the operation of charter air services, and in the Bilateral Non-scheduled Air Service Agreements, concluded by the U.S.A,(48) lets the country of origin rule prevail. For instance, Article 7 of the U.S.A. - Yugoslavia charter bilateral(49) provides:

> "Where both Parties have promulgated different rules governing the same specific service type, the rule of the Party in wose territory the enplanement occurs shall govern unless agreed otherwise."

This then leads to a discussion of bilateralism in the field of Government regulation of international charter air transportation. This bilateralism was initiated by the U.S.A. in 1972, when it concluded its first Memorandum of Understanding with Belgium.(50) The bilateral approach to the regulation of international charter transportation was already a feature of the 1970 U.S. Statement of International Air Transportation Policy.(51) The country of origin rule is the essence of all Memoranda of Understanding and bilateral charter Agreements, concluded by the U.S.A. With respect to TGCs and ABCs the legality of this country of origin rule was challenged by Pan Am and TWA before the U.S. Court of Appeals.(52) Amongst other things, the two airlines argued that, in allowing foreign originating charters into the U.S.A., the CAB might in fact give approval to charter services not falling under the Federal Aviation Act's definition of supplemental air transportation. This argument was rejected by the Court. It held country of origin rules to be valid, as long as substantially similar to U.S. TGC rules, and covered by bilateral international agreements.

While the bilateral approach is strongly advocated by the U.S.A., and certainly deserves encouragement, the multilateral approach should not be neglected.(53) With respect to North Atlantic charters ECAC has consistently urged its member States not to deal with the U.S.A. bilaterally, but rather multilaterally. On the insistence of the U.S.A., however, all bilateral North Atlantic charter agreements have so far been worked out bilaterally, rather than multilaterally.(54)

With respect to the multilateral approach, reference has already been made to two regional multilateral agreements: the Multilateral Agreement on Commercial Rights of Non-Scheduled Air Services in Europe, usually called the 1956 Paris Agreement, and the 1971 Multilateral Agreement on Commercial Rights of Non-Scheduled Air Services among the Association of South East Asian Nations.(55) The latter Agreement liberalizes those non-scheduled commercial flights within the Association of South East Asian Nations, which are not harmful to scheduled air services.(56) The Paris Agreement, reached within the framework of ECAC, completely liberalizes charter flights of a humanitarian or emergency nature, taxi-class passenger flights with a maximum seating capacity of six passengers, single entity charters and single flights of any other nature between the same two traffic centres, but with a maximum of one such flight per month for any operator.(57) Other international cargo charters, and passenger charters "between regions which have no reasonably direct connection by scheduled air services", are subject to the provision that they may be refused by States, when deemed "harmful to the interests of ..... scheduled air services.(58) Had this provision, or the provisions of Article 3 of the Agreement(59) been used extensively by ECAC member States, the rapid growth of ITCs(60) in Europe would never have become a fact. This rapid growth, however, did take place, and may, in part, have been due to the fact that many destinations served by ITCs were indeed previously not or almost not served by scheduled flights. In 1960, ECAC created its Non-Scheduled and Inclusive Tour (NSIT) study group. Amongst other things, its work resulted in a 1961 Recommendation by ECAC to its member States to "continue to adopt a liberal attitude toward flights exclusively reserved for inclusive tours."(61) This liberal attitude was indeed adopted, and as a result, in 1972, ITCs accounted for 38.5 percent of the total intra-European air traffic market.(62)

As shall be seen below, ECAC has also been active in the field of ABCs. With respect to that form of charter flights an important multilateral agreement was reached at Ottawa, on October 21, 1972. At that time Canada, ECAC member States and the U.S.A. adopted a "Text of Agreed Principles for North Atlantic Charter Flights",(63) setting out the basic conditions for the introduction of ABCs and TGCs by April 1, 1973. This multilateral agreement, which will be discussed hereunder, is usually referred to as the Ottawa Declaration.

The importance of IATA Traffic Conference Resolution 045(64) in the international charter field has already been underlined several times. The Resolution developed the affinity group charter concept, which would rule the bulk of the international charter market for some twenty years, from 1953 to 1972. Its real significance lies in the fact, that national aviation authorities adopted, in one form or another, the 045 rules as their national charter legislation, thus making those IATA developed rules not only applicable to IATA member airlines, but also to scheduled non-IATA and charter only airlines.

The history of Resolution 045 goes back to the year 1948.(65) In December of that year, an IATA proposal recommended that contracts between IATA airlines and charterers would stipulate that space on aircraft would not be resold to the public at less than IATA fares. The first version of Resolution 045 was issued on April 7, 1949, but it would not be until 1953, that the Resolution was adopted in the form which would dominate the international charter market until 1972. In essence the Resolution provides that IATA airlines may perform international charter air services, but if the price of such services, when reduced to a unit basis, is lower than the applicable IATA fare or rate, they will have to follow the rules of 045. These rules then allow three kinds of charters: the above-mentioned own use or single entity charters,(66) study group charters,(67) and, most importantly, affinity group charters.(68) IATA airlines' charter contracts shall be with one charterer, who, in the case of affinity charters, may sell space on the chartered aircraft to a group

> "which has principal purposes, aims and objectives other than travel and sufficient affinity prior to the application for charter transportation to distinguish it and set it apart from the general public",

subject to numerous detailed conditions. Besides the three above-mentioned charter types Resolution 045 also allows IATA airlines to perform military charters(69) within Traffic Conference 2 and Joint Traffic Conferences 1-2 and 1-2-3,(70) and ITCs within the Europe - Middle East - Africa region of Traffic Conference 2.(71) However, as far as such ITCs are concerned IATA members are under the obligation to ensure that the price for the tour, including accommodation and other services, shall not be less than the lowest applicable IATA economy class fare or scheduled inclusive tour price on the same route, whichever is lower.(72)

In the fifties, many national charter regulations were almost identical to Resolution 045,(73) thus extending its applicability to non-IATA airlines. Gradually, however, numerous Governments began to adopt more liberal international charter rules. The 1960s, for instance, saw the above-mentioned growth of ITCs in Europe. The U.S. CAB started to adopt a more liberal international charter attitude around 1961,(74) resulting, i.a., in a permission for split charters(75) in 1964, and for ITCs(76) in 1966. The growth of ITCs in the U.S.A. thus began later than in Europe, and never became as widespread. The reason for the ITCs limited success in the U.S.A. lies in the fact, that the CAB put numerous conditions on the performance of ITCs. Amongst other things, a three-stop-requirement(77) prevented the development of the European-type point to point ITCs. The latter were not introduced in the U.S.A. until 1975, and were then given the name One-stop-inclusive tour charters (OTCs).(78)

One of the consequences of Governments adopting more liberal international charter rules, was that IATA airlines remained bound by the strict 045 rules, whereas non-IATA airlines could operate under the often more liberal Governmental rules. A large number of European IATA airlines then formed separate charter subsidiaries, non-IATA airlines, which would not be bound by Resolution 045. Many of these charter subsidiaries later became united in ACCA.(79) By virtue of Section 401(d)(3) of the Federal Aviation ACT(80) this road to circumvent Resolution 045, was not open to U.S. airlines. This then became one of the reasons, which, in 1972, led the CAB to disapprove Resolution 045.

Because of the fact that, in the sixties, many national charter regulations became more liberal than the 045 rules, IATA airlines began to urge their Governments to make reservations and conditions to Resolution 045. As a consequence thereof Resolution 045 became one of IATA's most "conditioned" ones. Furthermore, since the affinity group rules proved to be extremely hard to enforce, bona fide affinity groups became the exception rather than the rule. All this, together with the development of advance booking charter rules in the U.K. and in the U.S.A., finally culminated in the June 1972 CAB disapproval of Resolution 045, thus making its provisions inapplicable to, i.a., the key North Atlantic charter market.(81)

In its disapproval of Resolution 045 the CAB noted, amongst other things that

> "the time had come to recognize new concepts of charter air transportation".(82)

This recognition then took the form of the above-mentioned multilateral Ottawa Declaration of October, 1972. Non-affinity ABCs, or in the American terminology, TGCs, would be introduced by April 1, 1973. Through tour organizers they would be open to non-affinity travel groups of at least 40 persons, for round-trips only. Passengers would have to make reservations at least 90 days before the date of departure,(83) pay a non-refundable deposit of 25 percent of the charter fare at the same time, and pay the balance at least 30 (ABCs)/60 days (TGCs) before departure. ABCs and TGCs were originally intended to replace North Atlantic affinity charters completely by the end of 1973. Only Canada adhered to this date. European origin affinity charters dropped sharply in number after 1973. ECAC has urged its member States to terminate all such prior affinity charters by the end of 1975, and has further been very instrumental in harmonizing the ABC rules of different European countries.(84) Although it originally intended to do so, the U.S.A. has as yet not abolished North Atlantic prior affinity group charters.(85) The larger part of U.S. originating North Atlantic charter flights are still in the form of affinity charters. The reason herefor lies in the fact that, whereas ABCs have proved to be very popular in Europe, the American TGCs never became widely accepted. This limited success of TGCs in the U.S.A. is probably due to an important regulatory difference with ABCs. Whereas ABCs may be marketed by the tour organizer at a fixed price, the cost of TGCs must be prorated among TGC participants.(86) In other words, under ABC rules it is the tour organizer, who bears the risk of loss in cases, where he is unable to fill up the chartered aircraft or part thereof. Under TGC rules it is the passenger, who bears this risk. If the TGC organizer is, for instance, only able to fill up 90 percent of the chartered aircraft or part thereof, the passengers will have to pay for the unoccupied 10 percent of the seats. In order to protect TGC participants against the financial risks of the pro-rata rule, TGC regulations further provide that at least 80 percent of the chartered aircraft must be filled. If not, the TGC must be cancelled.(87) These rules cause considerable price uncertainty for the TGC passenger, and make the marketing of TGCs in the U.S.A. extremely difficult. The proposed Low Cost Air Transportation Act,(88) introduced in the U.S. Senate by Senators Cannon and Kennedy on January 27, 1975, would have replaced TGCs by European type ABCs. In the meantime, the CAB itself issued a Notice of Proposed Rule-Making,(89) which would introduce European type ABCs in the U.S.A., and which would enable tour organizers to market these charters at fixed prices. These new charters were indeed introduced for a trial period of five years, until March 31, 1981, and are aimed at replacing affinity group charters and TGCs.

The present situation in the international air charter market is then as follows. North Atlantic charters between Canada and Europe are almost exclusively ABC charters. European originating North Atlantic charters are predominantly ABCs. U.S. originating North Atlantic charters are still mostly prior affinity group charters,(90) although the new American ABCs are rapidly becoming popular. TGCs never gained universal acceptance. The new U.S. OTCs and SECs will probably enlarge U.S. originating inclusive tour charter traffic considerably. Within Europe ITCs and SECs are the major charter types. ABCs have not been introduced in intra-European air traffic. In other parts of the world, the affinity group charter still exists, often performed in accordance with IATA 045 rules.

After this discussion of the regulatory framework, within which international charter flights function, and of the major types of international charter services available to the public, attention can now be focussed on international charter tariffs.

At the present time, there is no international mechanism, either private or public, for the determination of international charter tariffs. They are set by individual charter operators on the basis of the law of demand and supply. Prices for the transportation of charter passengers or cargo should, of course, by primarily related to the costs of such transportation. Factors which charter operators will take into account in determining their charter prices, should further include such things as distance of the charter trip, size and type of aircraft, geographical and metereological conditions, type of passengers or cargo, the possibility of "empty legs",(91) and, finally, competition and market situation.(92) To conclude from this that charter operators would be entirely free in their individual ratemaking practices, would be wrong. Many Governments exercise some form of tariff control over international charter flights, most frequently by expressing a minimum charter tariff in the form of a comparison with applicable IATA tariffs. The purpose of this form of Governmental tariff control is, of course, to protect scheduled international IATA airlines from too much charter competition. The above form of tariff control has, especially in the fifties, been used by some Governments with respect to affinity group charters. Gradually, however, affinity group charter tariffs have become largely free from Government intervention and control. Tariff control has been more widely used with respect to ITCs. In this context, it should be recalled that Resolution 045(8)(iv) obliges IATA members to assure that the all-in ITC price shall not be less than the lowest applicable IATA economy class fare or scheduled inclusive tour price on the same route, whichever is lower. This is the only instance of direct IATA involvement in charter tariffs, although it should be remembered that the above-mentioned all-in price relates to the total price of the ITC and not to the air transportation part thereof.(93) The provisions of Resolution 045(8)(iv) were taken over by many European Governments in their national aviation regulations, thus extending their applicability to non-IATA inclusive tour operators. Little by little European civil aviation authorities became more liberal with respect to minimum intra-European ITC prices. The system of minima was, for instance, completely abandoned in the U.K. and Scandinavia. Other European nations lowered the intra-European minima considerably. In the Netherlands, for instance, prices for intra-European ITCs of a duration of at least one week should not be less than 60 percent of the comparable IATA return fare during the summer, and 50 percent during the winter. For ITCs of a duration of less than one week, these percentages are 55 and 45 respectively.(94) U.S. ITC rules contain the following minimum price rule. The all-in price should not be less than 110 percent of the lowest available individual air fare offered by a scheduled carrier over the same route.(95) The same 110 percent rule was originally intended to apply to OTCs as well. The OTC regulations which were eventually adopted, however, fix the minimum OTC price at the level of the charter price, plus $15,00 for each night of the tour.(96) ECAC has consistently urged its member States to adhere to the 110 percent rule for European originating North Atlantic ITCs.(97)

On two occasions in 1974, Canadian, ECAC and U.S. representatives met to discuss North Atlantic charter tariffs. At a meeting, held in Paris on 22-23 May, 1974, they agreed that there should be a reasonable relationship between the lowest scheduled international air fares and charter fares, and that uniform minimum charter fares should be worked out between the carriers themselves, both scheduled and charter.(98) At an informal meeting, held in Montreal on September 27, 1974, during the 21st Session of the ICAO Assembly, Canadian, ECAC and U.S. representatives again reached the conclusion, that North Atlantic scheduled and charter carriers should, as soon as possible, reach an agreement on minimum North Atlantic charter tariffs, applicable to both IATA and non-IATA carriers, to both affinity charters, ABCs and TGCs. If such an agreement could not be reached, Governments would have to step in. As shall be seen hereunder in paragraph III, no agreement could be reached, and the negotiations between IATA and charter carriers broke off at San Diego (California) on October 8, 1974.

In view of the carriers' inability to reach agreement on North Atlantic minimum charter tariffs, Canada(99) and ECAC(100) had already, in 1973, taken action on minimum ABC tariffs. The U.S. CAB was more patient, and awaited the final collapse of inter-carrier negotiations at San Diego in October, 1974. On September 7, 1973, the CAB, under the new Subsection 1002(j) of the Federal Aviation Act,(101) had already issued a Notice of Proposed Rule Making,(102) containing minimum North Atlantic charter fares,(103) applicable to both affinity group charters and TGCs. On October 21, 1974, these minimum North Atlantic charter fares were made immediately effective.(104) Formally the CAB minimum charter fares were announced as mere "guidelines". Fares which would fall below the set "guidelines" would be investigated and suspended under Section 1002(j), unless adequately justified. The U.S. Department of Justice (Antitrust Division) issued the opinion that the CAB "guidelines" were <u>ultra vires</u> Section 1002(j). This Subsection gives the CAB suspension and rejection power over foreign air tariffs, but does not authorize the Board to prescribe such tariffs. According to the Department, the CAB had simply circumvented Section 1002(j) by issuing North Atlantic minimum charter fares, disguised as "guidelines". In practice the "guidelines" would be tantamount to a prescription of fares, a power not bestowed upon the Board under Section 1002(j).(105) The new CAB "guidelines" were also discussed during the so-called Kennedy Hearings of November, 1974.(106) Following the Hearings ACAP and NACA requested the U.S. Court of Appeals for the District of Columbia, to review the Board's "guidelines". The Court agreed to hear the case on February 14, 1975. Eight days before the scheduled Court hearing, the Board requested the Court to postpone it. The request was denied, and on February 11, 1975, the Board, in a sudden move, voluntarily withdrew its own "guidelines".(107) According to the Board the differential rates for different types of aircraft equipment and the general validity of data submitted to the Board by the airlines, could not be satisfactorily resolved. Furthermore, the Board noted that its "guidelines" came too late, since many charter contracts for the 1975 season had already been concluded, and sales to the public were already well under way, especially with respect to TGCs, requiring advance bookings. Whether the arguments raised by the Board, were its real reason for withdrawing the "guidelines" is difficult to say. One is tempted to see in the Board's withdrawal a degree of uncertainty about the outcome of the Court of Appeals' decision on the matter. The final result then of the Board's withdrawal was that no minimum charter fares were adopted for U.S. origin North Atlantic charter flights. Also the new regulations introducing European style ABCs in the U.S.A. make no mention of minimum charter fares.(108)

The situation in Europe is entirely different. Eleven ECAC member States have followed the Conference's Recommendations as to minimum North Atlantic ABC fares. Seven other ECAC member States,(109) however, have declined to do so, or have their own minimum North Atlantic ABC fares. ECAC's first Recommendation was issued in June, 1973.(110) The minimum ABC fares, contained therein, were revised and raised in <u>inter alia</u> January, 1974,(111) and November, 1974.(112) They are higher than the minimum charter fares, as proposed and withdrawn by the U.S. CAB.

III. Rapprochement between IATA and Charter Airlines

Charter competition between IATA and charter only airlines has generally been favourable for the aviation consumer. It has tended to bring air fares, both scheduled and non-scheduled down, especially on the North Atlantic market, where such competition has always been at its strongest. Notwithstanding this competition both IATA and charter airlines fared well financially until about 1970. After that time, however, inflation, overcapacity and the fuel crisis began to plague both classes of airlines, and as a consequence thereof certain attempts were made to limit price competition between IATA and charter airlines, so that perhaps both would be able to do better financially. IATA's unsuccessful attempt to open up the Association to charter only airlines must amongst other things be seen in that light.(113)

Furthermore, the above-discussed ECAC recommended minimum charter fares, and also the abortive U.S. CAB minimum charter fares should primarily be regarded as a Governmental attempt to shield financially troubled flag carriers from a too fierce form of charter price competition. It is not surprising to see that European Governments are more eager to impose such Governmentally determined minimum charter fares than is, for instance, the American Government. After all, most of Europe's scheduled international airlines are wholly or partially State-owned, and their financial well being is of direct interest to their owners, the Governments. In the U.S.A., where all airlines are privately-owned, the Government is certainly not irresponsive to the financial interests of its international air carriers, but, on the other hand, it is definitely less willing than European Governments to protect them, for instance, through a system of Governmentally determined minimum charter fares, aimed at limiting charter price competition.(114)

Charter only airlines have not been hostile to the idea of negotiating a system of minimum international charter fares with the scheduled international airlines. In doing so, they have, however, always insisted on preserving their own identity and independence. They have consistently resisted any attempt to be "wrapped up" by scheduled airlines. Such a course of events would perhaps not only be disastrous for the charter only airlines themselves, but certainly also for the aviation consumer. The latter definitely benefits from a certain degree of price competition between IATA and charter only airlines. In case of elimination of such competition, for instance, in the form of charter airlines being completely absorbed by IATA, it would probably be the aviation consumer, who would suffer most, since tariffs would then almost certainly rise for lack of any competitive incentive.

In this context reference should again be made to the "ideal regulatory framework of international ratemaking", discussed in Chapter I. Might future bilateral air transport agreements, or a standard ICAO tariff clause or clauses, delegate international ratemaking, both scheduled and non-scheduled to "an association or associations of international airlines", the danger exists that, when such an "association" would be IATA only, price competition between scheduled and charter airlines would disappear altogether. Therefore, it would perhaps be better to have two international ratemaking machineries, one scheduled - IATA - one non-scheduled - e.g., within the framework of IACA. The existence of an international non-scheduled ratemaking machinery would, of course, to a certain extent eliminate competition, but the fact that there would still be two international ratemaking machineries, competing with each other, would probably guarantee the aviation consumer the benefit of competition, which he has had to date.

In relation to scheduled - charter competition - it should further be remarked, that any form of predetermination of capacity for international air charter services would be disastrous for the consumer. Such capacity control, as suggested by, for instance, Gazdik and Lowenfeld,(115) would perhaps limit scheduled - charter competition even more than any form of price competition elimination. It seems that, at least, the U.S.A. is still firmly committed to only an *ex post facto* review of capacity.(116)

Inter-carrier negotiations on minimum charter fares have so far only taken place with respect to the key North Atlantic charter market. A request to hold such negotiations was filed with the U.S. CAB, on May 9, 1973, by NACA, the trade association of the five biggest U.S. supplemental air carriers.(117) NACA, at that time, was of the opinion that negotiations between scheduled and charter air carriers might produce certain minimum fare levels, which would preclude the evil of below cost operations.(118) NACA envisaged that the desired inter-carrier negotiations could either be held simultaneously with IATA Traffic Conference meetings, or at a separate place and time. After the necessary CAB approval under Section 412 of the *Federal Aviation Act*(119) had been obtained, on June 19, 1973,(120) the second alternative, namely, to hold the inter-carrier negotiations at a separate place and time, was chosen. In its approval the CAB noted that its action was a

> "departure from historical policy which left charter rates to the forces of the market place".(121)

Unlike some commentators the Board did not see a move towards an IATA type charter cartel in its own approval. Amongst other things, the Board noted that the proposed inter-carrier negotiations would not necessarily be of a permanent nature, and that no IATA type administrative secretariat or rules of procedure had been established. The Board's approval was of a limited duration,(122) and extended to all U.S. and foreign air carriers, holding certificate(123) or permit(124) authority to perform North Atlantic charter services.

After preparations by a steering committee, the first inter-carrier negotiations were held at Brighton (England), from July 27 - 31, 1973. Twenty-two scheduled and seventeen charter operators participated in the Conference. Notwithstanding a rather optimistic press release, issued at the end of the Conference,(125) the negotiations finished without an agreement on minimum North Atlantic charter fares having been reached. Not only did the actual level of minimum charter fares prove to be a stumbling block, but also the question of whether there should be different fare minima for different types of aircraft, and different seating configurations.

A renewed attempt at reaching an agreement on minimum North Atlantic charter fares was made in 1974.(126) On May 17 of that year, the CAB approved a request by NACA, Pan Am and TWA for renewed minimum North Atlantic charter fare negotiations between all North Atlantic air carriers.(127) The approval was valid for a period of ninety days. After a steering committee meeting at Geneva, on May 29-30, 1974, an inter-carrier conference was scheduled for Montreux (Switzerland) on July 16, 1974. After two separate sessions, negotiations ended in a tentative agreement on August 9, 1974. Certain issues, however, remained unresolved. Amongst them was the dissatisfaction of charter air carriers with the volume of APEX traffic, set aside by IATA carriers on their North Atlantic scheduled air services.(128)

On August 15, 1974, the CAB again renewed its approval of North Atlantic inter-carrier negotiations,(129) this time for a period of sixty days. The negotiations were then resumed at San Diego (California), and, on September 11, 1974, resulted in another tentative agreement.(130) One day later, however, four charter operators(131) announced that they considered the proposed minimum charter fares too high. A last attempt at reaching an agreement was made a few weeks later, again at San Diego. In the meantime, on September 27, Canadian, ECAC and U.S. representatives had met in Montreal to discuss the situation.(132) On the same day, the U.S. Department of Transportation had convened a meeting of scheduled and charter carriers, and had, like the Montreal meeting, urged them to reach agreement so as to avoid Government intervention. Notwithstanding all this, the San Diego meeting ended without an agreement having been reached, and the negotiations were broken off on October 8, 1974.(133)

Since October, 1974, no inter-carrier negotiations on minimum North Atlantic charter fares have taken place. Both in private and public circles in the U.S.A., the present attitude is against such minimum charter fares. ECAC, as noted before, has since recommended its own minimum North Atlantic charter fares to member States.(134)

The main impetus which brought scheduled and charter air carriers together in the above-discussed negotiations, was the rather bleak financial situation, in which both classes of carriers found themselves in the early seventies. Gradually international airlines are recovering from the depression, caused by inflation, overcapacity and the fuel crisis. Hand in hand therewith goes a decreasing interest on the part of the carriers to come to a system of minimum international charter fares. Instead it seems, that scheduled - charter competition is again on the increase. The latest development in the field is probably that IATA carriers are no longer satisfied with APEX fares as a means to combat charter competition. Although APEX and Super-APEX fares are the lowest available scheduled fares on the North Atlantic - they are lower than the traditional North Atlantic 22-45 day excursion fares, and only slightly higher than the average charter fares - they are, according to IATA carriers, not low enough to efficiently combat charter competition. IATA carriers now propose to introduce part charters on their scheduled international air services.(135) Part charters are charter groups, travelling together on regular scheduled air services. Might these charters become reality on the North Atlantic routes, IATA airlines would probably set a portion of their total scheduled capacity apart for such services. Part charter fares would be lower than APEX fares. Their introduction would mean an intermingling of scheduled and charter passengers on IATA airlines' flights. The British CAA has already licensed its two major scheduled international air carriers, British Airways and British Caledonian Airways, to perform part charters. Whether they will in fact be introduced on the key North Atlantic market depends largely on the attitude of the American and Canadian Governments towards this new charter type. As far as Canada is concerned, it seems that the new (individual) Super-APEX or Charter Class Fares have taken the wind out of the sails of the proposed (group) part charter fares. Charter Class fares are now available between Canada, Britain and a number of other European countries.

IV. Government Ordered International Air Tariffs

The above-discussed Governmentally set minimum charter fares, e.g., in relation to ITCs and ABCs, are examples of Government ordered fares relating to non-scheduled international air transportation. Also in scheduled international air transportation, there exist a considerable number of Government ordered tariffs. In the first place, it should be remarked that most foreign originating mail conveyance rates can be considered as Government ordered rates.(136) They are determined on an inter-governmental level by the UPU.(137) Furthermore, many scheduled and non-scheduled "cabotage" tariffs are, in fact, Government ordered tariffs. In this respect the term "cabotage" should not be taken in its traditional sense of "coastal navigation", but rather in the wider sense of traffic between a certain country and its overseas possessions. That latter kind of traffic is, although often involving long distances, not international traffic for the airline(s) of the mother country and its overseas possessions. More often than not, carriage of this type of traffic is reserved to the airline(s) of the mother country and/or of its overseas possessions. As far as scheduled tariffs on these "cabotage" routes are concerned, some Governments simply use IATA tariffs. Other Governments, however, have preferred to issue orders to their national air carriers containing specified, non-IATA tariffs for "cabotage" routes. There are also Governments, which, on their "cabotage" routes, apply IATA tariffs to non-residents of the mother country and its overseas possessions, but special, lower Government ordered tariffs to residents.(138)

In purely scheduled international air traffic, there are also a considerable number of Government ordered tariffs. These tariffs would normally be IATA tariffs. The Association, however, recognizes that Governments can issue orders to their national air carriers, and sometimes to foreign air carriers, to provide special tariffs for certain traffic categories of national importance.(139) Most of these orders are indeed related to traffic of national importance, such as the carriage of diplomatic and Governmental officials, emigrants, pilgrims, missionaries, refugees, diplomatic cargo and mail, Governmental printed matter, and so on. Some Governments issue considerably more Government ordered tariffs than others. Of the major aviation countries, the U.K. is on the top of the list with respect to Government orders, and the U.S.A. on the bottom. An increasing number of Government orders, however, do not truly relate to traffic of national importance, but are rather aimed at giving national air carriers a competitive advantage over their foreign counterparts. Some of these latter orders are difficult to distinguish from Governmental reservations and conditions to IATA Traffic Conference Resolutions.(140) Government ordered tariffs containing special fares for, e.g., excursion, group, inclusive tour, journalist, and travel agent traffic, are more promotional in nature than inspired by national interest. The prime example of a competition inspired Government order was the June 1971 order of the Belgian Government to Sabena to introduce special, very low, non-IATA youth/student fares on the North Atlantic.(141) The use of these special fares was not limited to Belgian residents. Consequently, North Atlantic air carriers became worried that a considerable part of their North Atlantic youth/student traffic would be diverted to Sabena. Many Governments quickly decided to help their national air carriers in this respect, and issued similar orders as the Belgian Government had done. As a consequence thereof the summer of 1971 saw a whole scale of Government ordered North Atlantic youth/student fares, none of which were IATA agreed fares.

In order to protect its uniform international tariff system, IATA has consistently urged Governments not to use the system of

Government ordered tariffs for promotional purposes. It has also urged Governments to limit the number of Government ordered tariffs aimed at foreign air carriers. As far as such orders to foreign carriers are concerned, it is indeed true, as IATA argues,[142] that they may often contravene applicable bilateral air transport agreements, delegating international ratemaking, in the first instance, to the airlines concerned and/or IATA.

(1) For percentages, see _supra_, Introduction.

(2) International charter flights are performed both by IATA and non-IATA, both by scheduled and by non-scheduled airlines (see also _supra_, Introduction). Of the 1972 total international _passenger_ charter traffic 37 percent was performed by scheduled airlines, whereas 63 percent was performed by charter only airlines. It should be noted that of this total international passenger charter traffic carried by _scheduled_ airlines (37%), almost 15 percent was carried by non-IATA scheduled airlines (_Source_: "A Review of the Economic Situation of Air Transport (1963-1973)", _op.cit._, at 22-23).

(3) See _supra_, Ch. III, para. I.

(4) For the percentage relationship between _scheduled_ international passenger and _scheduled_ international cargo traffic see _supra_, Ch. V, para. II. In the 1972 international charter field 82 percent of the total number of tonne-kilometres performed were passenger kilometres, and 18 percent cargo and mail kilometres. It should be noted that _charter_ traffic is essentially international in nature. For instance, of the 1972 world total international _charter_ air traffic 89 percent was international in terms of tonne-kilometres, whereas in the 1973 _scheduled_ international field, 43 percent was international in terms of tonne-kilometres. Of the remaining 57 percent _domestic scheduled_ tonne-kilometres, 83 percent was accounted for by U.S. and USSR domestic air services (_Source_: "A Review of the Economic Situation of Air Transport (1963-1973)", op.cit., at 51 and 21).

(5) For instance, in 1960, 15.5 percent of the total North Atlantic air traffic was charter traffic, whereas in 1973, this percentage had risen to 28.4 percent. The highest percentage was attained in 1971: 30.8 percent. Some 25 percent of total international air traffic now consists of charter flights. See _supra_, Introduction.

(6) See _supra_, Introduction.

(7) In terms of both domestic and international air services, Aeroflot is the world's biggest airline.

(8) Civil Aviation Administration of China.

(9) Exceptions to this rule are, for instance, the very low scheduled tariffs of Aeroflot and Interflug between East Berlin and Moscow and between these two cities and a number of points in the Middle East. On Eastern European air tariffs see also, Dirlewanger, _op.cit._, at 227 et seq.

(10) _Example_: when the flag carriers of countries A and B are IATA members, tariffs between countries A and B will be IATA tariffs. When countries A and B would then allow the non-IATA flag carrier of country C to fly to their respective territories at lower than IATA tariffs, this non-IATA airline could, by combining services between countries A and C, C and B and v.v., undercut the direct IATA tariffs between countries A and B, thus causing severe competition for the IATA flag carriers of countries A and B.

(11) See _supra_, Ch. I, para. II.

(12) _Loftleidir_ has now merged with Icelandair, itself an IATA member.

However, Loftleidir, as part of Loftleidir/Icelandair, remains outside IATA.

(13) Cf. Dirlewanger, op.cit., at 223 et seq.

(14) In this context it should be recalled that, until 1972, CAB power over foreign air tariffs was rather limited. See supra, Ch. IV, para. III.

(15) In November, 1975, a non-IATA airline, Royal Air Maroc, started scheduled air services from Casablanca to New York and Montreal. On these services the company charges fares which are comparable to those of IATA for the same North-Altantic route. Pan American World Airways charges identical tariffs on its New York - Morocco air services. There are also some Latin American airline companies, such as Air Panama, which have remained outside IATA.

(16) Cathay Pacific Airways (Hong Kong), China Airlines (Taiwan, formerly an IATA member), Korean Airlines, Malaysian Airlines System, Singapore Airlines, Thai International.

(17) See Politics, Downturn Hit Far East, AWST, Jan. 13, 1975, at 26 et seq.; IATA: Seeking a new image for changing times, Montreal Star, Jan. 24, 1976.

(18) Resolutions 115, 115 A, 115 B, 115 C, 115 D, 115 E, 115 F.

(19) See British Air Transport in the Seventies, op.cit., at 57. For the definition of load factor, see supra, Ch. III, para. I.

(20) In addition hereto overhead costs of scheduled airlines tend to be higher than those of charter airlines. Like operating costs, overhead costs are passed on to the user.

(21) See, Review of the Economic Situation of Air Transport (1963-1973), op.cit., at 57.

(22) Ibidem, at 26 and 28.

(23) The October, 1975, average load factor of IATA airlines on the North Atlantic routes, for instance, was 61.8 percent (Source: AWST, Feb. 16, 1976, at 34).

(24) See supra, Ch. II, para. II.

(25) For instance, it was reported that the average 1974 load factor on the US supplemental airline World Airways' Boeing 747 services was only 79.69 percent (Source: Gazdik, The Distinction between Scheduled and Charter Transportation, 1 Air Law, 66 at 69 (1976).

(26) See supra, Ch. V, para. I.

(27) See, e.g., An Analysis of International Air Charters Undertaken at the Request of the European Civil Aviation Conference. Prepared by IATA, Geneva, Switzerland, Feb. 1972; Gazdik, Co-Existence of Scheduled and Charter Services in Public Air Transport, 77 The Aeronautical Journal, 32 at 36 and nt 22 (1973); Detière, Competition between Scheduled and Charter Services, 11 ITA Bull., 247 at 250 - 251 (March 1973); Agreeing Fares and Rates, op.cit., at 69.

(28) See supra, Ch. V, para. I.

(29) For an explanation of these charter types, see infra.

(30) It did, however, also have the objectionable by-effect of making the IATA fare structure very complicated (See supra, Ch. V, para. I).

(31) Saturn Airways, Inc. v. CAB, USCA, D.C. Circ., July 11, 1973, 12 AVI 17.986.

(32) See supra, Ch. I, para. I.

(33) This Governmental permission is usually exchanged in bilateral air transport agreements; see supra, Ch. I, para. II.

(34) ICAO Doc. 6894 - AT/694 (1949).

(35) See supra, Ch. I, para. I: Definition of a Scheduled International Air Service, op.cit., at 12.

(36) For more details see infra, and Van den Assum, International Air Charter Transportation: Its Legal Rules and Implications, unpublished thesis, McGill Univ., Montreal, 1975, at 98 et seq.

(37) Definition of a Scheduled International Air Service, op.cit., at 3.

(38) See, e.g., Gazdik, op.cit., 77 The Aeronautical Journal, 32 at 36 (1973); Gazdik, op.cit., 1 Air Law 66 at 67 (1976).

(39) See, Non-Scheduled Services in International Air Transport, ICAO Doc. 8744 - AT/717 (1962).

(40) The definition of "supplemental air transportation" (i.e., charter air transportation) in Section 101(34) Federal Aviation Act, 72 Stat. 731, as amended, 49 U.S.C. 1301, does not contain the distinction between "individually ticketed" and "group" travel, except for ITCs (added by amendment: Public Law No. 90-514, Act of Sept. 26, 1968, 82 Stat. 867). The distinction is, however, clearly made in the CAB's Economic and Special Regulations (14 C.F.R.).

(41) The original British ABC rules allowed the carrier to market ABCs directly to the public. This rule was later changed pursuant to a 1972 ECAC Recommendation (ICAO Doc. 9044, ECAC/INT. S/5 (SP) at 8-12). British rules now provide that ABCs must be sold to the public through travel organizers (CAA Off. Records, Series I, Amendment 30, Schedule 5, Art. 1(1)).

(42) For TGCs see, Saturn Airways, Inc. v. CAB, cit. supra. For US domestic ITCs, see American Airlines, Inc. v. CAB (No. II), USCA, D.C. Circ., July 9, 1966, 9 AVI 18.230. The contrary decision, namely, that ITCs contravene the "group" vs. "individually ticketed" travel distinction, was reached with respect to foreign ITCs by the USCA, 2nd Circ., in Pan American World Airways, Inc. v. CAB, July 20, 1967, 10 AVI 17.399. The decision was affirmed by the US Supreme Ct., but its effect was annulled by quick Congressional Action bringing ITCs under the Federal Aviation Act's definition of "supplemental air transportation" (PL 90-514, cit. supra.). As early as 1965, the USCA had already decided that split charters preserve the "group" vs. "individually ticketed" travel distinction: American Airlines Inc. v. CAB (No. I), USCA, D.C. Circ., March 4, 1965, 9 AVI 17.451. Split charters are charters, whereby the total capacity of the aircraft is not chartered by one, but by several intermediaries. They have been allowed in the U.S.A. since 1964 (ER-408, 29 Fed. Reg. 6005).

(43) British Air Transport in the Seventies, op.cit., at 55-60.

(44) Statement of July 20, 1970, op.cit., at 88.

(45) AWST, Feb. 16, 1976, at 32.

(46) Laker Airways v. Department of Trade, Q.B.D., July 30, 1976; appeal dismissed; see 2 Air Law 31-34 (1977).

(47) See, Van den Assum, op.cit., at 98 et seq.

(48) See supra, Ch. I, para. II.

(49) TIAS 7819.

(50) TIAS 7479.

(51) Statement of July 20, 1970, op.cit., at 88. The bilateral approach is strongly advocated by, i.a., Browne, The International Angle, op.cit., and by Lichtman, Regularization of the Legal Status of International Air Charter Services, 38 JALC 441 (1972). Scoutt and Costello advocate a bilateral approach for a trial period of five years; thereafter a multilateral approach should be adopted: The New Mode: Setting A New Course for International Air Transportation, 39 JALC 1 at 24-25 (1973).

(52) Pan American World Airways, Inc. and Trans World Airlines, Inc. v. CAB, USCA, 2nd Circ., May 22, 1975, 13 AVI 17.856.

(53) Houston, Lay and Menke go so far as to propose the creation of an international organization in the field of international charter transportation, called the International Charter Enforcement Organization (ICEO). See International Charter Flight Standings: Proposals for Multinational Regulation, 3 Cal. Western Int. L.J. 333 at 339 et seq. (1973).

(54) See AWST, Dec. 1, 1975, at 34.

(55) See supra, Ch. I, para. III.

(56) Preamble and Art. 2 of the Agreement.

(57) Article 2(1) of the Agreement.

(58) Article 2(2) of the Agreement.

(59) In accordance with Article 3 of the Agreement, all air charter services not covered by Article 2 remain subject to the "regulations, conditions or limitations" rule of Article 5(2) of the Chicago Convention.

(60) ICAO Doc. 8244-AT/717, op.cit., defines an inclusive tour as "a round trip or circle-trip performed in whole or in part by air for a comprehensive price which includes accommodation for the period the participants are away from the starting point of the journey. It may also provide for additional facilities and may be undertaken either on normal scheduled air services or on aircraft especially hired for that purpose. A tour is normally for a predetermined period and to an announced destination or destinations."

(61) Rec. No. 6. ECAC Fourth Session, July 1961 (ICAO Doc. 8185, ECAC/4-1). ECAC has no decision-making power. It can only recommend certain actions to its member States.

(62) Non-Scheduled Air Traffic Within and From the "EU-MED" Region, 1972, ITA Study, 1974/1.

(63) 68 Dept. of State Bull. 20 (1973).

(64) "Passenger Charters".

(65) See, Goldklang, Transatlantic Charter Policy - A Study in Airline Regulation, 28 JALC 99 at 105 et seq. (1961/1962).

(66) Res. 045(4)(a).

(67) Res. 045(4)(c).

(68) Res. 045(4)(b).

(69) Res. 045(9).

(70) For the definition of TC and JT areas see supra, Ch. III, para. II.

(71) Res. 045(8).

(72) Res. 045(8)(iv).

(73) E.g., the 1950s editions of Part 207 of the CAB's Economic Regulations, 14 C.F.R. Part 207. Until 1960, the British regulations merely referred to Res. 045.

(74) See Keyes, The Transatlantic Charter Policy of the United States, 39 JALC 215 at 219 et seq. (1973).

(75) See American Airlines, Inc. v. CAB (No. 1), cit. supra, and ER-408, 29 Fed. Reg. 6005, cit. supra.

(76) See American Airlines, Inc. v. CAB (No. II), cit. supra, and PL 90-514, cit. supra.

(77) 14 C.F.R. Part 378.2(b)(2).

(78) 14 C.F.R. Part 378 A, effective Sept. 13, 1975. At the same time that OTCs were introduced, the CAB also introduced Special Event Charters (SECs) as a special type of OTCs (14 C.F.R. Part 378 A.101-103). SECs, used for charter air transportation to (and accommodation at) special events such as sports events, fairs and conventions, have been in existence in Europe for a considerable number of years.

(79) See supra, Introduction.

(80) 49 U.S.C. 1371: a scheduled operator cannot also hold a certificate

of public convenience and necessity for supplemental air transportation.

(81) Res. 045 is still valid in other parts of the world. Res. 045c (cargo charters) is still generally valid. In April, 1975, the third session of the African Civil Aviation Conference (AFCAC) decided to continue to endorse Resolution 045.

(82) Order 72-6-91, June 21, 1972, at 4.

(83) This period was later, for both ABCs and TGCs, brought down to 60 days. The same period applies to IATA's special APEX fares.

(84) See, i.a., ICAO Doc. 9044, ECAC/INT. S/5 (SP), Nov. 1972; ECAC/ECO-II/7, April 1974.

(85) CAB Docket 24908. The latest postponement of the suspension of prior affinity charters can be found in EDR-237E, Jan. 30, 1975.

(86) 14 C.F.R. Part 372A.10(g) and 14.

(87) 14 C.F.R. Part 372A.10(f) and 15.

(88) S.421, 94th Cong., 1st Sess.; see also, H.R. 6625, 94th Cong., 1st Sess.

(89) EDR-294/SPDR-42/ODR-12, Feb. 10, 1976.

(90) Performed in accordance with relevant CAB regulations (see 14 C.F.R. Parts 207, 208, 212).

(91) Return charter flights without passengers or cargo.

(92) Cf. Cirlewanger, op.cit., at 213 et seq.; ICAO's Survey of International Air Transport Fares and Rates, op.cit., only gives partial and scattered information on non-scheduled international fares and rates.

(93) Unrealistic as it may sound now, the US CAB, in 1950, urged IATA to begin determining international charter tariffs. At that time, most IATA airlines felt that such action would be premature. Consequently, the CAB proposal was not implemented.

(94) AIP Neths. FAL -1-3-2/3, Art. 5 A/B.

(95) 14 C.F.R. Part 378.2(b)(4).

(96) 14 C.F.R. Part 378A.10(g).

(97) See i.a., ICAO Doc. 9086, ECAC/INT.S/6 (SP) at 14 (1974).

(98) ECAC Press Rel. No. 26E, May 24, 1974.

(99) Unilaterally through the CTC.

(100) Multilaterally in the form of Recommendations to member States.

(101) See supra, Ch. IV, para. III.

(102) PSDR-37, Docket 25875.

(103) 2.2 ¢ per seat mile for midweek charters; 2.4 ¢ per seat mile for weekend charters.

(104) Order 74-10-106, Oct. 21, 1974: 3.1 ¢, 3.4 ¢, 4.1 ¢ per seat mile for aircraft with less than 230 seats (in low, shoulder and peak season respectively); 2.4 ¢, 2.7 ¢, 4.1 ¢ per seat mile for aircraft with more than 229 seats (in low, shoulder and peak season respectively).

(105) See supra, Ch. IV, para. III.

(106) Hearings before the Subcommittee on Administrative Practice and Procedure, Committee on the Judiciary, U.S. Senate, 93rd Cong., 2nd Sess., Nov. 7 and 8, 1974 (Airline Charter Fares).

(107) CAB Press Rel. No. 75-34, Feb. 11, 1975.

(108) See EDR-294/SPDR-42/ODR-12, Feb. 10, 1976, at 11.

(109) Belgium, Denmark, Italy, Norway, Sweden, Switzerland, the United Kingdom.

(110) ICAO Doc. 9062, ECAC/8, at 12: 2.2 ¢ per seat mile during the off season, and 2.5 ¢ during the peak season.

(111) ICAO Doc. 9086, ECAC/INT. S/6 (SP) at 10-11: 2.9 ¢ per seat mile during the off season, and 3.3 ¢ during the peak season.

(112) ECAC Doc./INT. S/8 at 26-27: 3.34 ¢ per seat mile during the

off season, 3.57 ¢ during the shoulder season, and 4.39 ¢ during the peak season. These amounts, like the above-mentioned ones, apply to the eventual retail price to be paid by the passenger. The following wholesale prices were recommended as between carriers and tour organizers: 2.85 ¢ per seat mile during the off season, 3.05 ¢ during the shoulder season, and 3.75 ¢ during the peak season. ECAC further urged member States to apply these wholesale prices also to charters other than ABCs or ITCs (thus, to affinity group charters). The above Recommendation came into force on 1 April, 1975, with 31 March, 1976 as expiry date.

(113) See _supra_, Ch. III, para. I and II.

(114) Another example of U.S. Governmental reluctance to help its international flag carriers financially, this time in a more direct fashion, was President Ford's refusal to grant financial aid to Pan American World Airways, when, in 1974, the company was on the brink of bankruptcy.

(115) Gazdik, _op.cit._, 1 Air Law 66 at 68 and 72 (1976); Lowenfeld, _op.cit._, 54 Foreign Affairs 36 at 48 (1975).

(116) _AWST_, Dec. 15, 1975, at 26-27.

(117) See _supra_, Introduction.

(118) Like IATA tariffs, officially minima (see _supra_, Ch. V) possible minimum charter tariffs are also likely to become the actual, uniform tariffs.

(119) See _supra_, Ch. II, para. II and Ch. IV, para. III.

(120) Order 73-6-79.

(121) _Ibidem_, at 3.

(122) 120 days.

(123) For US air carriers, Section 401 _Federal Aviation Act_, 72 Stat. 731, 49 U.S.C. 1371.

(124) For foreign air carriers, _ibidem_, Section 402, 49 U.S.C. 1372.

(125) "While no specific agreement was reached, notable progress was made. The Conference enabled the delegates to exchange views for the first time on the make up of an acceptable package covering charter rates and services, and while the views differed, many common approaches were found. Notable among these was the agreement in principle on a programme covering standards of services which would become an integral part of a rate understanding." See: _Annual Report of the Director General of IATA_, 29th AGM, Auckland, Nov. 1973, at 6-7.

(126) In the meantime, ECAC's minimum charter fares had come into force and the CAB had adopted its Notice of Proposed Rule Making regarding minimum North Atlantic charter fares. See _supra_, para. II.

(127) Order 74-5-89. Approximately at the same time, on May 15, US carriers requested prior CAB approval for a plan to create a special Charter Conference within IATA. The plan never materialized. See _supra_, Ch. III, para. II.

(128) See _infra_, Ch. VII, para. III.

(129) Order 74-8-62.

(130) Proposed were: a) for narrow-bodied aircraft 3.1 ¢, 3.4 ¢ and 4.1 ¢ per seat mile (in low, shoulder and peak season respectively); b) for wide-bodied aircraft 2.75 ¢, 3.05 ¢ and 3.75 ¢ per seat mile (in low, shoulder and peak season respectively).

(131) Capitol Airways, Overseas National Airways, Saturn Airways, Wardair.

(132) See _supra_, para. II.

(133) For the exact chronology of events see also: Driscoll, Pres., NACA, Statement during 1974 Kennedy Hearings (Airline Charter Fares), _op.cit._, at 4 et seq.

(134) See _supra_, para. II.

(135) See, <u>Montreal Star</u>, Feb. 4, 1976; AWST, Oct. 4, 1976 at 27.

(136) Most international mail is carried on scheduled flights. It can, of course, also be carried on non-scheduled flights. For instance, in intra-European air traffic a considerable amount of international mail is carried on non-scheduled flights, mostly ITCs, and especially to holiday resorts which are exclusively or almost exclusively served by charter flights.

(137) See *supra*, Ch. III, para. III.

(138) For instance, IATA tariffs apply to scheduled air traffic by non-residents between the Netherlands and the Netherlands Antilles. Special, lower Government ordered tariffs apply to such traffic by residents of the Netherlands and the Netherlands Antilles.

(139) See, *Agreeing Fares and Rates*, *op.cit.*, at 76 et seq.

(140) See *supra*, Ch. IV, para. II.

(141) See also *infra*, Ch. VII, para. III.

(142) *Agreeing Fares and Rates*, *op.cit.*, at 77.

CHAPTER VII: THE NORTH ATLANTIC BATTLEFIELD

A special study of North Atlantic air fares and rates is warranted, when one considers that some twenty-five percent of the world's total international air traffic is carried on the North Atlantic air routes from Europe to the U.S.A. and Canada.(1) Twenty-three IATA airlines, of which 5 North American,(2) 16 European,(3) and 2 Asian(4) fly between European and North American points. Four non-IATA international airlines also perform North Atlantic scheduled air services.(5) In addition, there are numerous charter only airlines, most of which are ACCA, IACA and NACA members,(6) which fly the North Atlantic air routes.

It is not only the magnitude of North Atlantic air traffic, which warrants a special study of North Atlantic air tariffs, but also the fact that the North Atlantic market has traditionally been the battlefield between IATA and charter only airlines, and that Governmental tariff intervention, especially by the U.S. CAB, has been stronger here than anywhere else in the world. It is in particular the strong North Atlantic charter competition, which is responsible for the comparatively low level of North Atlantic air tariffs.(7)

North Atlantic tariffs are not only important for the North Atlantic market as such but also for the tariff structure in the rest of the world. It proves to be extremely difficult to determine scheduled international air tariffs elsewhere in the world, when North Atlantic scheduled air tariffs have not first been agreed upon. IATA, therefore, usually schedules its JT 12 meetings before any other Traffic Conference meetings.(8)

In studying North Atlantic air tariffs from 1945, when North Atlantic air services first began on a truly regular basis, until today, one can distinguish three periods: the periods between 1945 and 1960, between 1960 and 1970, and between 1970 and now. These periods will be studied in three consecutive paragraphs. The first period can be qualified as the period of growth of North Atlantic air services. During that period North Atlantic air traffic was almost exclusively scheduled in nature, and was characterized by a slowly declining tariff level. The end of the fifties, and the beginning of the sixties saw the replacement of propeller aircraft by jet aircraft (DC 8, Boeing 707), and an initial overcapacity problem connected therewith. The second period, the sixties, was the period of consolidation of North Atlantic jet aircraft services, and of the birth of true charter competition. The end of this period then saw the introduction of wide-bodied jets (DC 10, Boeing 747, L1011) on the North Atlantic air routes, and again an overcapacity problem. During the early seventies, this overcapacity problem was aggravated by inflation and the fuel crisis, bringing both scheduled and non-scheduled airlines into financial difficulties. Gradually airlines seem to be recovering from this depression. The latest development on the North Atlantic is the introduction of supersonic scheduled air services.(9)

In this Chapter, as in the preceding one, heavier emphasis will be put on international air fares than on international air rates. Although the transportation of air cargo is percentage-wise more voluminous on the North Atlantic air routes than anywhere else,[10] major North Atlantic tariff developments have taken place rather in the international fares than in the international rates field. Scheduled North Atlantic cargo rates have been lower than international cargo rates elsewhere in the world.[11]

I. Period 1945 - 1960

As stated earlier, the period between 1945 and 1960 can be described as the period of growth of North Atlantic air services. These services were predominantly scheduled ones, and were performed with propeller aircraft. During this period North Atlantic air tariffs slowly declined. The declining level of air tariffs was mainly due to the gradual introduction of larger and more efficient aircraft.[12] Within the IATA Traffic Conferences the period was characterized by a difference of opinion between American and European carriers. The former, with the support of the U.S. CAB, generally pushed for lower tariffs, whereas the latter generally advocated higher tariffs. The reason behind the difference in American and European pricing policies lay in the fact that, especially after the second World War, the unit operating costs of American carriers were lower than those of their European counterparts. American carriers generally oeprated with newer and more efficient aircraft than did European carriers. They were generally more efficiently managed than European airlines, and, furthermore, capital was more readily available in North America than in Europe.

The first time that the U.S. CAB approved a New York - London IATA fare was in 1946.[13] At that time the one-way New York - London fare was $325,00, thus, disregarding the enormous rise in general price levels between 1946 and 1976, approximately equal to the present New York - London one-way economy class fare.[14] This 1946 New York - London fare was thirteen percent lower than the previously applicable fare, but eighteen percent higher than the one proposed by Pan American.[15] Until 1952 all North Atlantic IATA services were first class services. Cheaper tourist class services were introduced in May, 1952, almost three years after Pan American's original proposal to that effect.[16]

The first time that the CAB seriously considered disapproval of an IATA North Atlantic fare package, which it considered too highly priced, was in 1956. The package proposed to raise first class fares by ten percent. The CAB was of the opinion that, when increasing first class fares, IATA airlines should, at the same time, decrease tourist class fares, and should introduce a higher seating density on tourist class services.[17] After vehement protests by carriers and European Governments, the CAB soon gave in, and approved the ten percent fare increase.[18] During the same year, 1956, Pan American proposed the introduction of a new, more inexpensive service on the North Atlantic market, i.e., economy class service. Pan Am's proposal was not implemental until April 1, 1958, and then at fare levels which were considerably higher than the ones originally proposed.[19]

A major IATA Traffic Conference crisis broke out in the fall of 1959, soon after the introduction of jet aircraft on the world's important air routes. The 1959 Honolulu Composite Traffic Conference foundered upon basically two issues, not only related to the North Atlantic market, but rather to the world's air routes as a whole. The first issue was, whether a tariff surcharge should be introduced for travel on the new jet aircraft services. The second issue was the insistence of British carriers, with the strong support of their Government and also of a number of flag carriers of other Commonwealth countries, upon very low international air fares. Half a year after the Honolulu Conference, and after a change of Government in Britain, the IATA Traffic Conference machinery was able to solve its internal problems. For the future, there were to be only two classes of service on the world's trunk air routes: first class and economy class service. The tariff structure should be based on the use of jet aircraft. Discounts for travel on propeller aircraft were provided for in the form of either lower fares or more liberal service conditions.[20]

II. Period 1960 - 1970

The replacement of propeller aircraft by jets had two important economic consequences. On the positive side, the new and more efficient aircraft reduced unit operating costs. On the negative side, the new and bigger aircraft caused an overcapacity problem. The increase in capacity resulting from the introduction of jets, outpaced the increase in traffic, thereby dangerously lowering the international airlines' average load factors and earnings. To remedy the overcapacity problem, American airline companies proposed lowering tariffs in order to attract additional traffic. European airlines, on the other hand, were of the opinion that only an increase in tariffs could improve the situation. The clash came at the IATA Composite Traffic Conference, held at Chandler (Arizona) in the fall of 1962. The international confrontation resulting from the Chandler Conference, is generally known as the Chandler Fare Controversy.[21] The Chandler Conference had decided to adopt a worldwide fare increase in the form of a reduction in the then existing round-trip discount from ten to five percent. The U.S. CAB, which had expected that, in view of the differing pricing policies of carriers, the Chandler Conference would decide upon a maintenance of the status quo in the international fares field, announced its intention of disapproving portions of the Chandler fare package, inter alia, with respect to North Atlantic fares.[22] Although the IATA adopted reduction in the round-trip discount would not apply to North Atlantic first class fares, but only to North Atlantic economy class fares, it would nevertheless have the consequence of increasing most North Atlantic round trip fares, since the bulk of North Atlantic traffic already moved in economy class service. The CAB made its intended disapproval definite thirteen days before the Chandler fares were to become effective on April 1, 1963.[23] IATA, a number of foreign carriers and their Governments voiced fierce protests, and warned the CAB against the adverse effects of a possible open fare situation on the North Atlantic. Nevertheless, that open fare situation became a fact on April 1, 1963. In its final disapproval the Board noted that, in its opinion, the pre-Chandler fares were adequate to produce fair earnings for the carriers at reasonable load factors, and that the proposed fare increase to offset low load factors would be unfair to the travelling public.

As explained earlier,[24] before the introduction of Section 1002(j) of the U.S. Federal Aviation Act in 1972, CAB disapproval of IATA tariffs under Section 412 still left carriers the freedom to file individual tariffs, over which the Board had then virtually no control. After April 1, 1963, European carriers indeed began to file individual tariffs with the CAB, which incorporated the Chandler fares. Upon the insistence of the Board, Pan Am and TWA, however, filed the cheaper, pre-Chandler fares. The U.S. State Department then sent diplomatic notes to fourteen countries, in which dissatisfaction was voiced with the tariffs filed by the flag carriers of these nations. Due to a lack of real power over international air tariffs, however, the State Department and the CAB found themselves in a rather poor bargaining position. Whereas the applicable type (f) Bermuda rate clause gave the U.S. Government the international authority to "take such steps as it may consider necessary", this provision was generally considered to remain ineffective, as long as Congress had not granted the CAB real domestic power, in other words a Section 1002(j) power, over international air tariffs.(25) As a consequence thereof, when European carriers continued to apply the Chandler fares, and when their Governments began to order Pan Am and TWA to apply the Chandler fares as well - the British Government even threatened to bar U.S. air carriers from British airports - the State Department and the CAB gave in to the pressure. Pan Am and TWA were instructed by the Board to apply the Chandler fares.

A special IATA Traffic Conference, which was subsequently convened at Montreal, attempted to heal the scars caused by the Chandler Fare Controversy, and adopted a compromise fare package, which, by mid-July, 1963, would reduce the Chandler fare increase by approximately fifty percent.(26)

With the unpleasant experience of the Controversy still in mind, Governmental aviation authorities from twenty-two countries met at Ottawa, in July, 1963, to study procedural improvements in the relationship between Governmental aeronautical authorities and IATA. The Conference ended with the adoption of a set of rather vague recommendations. In an explanatory statement the U.S.A. indicated some general tariff changes, which it would wish to see implemented. Among them were a substantial general reduction in tariffs, the introduction of a super-economy service, sharp reductions in off-season fares, and the introduction of directional and group fares.(27)

The most important consequence of the Chandler crisis was probably the adoption in the U.S.A., both by the CAB and by Congress, of a more liberal attitude towards charter flights.(28) This attitude resulted in a growing availability of North Atlantic charter flights at ever lower prices. This, in its turn, forced IATA and its member carriers to adopt lower special fares(29) in order to match the charter competition.

Between 1963 and 1970 both IATA's normal economy and special North Atlantic fares went down. Charter flights increased in number and decreased in price. Due to a satisfactory average annual traffic growth of approximately sixteen percent,(30) the IATA airlines' initial overcapacity problem was soon solved, and notwithstanding fierce competition between the two classes of carriers, both IATA and charter carriers did well financially on the North Atlantic between 1963 and 1970. No major IATA North Atlantic fare crises occurred during this period. It may, however, be worthwhile to mention a conflict, which broke out over IATA service standards in 1964, and which might well have caused a major fare crisis. The conflict was related to the introduction of visual inflight entertainment on the flights of IATA airlines.(31) TWA was the first international airline to introduce such service on its flights. Its example was followed by a number of other airlines. At the IATA Composite Traffic Conference, held at Athens (Greece) in the fall of 1964, a difference of opinion arose between the "haves" and the "have-nots". The latter, not offering visual inflight entertainment, felt that those IATA airlines which had begun to offer the service, were causing them undue competition. Strong pressure was put on the "haves" to abandon their visual inflight entertainment, but no unanimous agreement was reached in that respect at Athens. Two special IATA meetings in the spring of 1965, however, did solve the issue, and a Resolution was adopted which would completely ban visual inflight entertainment from the flights of IATA airlines. Airline companies, which had already introduced the service, would be indemnified. The Resolution was tied in with the general fare package, already adopted at Athens. On June 1, 1965, the U.S. CAB disapproved the Resolution as being contrary to the public interest(32) thereby causing an open fare situation. After a maintenance of the status quo during the summer of 1965, an IATA JT 12 and JT 123 Conference, held at Bermuda in the fall of 1965, succeeded in producing a new fare package. Soon thereafter a special IATA meeting adopted another Resolution, which would allow IATA airlines to offer visual inflight entertainment, but at a charge of $2,50 per passenger wanting to use the service.(33) This Resolution, tied in with the Bermuda fare package, was approved by the CAB on May 1, 1966,(34) and is still valid.(35)

III. Period after 1970

History repeats itself. At the end of the fifties, jet aircraft began to replace propeller aircraft on the world's trunk air routes, thereby causing an overcapacity problem. At the end of the sixties, wide-bodies jets (DC 10, Boeing 747, L1011), made their appearance on long haul air routes, and again an overcapacity problem arose. Traffic growth could not keep pace with the increased capacity. This time, however, the situation became further complicated by a number of other factors: the inflationary pressures, and currency devaluations and fluctuations of the early seventies. Consequently airline operating costs began to rise sharply. The answer of IATA airlines to these rising operating costs was a gradual increase in tariffs. Due to the presence of strong charter competition, such IATA tariff increases on the North Atlantic air routes were not as steep as those elsewhere in the world.

With the overcapacity, inflation and currency problems of the early seventies, the fuel crisis of 1973 came as a serious blow to all international airlines. Notwithstanding the fact that increased fuel prices were generally passed on to the consumer in the form of higher tariffs, the crisis brought most international airlines, both scheduled and non-scheduled, in the red. Only now, in 1976-1977, do airlines seem to be recovering from their financial difficulties.

Overcapacity, inflation, currency problems and the fuel crisis made the period from 1970 until now a particularly tumultuous one on the North Atlantic. IATA encountered difficulties in trying to agree on North Atlantic fare packages. Governments became actively, but not very successfully involved in North Atlantic ratemaking. Finally, as discussed earlier, several fruitless attempts were made to come to a system of inter-carrier agreed minimum North Atlantic charter fares. Highlights of North Atlantic fare developments after 1970 are discussed below.

During the overcapacity period of the early sixties, North American airline companies had favoured a general tariff reduction in order to attract additional traffic, and thereby to solve the overcapacity problem. During the overcapacity period of the early seventies a number of European, rather than American carriers adopted this policy. In April, 1971, the Belgian flag carrier Sabena introduced a low cost North Atlantic youth fare for students under thirty years old.(36) The carrier adopted the fare after having been "ordered" to do so by the Belgian Government. As of April 1, 1971, an open fare situation was already a fact on the North Atlantic, since the same Belgian Government had not approved the North Atlantic fare package, agreed upon at the Geneva Traffic Conference of December, 1970. Whereas after the Belgian Governmental disapproval, North Atlantic air carriers had originally intended to maintain a tariff status quo from April 1, 1971 to March 31, 1972, the new Sabena youth fare forced them to introduce special low youth fares themselves in order to avoid a diversion of youth traffic to Brussels.(37) Hence, the summer of 1971 showed a variety of youth fares on the North Atlantic.

IATA, unhappy with this situation, convened another Traffic Conference at Montreal, in July, 1971. At the Conference the idea was put forward to introduce a new, low special fare on the North Atlantic, the APEX fare.(38) This plan, however, did not materialize. One IATA carrier, Lufthansa, opposed it, exercised its veto right, and as a consequence the Montreal Conference broke down in August, 1971, without having reached agreement on a new North Atlantic fare package. In fact, Lufthansa was at the time of the opinion that there should be only three kinds of fares on the North Atlantic: normal fares, low 14/28 day excursion fares(39) and special youth fares for persons under 21 years old.

Lufthansa's proposed low excursion fares were considered as uneconomic by U.S. air carriers. The fear of introduction of such low excursion fares was one of the factors, which induced the U.S. Congress to pass its 1972 legislation, giving the CAB more power over international air tariffs.(40) In the meantime, on September 24, 1971, the CAB had issued a Statement on International Air Fares,(41) in which it indicated that, like Lufthansa, it wished to see the implementation of a simplified fare structure, but then at fare levels, which would cover the full costs of the air services offered. What the CAB really wanted, was lower normal fares, and fewer and higher special fares.

After a series of Traffic Conference meetings, IATA finally succeeded in adopting a North Atlantic fare package for the period April 1, 1972, to March 31, 1973. Besides normal fares, the package showed, inter alia, both 14/28 and 22/45 day excursion fares, and also special youth fares for persons under 21 years old, at the same level as the 22/45 day excursion fares. Grudgingly, the CAB approved the package.(42)

At Montreux, in July, 1972, IATA's North Atlantic ratemaking machinery broke down altogether. No agreement could be reached on North Atlantic air fares for the period commencing April 1, 1973. Faced with this situation, carriers began to file individual tariffs for the summer of 1973. European carriers generally field tariffs, which would maintain the existing low excursion fares. Tariffs filed by U.S. carriers followed the CAB Statement of September, 1971, and raised excursion fares, while at the same time lowering normal fares. In January, 1973, the CAB approved the North Atlantic fares filed by U.S. air carriers.(43) During the following months, however, it disapproved, under the new Section 1002(j) of the Federal Aviation Act, the North Atlantic air fares filed by nine European air carriers.(44) The Board considered these fares as bearing little or no relation to costs, and as having an adverse effect upon the yield to carriers.

A major North Atlantic fare cirsis was now imminent. After the failure of several rounds of informal inter-governmental negotiations, IATA hammered out a last minute fare package at London, in March, 1973. The package would revalidate and extend the existing North Atlantic IATA fare structure for the period April 1 to December 31, 1973, subject to an across-the-board six percent fare increase for

Eastbound originating traffic effective April 13, 1973, to reflect the recent devaluation of the U.S. dollar. With misgivings, the CAB approved the package.(45) It noted that the IATA agreement did nothing "to simplify the fare structure or to produce the revenue improvement all consider necessary". Nevertheless, the Board was of the opinion that a maintenance of the status quo, as laid down in the fare package, was in the public interest, since lack of agreement and an open fare situation would cause the travelling public and those who sell air transportation "considerable inconvenience". With the CAB's reluctant approval the existing North Atlantic fare structure was thus again extended until December 31, 1973. A Court action by ACAP against the Board approval was successful, but did not come timely enough to invalidate the North Atlantic fare package. In Pillai, Goldwyn, ACAP v. CAB(46) the U.S. Court of Appeals decided that the Board's findings as to the predicted inconvenience of an open fare situation for the travelling public were unsupported by substantial evidence,(47) and constituted an abuse of agency discretion.(48) Shortly after the Court's decision, the CAB issued an Order,(49) inviting interested persons and Governmental authorities to submit their views and comments as to what action the Board ought to take. Out of the two alternatives, namely, to require air carriers to file new individual air tariffs or to reapprove the agreement, the Board chose the latter. In this action, which was taken on October 15, 1973,(50) the Board was supported by most carriers and by ECAC. The U.S. Departments of Justice and Transportation, and ACAP, however, would have favoured the former action.(51) In its Order, reapproving the March 1973 Order the CAB went into great detail concerning the history which had led to the original April 1973 approval. It was also very careful in observing the "substantial evidence" requirement, as ordered by the Court of Appeals. No action followed the Board's reapproval of October 15, and consequently the controversial IATA North Atlantic fare package remained in force until its expiry date, December 31, 1973.

In the meantime, at Monaco, in October 1973, IATA carriers had reached agreement on a new North Atlantic fare package for the period of January 1, 1974, through October 31, 1974. The package maintained the existing North Atlantic fare structure of normal and special fares, but introduced a gradual scale of fare increases, averaging approximately six percent, in order to meet rising fuel costs and to offset currency losses. With the Court of Appeals decision and its own 1971 Statement in mind, the CAB disapproved the youth/student fares contained in the package as being discriminatory,(52) disapproved the proposed increases in normal economy class fares, and deferred action on the proposed 22/45 day excursion fares, which it considered as being too low.(53) In a spirit of cooperation IATA soon revised the package in accordance with the wishes of the Board.(54) The revised package, maintaining the normal economy class fares at the 1973 levels, increasing the 22/45 day excursion fares, and eliminating the youth/student fares, was approved by the Board on December 26, 1973,(55) as "a material first step towards setting in motion a series of alterations in the North Atlantic fare structure which could and should culminate in a cost-oriented pattern of fares for the longer term.(56)

One facet of the thus approved North Atlantic fare structure for 1974 was of great concern to U.S. air carriers. They were worried that, since youth/student fares had been eliminated between the U.S.A. and Europe, U.S. originating youth and student traffic would be diverted to Canada, from where special youth/student fares to Europe were available. Such a diversion of traffic did indeed occur, but nevertheless the CAB, in June, 1974, refused to approve tariffs, filed by TWA, Pan American, National Airlines and a number of foreign air carriers, which would have reinstated youth fares from the U.S.A. to Europe.(57) A motion by TWA to the same effect was also denied by the Board.(58) The following North Atlantic IATA fare package, however, brought a solution to most of the diversion concerns of U.S. air carriers. Beginning November 1, 1974, youth fares from Canada to Europe would, during the peak season, not be available to holders of U.S. passports, unless they could prove to be Canadian landed immigrants, holders of a Canadian student visa, or of documentary proof of at least three months' residence in Canada.(59)

During 1974, a series of attempts was made to arrive at a truly new North Atlantic fare structure. American, Canadian and European Government officials met at Paris, in the spring of 1974, and agreed on a number of guidelines for future ratemaking in the North Atlantic market.(60) Minimum charter fares should be agreed upon on an inter-carrier basis.(61) Fares should generally be cost-related, and capacity should be brought more closely into line with demand. The same principles were later enunciated by the CAB in its Policy Statement of June, 1974.

IATA scheduled a North Atlantic Traffic Conference at Fort Lauderdale (Florida), for June 11, 1974.(62) Plans were studied to replace the IATA three-season North Atlantic fare structure (low, shoulder, peak) by a two-season fare structure (winter fares at the previous shoulder levels, and summer fares at the peak levels). The proposal to have only three North Atlantic IATA fares: normal, excursion and APEX, was also under consideration. The Fort Lauderdale Conference ended without an agreement on a specific North Atlantic fare package. The Conference decided to await the results of the inter-carrier charter Conference of Montreux, to be held in July. The Fort Lauderdale Conference did, however, decide upon another fuel-related fare increase of five percent, effective August 1, 1974.(63)

Since the above-mentioned Montreux charter Conference did indeed reach agreement in principle on a system of minimum North Atlantic charter fares,(64) IATA then proceeded with the convening of another North Atlantic Traffic Conference, also to be held at Montreux, during the month of August, 1974. The Conference did not adopt a two-season fare structure or a system of only three North Atlantic IATA fares, but rather maintained all existing fares while raising them by an average of ten percent. In addition, cheaper APEX fares would be introduced.(65) The minimum charter fares tentatively adopted by the inter-carrier Conference of July, were included in the fare package as a Recommended Practice.(66) An escape clause in the package further provided that, might the minimum charter fares not become effective, a new meeting should be held. The package was due to become effective on November 1, 1974.(67) The CAB approved it on October 21, 1974,(68) noting, *inter alia*, that "the agreement before us does accomplish in small measure some of our stated objectives."(69)

In view of the final breakdown of inter-carrier charter negotiations at San Diego, in October, 1974,(70) the escape clause in the fare package did indeed become effective, and a series of new IATA meetings became necessary. These meetings were held at Geneva, in late October, 1974, and resulted in the adoption of a North Atlantic fare package for the three months' period November 1, 1974, to January 31, 1975. The package abandoned the adopted APEX fares and the recommended minimum charter fares. Other fares, agreed upon at Montreux, in August, 1974, were maintained. The CAB approved the interim package as an emergency measure.(71)

After the largely unsuccessful 1974 attempts to arrive at a revised IATA North Atlantic fare structure, and to tie that in with inter-carrier agreed minimum charter fares, the year 1975 was a relatively uneventful period in the North Atlantic fares field. The abovementioned interim fare package, which went into effect on November 1, 1974, had to be extended for another two months, from February 1, 1975 to March 31, 1975,(72) in view of the inability of IATA carriers to settle the question of the possible introduction of APEX fares.

In January, 1975, IATA carriers were then finally able to agree on a North Atlantic fare package for the period April 1, 1975, to March 31, 1976. The agreement maintained the fare levels, adopted at Montreux, in August, 1974, and already laid down in the two abovementioned interim agreements (November 1, 1974, through March 31, 1975).(73) The APEX fares, agreed upon at Montreux, would also finally go into effect, at a slightly lower level than originally determined. Of course, under the circumstances, the recommended minimum charter fares, adopted at Montreux did not form part of the package. It was, however, decided that youth fares would be reinstated between the U.S.A. and Europe. On March 27, 1975, the CAB approved the whole package.(74) Although it certainly did not live up to the Board's expectations regarding a revised North Atlantic fare structure, its approval seemed warranted as the only possible compromise at the time, and in view of the fact that the financial results of carriers were slowly improving. The Board also approved the reinstatement of youth fares between the U.S.A. and Europe, arguing that the Canadian residence requirements during the peak season could not be adequately enforced, and did thus not give American carriers enough protection against diversion of youth traffic to Canada.

The IATA North Atlantic fare package for the summer of 1976,(75) again showed a maintenance of the existing North Atlantic fare package, coupled with the introduction of special first class fares for supersonic air services(76) and a new "super APEX" or "Charter Class" fare at the level of ABC fares between Canada and Europe.(77) Existing fares were raised in amounts varying up to ten percent. The package was approved by Canadian and European Governmental aviation authorities. The CAB approved only part of the package.(78) It disapproved _inter alia_ the increase in normal fares(79) and _all_ fares between Miami and London.(80) It considered the proposed APEX fares from the U.S.A. to Europe as being too low, but did not disapprove them for fear of diversion of APEX traffic to Canada.

The latest IATA North Atlantic fare package came, at least partially, into force on April 1, 1977 with March 31, 1978 as expiry date.(81) Three changes can be noted, when compared with the summer 1976 agreement: the initiation of a two-season structure (low and peak), the relaxation of APEX eligibility requirements and the change from a 21/45 to a 14/45 days excursion fare. Fare increases ranged from one to nineteen percent. Finally the 1977-78 package is the first species of the new IATA "limited agreement".(82)

On balance, the IATA North Atlantic fare structure is, except for the new APEX fares, and the new two-season structure, still based on the system of the sixties, i.e., relatively high normal fares and a multitude of different lower special fares. Attempts at revising this structure more thoroughly have so far been fruitless.

(1) A Review of the Economic Situation of Air Transport (1963-1973), op.cit., at 15 and 22.
(2) Air Canada, CP Air, National Airlines, Pan American, TWA.
(3) Aer Lingus, Air France, Alitalia, British Airways, British Calidonian Airways, CSA, Finnair, Iberia, KLM, LOT, Lufthansa, Olympic Airways, Sabena, SAS, Swissair, TAP.
(4) Air India, El Al.
(5) Aeroflot, Air Bahama, Loftleidir, Seaboard World Airways (All-cargo airline).
(6) See supra, Introduction.
(7) Average scheduled revenue per passenger kilometre: a) on North Atlantic routes 2.7¢; b) on intra-European routes 6.5¢; c) on routes between Canada, Mexico and the USA 3.9¢. Average non-scheduled revenue per passenger kilometre: a) on North Atlantic routes 1.4¢; b) on intra-European routes 1.8¢. Source: Survey of International Air Transport Fares and Rates, op.cit., at 40, 58, 88.
(8) See supra, Ch. III, para. II.
(9) See supra, Ch. V, para. I.
(10) Whereas in 1973, 26.2% of the total international passenger air traffic was carried on the North Atlantic air routes, this percentage was 34.5% for total international cargo air traffic. Source: A Review of the Economic Situation of Air Transport (1963-1973) op.cit., at 15.
(11) Average scheduled revenue per tonne-kilometre: a) on North Atlantic routes 13 ¢; b) on intra-European routes 38.5 ¢; c) on routes between Canada, Mexico and the USA 19 ¢. Source: Survey of International Air Transport Fares and Rates, op.cit., at 40, 58, 88.
(12) E.g., the DC 7 and Lockheed Super Constellation.
(13) 6 CAB Reports 845, 850 (1946).
(14) In low season and in shoulder season $323; in peak season $387.
(15) Keyes, The Making of International Air Fares and the Prospects for their Control, 30 JALC 176 (1964).
(16) Ibidem, at 177.
(17) Order E-9969, Feb. 2, 1956.
(18) Order E-10017, Feb. 20, 1956; Keyes, The Making of International Air Fares and the Prospects for their Control, op.cit., at 180-181; Lowenfeld, Aviation Law, op.cit., at III - 20-21.
(19) Keyes, The Making of International Air Fares and the Prospects for their Control, op.cit., at 177, 181.
(20) Lowenfeld, Aviation Law, op.cit., at III - 17-19 (reprinted from Cohen, Crisis in the Conferences, op.cit.); Wood, op.cit., at 8-9.
(21) See Goodwin, The Role of the U.S. in the 1963 Transatlantic Air Fare Crisis, 30 JALC 82 (1964); Keyes, The Making of International Air Fares and the Prospects for their Control, op.cit., at 181-183; Chayes, Ehrlich, Lowenfeld, op.cit., at 489 et seq.; Lowenfeld, Aviation Law, op.cit., at III - 31-78.
(22) Order E-19294, Feb. 12, 1963, 38 CAB Reports 1068 (1963).
(23) Order E-19385, March 18, 1963, 38 CAB Reports 1063 (1963).
(24) See supra, Ch. IV, para. III.
(25) See Hearings on International Air Transport Rates and S.1539 and

S. 1540 before theComm. on Commerce, US Senate, 88th Cong., 1st Sess., 1-48 (1963); see also *supra*, Ch. IV, para. III.

(26) See Lowenfeld, *Aviation Law*, *op.cit.*, at III-78-79.

(27) See Lowenfeld, *Aviation Law*, *op.cit.*, at III-78-80.

(28) See *supra*, Ch. VI, para. II; Keyes, *The Transatlantic Charter Policy of the United States*, *op.cit.*, at 219 et seq.

(29) See *supra*, Ch. V, para. I.

(30) See, *A Review of the Economic Situation of Air Transport (1963-1973)*, *op.cit.*, at 19 (1974).

(31) See Edles, *IATA, The Bilaterals and International Aviation Policy*, 27 Fed. Bar J. 291 at 301-302 (1967).

(32) Order E-22240, June 1, 1965, 42 CAB Reports 902 (1965).

(33) The charge is levied for the use of inflight entertainment equipment (ear-phones).

(34) Order E-23708, May 1, 1966, 44 CAB Reports 823 (1966).

(35) Res. 100 (Conditions of Service - Inflight Entertainment).

(36) New York - Brussels and return for $220. See also *supra*, Ch. VI, para. IV.

(37) These youth fares went down as low as $199 return.

(38) See *supra*, Ch. V, para. I.

(39) Frankfurt - New York and return for $210 in the off season, and $270 in the peak season.

(40) See *supra*, Ch. IV, para. III.

(41) See *Hearings before the Subcomm. on Aviation of the Comm. on Commerce*, U.S. Senate, 92nd Cong., 1st Sess., on S.2423, *op.cit.*, at 31-32 (1971).

(42) Order 72-3-104, March 30, 1972.

(43) Order 73-1-76, Jan. 26, 1973.

(44) Alitalia, BOAC, Lufthansa, Olympic Airways, Aer Lingus, CSA, Finnair, Iberia, TAP (see Order 73-10-55, Oct. 15, 1973, at 21 note 19).

(45) Order 73-4-64, April 13, 1973.

(46) USCA, D.C. Circ., Aug. 22, 1973, 12 AVI 18.036; see also *supra*, Ch. II, para. II, and *Pillai v. Civil Aeronautics Board - CAB Regulation of International Air Fares*, 47 Temple Law Quarterly, 620 (1974).

(47) *Administrative Procedure Act*, Act of Sept. 6, 1966, 80 Stat. 378, as amended, para. 10(e)(2)(E), 5 USC 706.

(48) *Ibidem*, para. 10(e)(2)(A).

(49) Order 73-8-131, August 28, 1973.

(50) Order 73-10-55, Oct. 15, 1973.

(51) *Ibidem*, at 6 et seq.

(52) Order 73-11-131, Nov. 28, 1973.

(53) Order 73-11-132, Nov. 28, 1973.

(54) The changes only affected traffic between Europe and the USA. The original package remained unchanged for traffic between Canada and the USA.

(55) Order 73-12-104, Dec. 26, 1973.

(56) *Ibidem*, at 3.

(57) Order 74-6-75, June 14, 1974.

(58) Order 74-8-12, Aug. 7, 1974.

(59) Order 74-10-106, Oct. 21, 1974 at 2.

(60) AWST, June 3, 1974, at 24.

(61) See *supra*, Ch. VI, para. II.

(62) In the meantime, a new seven percent IATA fuel surcharge had gone into effect on April 1, 1974. See CAB Press Rel. No. 74-161, July 31, 1974.

(63) Approved by the CAB on July 30, 1974, Order 74-7-141.

(64) See *supra*, Ch. VI, para. III.

(65) Sales of APEX fares would be limited to not more than 20% of an airline's total North Atlantic capacity on a particular route. They would be available under a 60 days advance booking and payment requirement.
(66) Recommended Practice 1045.
(67) AWST, Sept. 2, 1974, at 27.
(68) Order 74-10-106, Oct. 21, 1974.
(69) Ibidem, at 5.
(70) See supra, Ch. VI, paras. II and III.
(71) Order 74-10-151, Oct. 30, 1974.
(72) Approved by the CAB in Order 75-1-24, Jan. 7, 1975.
(73) An exception was made for 22/45 day excursion fares, which would go down slightly.
(74) Order 75-3-101, March 27, 1975.
(75) Valid from May 1 to October 31, 1976.
(76) See supra, Ch. V, para. I.
(77) The capacity set aside by IATA airlines for APEX traffic from the USA to Europe was raised from 20 to 25 percent. The capacity limitation for APEX traffic from Canada to Europe (previously 20 percent) was eliminated.
(78) Order 76-4-175, April 30, 1976.
(79) Normal fares between the U.S.A. and Europe will be maintained at the previously existing level.
(80) According to the CAB, National Airlines was making excessive profits on the Miami-London route. National and British Airways are the only two carriers on this route. A petition for reconsideration of this decision, made by National Airlines, was denied by the Board: Order 76-5-61, May 14, 1976.
(81) Order 77-3-54, March 9, 1977.
(82) See infra, Ch. VIII, para. III.

CHAPTER VIII: ALTERNATIVES TO THE PRESENT INTERNATIONAL RATEMAKING SYSTEM

In the final Chapter of this book possible changes to the present international ratemaking system will be discussed under three headings: free competition, intergovernmental involvement in international ratemaking, and a restructuring of IATA.

I. The Free Competition Alternative

Many advocates of the interests of those who use international air transport have brought forward the idea that IATA's ratemaking machinery should be dismantled and replaced by a system of free competition. IATA's system of uniform scheduled international tariffs and standardized service conditions does, to a very great extent, eliminate competition between scheduled international airlines. Such competition is, therefore, mainly limited to a competition in the scheduling of flights. Under the existing Bermuda - type bilateral air transport agreements there is in principle no a priori determination of capacity, leaving it up to the airlines themselves to decide upon the capacity and frequencies of their air services.(1) As far as pure tariff competition is concerned, it should, however, be remembered that IATA's uniform scheduled air tariffs, as a whole, compete with international charter tariffs, which are generally determined by the free forces of the marketplace.(2)

Would a dismantling of IATA's uniform tariff system and its replacement by a system of free competition really be to the benefit of the international aviation consumer? In the first place, it should be noted that in order to arrive at a system of truly free tariff competition, it is not only the IATA ratemaking machinery which should be dismantled, but also the presently existing system of Governmental control of international air tariffs. Existing bilateral air transport agreements would have to be changed to that effect. It is very doubtful whether Governments would be willing to do so. Most Governments, in one form or another, have a direct financial interest in their flag carriers,(3) and are presumably not ready to give up tariff control over these carriers. The only nation where public and Governmental opinion would probably be susceptible to eliminating Government control over international air tariffs, is the U.S.A.(4) All U.S. international airlines are privately owned, and in the U.S.A. heavy emphasis has always been put on the notion of free(tariff) competition between airlines. As yet, however, there are no clear indications that the U.S.A. would indeed want to abolish Governmental control over international air tariffs, and even if it wished to do so, it could practically not accomplish that aim without the consent of a sizeable number of other nations.(5)

Adopting, for the purpose of discussion, the hypothesis that both IATA and Governmental tariff control would be dismantled, what would then be the result for the international aviation consumer? The oligopolistic character of the airline industry would force airlines to choose between two alternatives. They could, on an informal basis, agree upon maintaining an IATA-like system of uniform tariffs. This, however, would probably be contrary to many existing antitrust laws. Their second alternative would be to initiate individual price experiments in the form of lower tariffs in order to attract more passengers and cargo. In an oligopolistic industry, like the airline industry, such price experiments could possibly lead to a real tariff war between airlines. The immediate effect of such a tariff war would be lower fares and rates for the consumer. In the long run, however, it would drive many airlines out of business. The few remaining airlines would then probably form a *de facto* monopoly resulting in either unchanged or higher tariffs for the international aviation consumer.

In the unlikely event that IATA's ratemaking machinery and Governmental tariff control would be abolished, consumers could thus, in the short term, possibly benefit from lower air tariffs. In the long term, however, free competition would be of little avail to them. In this context it should also be remarked that elimination of Governmental tariff control would be contrary to the public utility character of international air transportation.(6)

It is the author's opinion that an improvement in the consumer's position as to international air tariffs can be better and more adequately achieved through a more user-oriented system of intergovernmental tariff control.

II. The Intergovernmental Alternative

Governmental control over international air tariffs is presently exercised on an almost exclusively *national* basis,(7) either in accordance with applicable bilateral air transport agreements or unilaterally. No true intergovernmental system of international tariff control exists.

It is submitted that many international tariff problems could be solved or avoided through a more adequate system of intergovernmental tariff control. It is not suggested, however, that ICAO or any other intergovernmental organization would take over the task of international ratemaking. Intergovernmental organizations do not seem to be the proper forum for a highly technical, complicated and economic activity such as international ratemaking.(8) It is rather suggested that airlines themselves, either individually or through an organization or organizations like IATA, continue to determine their own tariffs in the first instance. In addition hereto, however, these (inter -) carrier determined tariffs should not only be subjected to national tariff control, as is the case now, but also to some form of intergovernmental control. National tariff control is mainly of a repressive, *ex post facto* nature. It is exercised by Governmental aviation authorities after the airlines themselves have determined their own tariffs. Intergovernmental tariff control could very well be of a preventive, *a priori* nature. Taking into account the interests of both the airlines and the consumers, such control could take the form of recommended or binding tariff guidelines to airlines, before they begin to determine their tariffs either individually or on an inter-carrier basis.(9) It could further be accomplished on a global basis through ICAO and/or on a regional basis. For example, as far as regional intergovernmental tariff control is concerned, the already existing *ad hoc* meetings between Canadian, ECAC and U.S. representatives(10) could easily be formalized into an ongoing intergovernmental tariff consultation and recommendation machinery for the North Atlantic market.

The choice between a system of binding or recommended intergovernmentally determined tariff guidelines is a difficult one. From the practical point of view, as far as international charter tariffs are concerned, there seems to be no objection to binding guidelines. The situation with respect to scheduled international air tariffs is different. As long as IATA's unanimity rule, even in its amended form,(11) has not been relaxed, binding guidelines could make the presently existing bargaining process within the Traffic Conferences almost impossible.

The choice between recommended and binding intergovernmental tariff guidelines also depends on one's economic philosophy. Nations with a traditional free market system would probably be more inclined to recommended guidelines, whereas nations with a mixed or socialist economy would be more inclined to binding guidelines. It is the author's opinion that a system of intergovernmentally determined recommended guidelines is preferable in view of the fact that a system of binding guidelines would almost be tantamount to transferring ratemaking power to an intergovernmental organization or organizations, an idea rejected earlier. It is furthermore doubtful, whether a system of binding guidelines would not contravene the letter, or at least the spirit of most existing bilateral air transport agreements, which delegate international ratemaking in the first instance to the airlines themselves.

ICAO, although for many years almost entirely inactive in the international ratemaking field,(12) now seems to take an active interest in the subject of international air fares and rates.(13) Pursuant to Resolution A 18-17, adopted by the ICAO Assembly during its Eighteenth Session in 1971, the ICAO Secretariat, in 1974, published its Survey of International Air Transport Fares and Rates.(14) The ICAO Assembly, during its Twenty-First Session, in 1974, then decided that this Survey should be published and updated annually.(15) The same Twenty-First ICAO Assembly also decided that within the triennium 1975 - 1977, a small panel of experts should meet to examine the machinery for the establishment of international air fares and rates.(16) In addition, the Assembly decided to convene a special Air Transport Conference or an ordinary or extraordinary Session of the ICAO Assembly to discuss air transport problems on a worldwide basis.(17) Finally, the Assembly directed the ICAO Council "to instruct the Secretary General to undertake a study of existing bilateral tariff clauses with a view to exploring the feasibility and relative benefits of either an international ICAO standard tariff clause or an international agreement embodying such a clause.(18) Upon the recommendation of ICAO's Air Transport Committee, the Council contracted this feasibility study out to the Institut de Transport Aérien (ITA) in Paris. The study was published in May, 1975 and is presently being considered by ICAO's Air Transport Committee.(19)

With respect to the feasibility study, the opinion has already been put forward(20) that an ideal framework of international ratemaking should be based upon an ICAO standard tariff clause of agreement, not only covering tariffs for scheduled air services, as envisaged by the present study, but also tariffs for charter air services. Such a clause or agreement should then, in the first instance, delegate international ratemaking to the airlines concerned. Under the clause or agreement airlines should be allowed to determine tariffs either individually or on an inter-carrier basis, through one or more associations of airlines. The IATA Traffic Conference machinery could thus function for the determination of scheduled international air tariffs alone, or also for the determination of international charter tariffs. Alternatively charter airlines could create their own international ratemaking machinery, for instance within the framework of IACA.(21) It would also be possible to retain the status quo with regard to international charter tariffs, namely, the system, whereby these tariffs are set by charter airlines themselves on the basis of the free forces of the marketplace. At any rate, after their initial determination by airlines, all tariffs should be subject to national Governmental control. Might the above-advocated proposal for preventive, a priori intergovernmental tariff control be followed, then it would only be necessary to mention this control mechanism in the ICAO standard tariff clause or agreement, in the event that intergovernmentally determined tariff guidelines would be binding upon the airlines concerned. Objection to such binding guidelines can certainly be expected from States, like the U.S.A., where national air carriers are not State-owned, and thus not or more moderately State-controlled.

In the meantime the first meeting of the above-mentioned panel of experts and a Special Air Transport Conference were held at ICAO Headquarters in Montreal,(22) respectively in December, 1976 and in April, 1977. The panel of experts adopted a number of tentative recommendations, which were subsequently studied and elaborated upon at the Special Air Transport Conference.(23) The Special Conference also considered matters such as capacity in international air services and the role of charters in international air transport. Amongst the recommendations finally adopted by the Special Conference in the international ratemaking field are the following. In the future ICAO representatives would sit as observers at IATA Traffic Conferences. In the interest of airline users and of the airlines themselves scheduled and non-scheduled air carriers are encouraged to establish regular discussions for the purpose of coordinating tariff policies. Finally, the ICAO Council has been requested to conduct a study of the necessity or not of creating a new intergovernmental machinery for the establishment of fares and rates. ICAO's ratemaking work will continue at the forthcoming Assembly Meeting in the fall of 1977, at a second meeting of the panel of experts and at a second Special Air Transport Conference.

III. The "New IATA" Alternative

Before discussing a possible restructuring of IATA, the question must be asked, whether IATA's ratemaking machinery is really indispensable. Would it not be better to abolish IATA's ratemaking machinery, and limit the Organization's activities to true trade association functions? In other words, could scheduled international airlines not determine their tariffs individually, only subject to national Governmental control? Since most bilateral air transport agreements do not make the use of the IATA ratemaking machinery compulsory,(24) there seems to be no legal objection to abolishing it. On the other hand, most international airlines and, more importantly, their Governments support the continuing existence of the IATA Traffic Conference machinery. Furthermore, its abolition, coupled with a retention of Government control over international air tariffs, would force national Governmental aviation authorities to take a much more active part in international ratemaking than before, something which they are generally unwilling or unable to do. Might national Governmental authorities not become more active in international ratemaking after the abolition of the Traffic Conference machinery, then the same development as in a system of complete free competition would probably occur: either a maintenance of the status quo, if allowed under antitrust laws, or initially lower, but later again stable or even higher tariffs.(25)

The idea of completely abandoning the IATA ratemaking machinery should, therefore, be rejected on both practical and economic grounds.

IATA once having tried to open up its doors to charter only airlines,(26) it now becomes necessary to decide, whether it it desirable that IATA enter the international charter ratemaking field. Charter only airlines have so far not showed any interest in joining IATA. Upon the basis of the already suggested ICAO standard tariff clause or agreement it would indeed be possible for IATA to engage in charter ratemaking. Nevertheless, it is submitted that such action would, at least for the time being, be undesirable. To-date, competition between scheduled IATA tariffs and non-IATA charter tariffs has been to the benefit of the aviation consumer, and in view of the fact that airlines have until now survived this competition financially, it seems worthwhile to retain it.(27) Another issue is, whether charter airlines should create their own ratemaking machinery, open either to charter only airlines exclusively, or also to scheduled airlines which perform charter services on the side. Although at the present time, there are no plans to create such a machinery, there would not be any major objection to it, as long as for the benefit of the consumer scheduled international IATA tariffs and inter-carrier agreed charter tariffs continue to compete with each other.

Whereas a restructuring of IATA in the form of an Association open to both scheduled and charter only airlines has thus been rejected, the idea of somewhat modifying the present Traffic Conference machinery should be encouraged, in particular with respect to the unanimity rule.(28) IATA's Thirty-First Annual General Meeting, held at Oslo from September 29 to October 2, 1975, decided that the Provisions for the Regulation and Conduct of the IATA Traffic Conferences should be amended so as to make place for "limited agreements", in which less than all Traffic Conference members participate and which bind only those participating members. Furthermore, it was decided that sub-areas should be created within the three existing Traffic Conference areas, wherein third, fourth and fifth freedom carriers(29) would exercise primary voting rights, and wherein carriers with an indirect interest would be limited in their veto rights.(30) Both proposals have in the meantime been implemented.(31) The system of "limited agreements" will solve at least part of the bargaining problem, caused by the existence of the unanimity rule.(32) Creating sub-areas will perhaps eliminate the anomaly that airlines, members of a Joint Traffic Conference by virtue of their membership in one of the Traffic Conferences constituting the Joint Conference, can veto tariffs within that Joint Conference, whereas they do not themselves perform air services between the Traffic Conference areas constituting the Joint Traffic Conference.(33) Amending the unanimity rule in these ways would also facilitate intergovernmental tariff control in the form of either binding or recommended tariff guidelines to airlines.(34)

(1) See *supra*, Ch. I, para. II. It should, however, be remembered that there are certain bilateral air transport agreements, which do contain capacity predetermination clauses (see *supra*, Ch. I, para. II) and that freedom of scheduling may be limited by the existence of pooling and capacity reduction agreements (see *supra*, Ch. II, para. II).

(2) See *supra*, Ch. VI, paras. II and III.

(3) See *supra*, Ch. II, para. I.

(4) Cf. developments in the US domestic air tariff field, *supra*, Ch. IV, para. III.

(5) See *supra*, Ch. IV, para. III.

(6) See *supra*, Ch. IV, para. I.

(7) See *supra*, Ch. IV and Ch. VI, para. II.

(8) It should, however, be remembered that foreign origin air mail conveyance rates are indeed determined by an intergovernmental body, namely, the UPU. See *supra*, Ch. III, para. III.

(9) E.g., in the form of a standard rate per kilometre for a certain route or area. See *supra*, Ch. V, para. I.

(10) See, e.g., Ch. VI, para. II; Ch. VII, para. III.

(11) See *infra*, para. III.

(12) See Pillai, *op.cit.*, at 122 et seq.

(13) See also *supra*, Ch. I, para. III.

(14) ICAO Circ. 123 - AT/33 (1974), *op.cit*.

(15) Res. A 21-26, para. 1(a). See Appendix D.

(16) Res. A 21-26, para. 1(c). See Appendix D.

(17) Res. A 21-25. See Appendix D.

(18) Res. A 21-27. See Appendix D.

(19) See *supra*, Ch. I, para. III.

(20) *Ibidem*.

(21) IACA could limit membership of its hypothetical ratemaking machinery to charter only airlines, or could also make scheduled airlines performing charter services eligible for membership.

(22) See Report of the First Meeting of the *Panel of Experts on the Machinery for the Establishment of International Fares and Rates*, ICAO Doc. FRP/1-Report (1976); *Special Air Transport Conference*, ICAO Doc. SATC, Report Folder (1977). See also Wassenbergh, *The Special Air Transport Conference of ICAO*. April 1977: A new basis for the trade in traffic rights for international air services? 42 JALC 501 (1976).

(23) See Documents, *cit. supra* nt 22.

(24) See *supra*, Ch. I, para. II.

(25) See *supra*, para. I.

(26) See *supra*, Ch. III, para. I.

(27) See *supra*, Ch. VI, para. III.

(28) See *supra*, Ch. III, para. II.

(29) See *supra*, Ch. I, para. I.

(30) For further details see Larose-Aubry, *op.cit.*, at 135.

(31) See the new sections 3-5 of Article VII Provs. for the Regulation and Conduct of IATA TCs.

(32) See *supra*, Ch. III, para. II.

(33) See *supra*, Ch. III, para. II.
(34) See *supra*, para. II, and Ch. V, para. I.

POSTSCRIPTUM

On 23 July 1977, the U.S.A. and the U.K. signed a new bilateral air transport agreement, commonly called Bermuda 2. It replaces the Bermuda Agreement of 1946 (Bermuda 1), discussed in Chapter I of this Book. The new Agreement maintains, although in a strongly eroded form, the above-discussed principles of Bermuda 1, namely *ex post facto* review of capacity and frequency of flights coupled with a system of Governmental approval of tariffs. When compared with Bermuda 1, the new tariff provisions of Bermuda 2 have been considerably streamlined and brought into line with post-Bermuda 1 practices.

Article 12 of Bermuda 2 provides that tariffs for scheduled air services shall be established "at the lowest level consistent with a high standard of safety and an adequate return to efficient airlines operating on the agreed routes" (Art. 12, para. 2). Each tariff shall be based on the costs of providing a particular air service "assuming reasonable load factors" (Art. 12, para. 2). The inclusion of a reference to reasonable load factors is new and in accordance with the tariff procedures of the U.S. CAB. Other factors to be taken into account in construing a fare or rate include competition from scheduled or charter air services and the prevention of unjust discrimination and undue preferences or advantages. The introduction of innovative, cost-based tariffs is encouraged (Art. 12, para. 2). Tariffs for carriage of traffic between the territory of Contracting Party B and a third State by the airline(s) of Contracting Party A (thus, *inter alia*, for fifth freedom traffic) shall need the approval of Contracting Party B and the third State in question (Art. 12, para. 3). All inter-carrier agreed tariffs, including those agreed upon by IATA, need prior Governmental approval in order to become effective (Art. 12, para. 4). Furthermore, all tariffs for transportation between the territories of the Contracting Parties must be properly filed with the competent aeronautical authorities. In the event of dissatisfaction with a proposed tariff each Contracting Party may require consultations to be held. If no notice of dissatisfaction is given within the delay provided for in the Agreement, a proposed tariff shall be deemed to be approved. Whenever the above-mentioned consultations lead to an agreement between the Contracting Parties, each Party "shall exercise its best efforts to put such tariff into effect". If not, the Party which raised the objection "may take action to continue in force the existing tariff" beyond its normal expiry date. In that event the other Party shall take similar action (Art. 12, para. 5, 6, 7).

New in Article 12 is the firm commitment of the Contracting Parties to combat the widespread system of airline rebates (Art. 12, para. 8) and the creation of a Permanent Tariff Working Group to avoid tariff disputes (Art. 12, para. 9,a). The Working Group shall, in accordance with the provisions of Annex 3 to the Agreement, make recommendations on load factor standards and other ratemaking criteria for use by the Contracting Parties in reviewing IATA tariffs (Annex 3, para. 4, 5). The Contracting Parties shall also keep each other informed on guidelines given to their airlines prior to and during IATA Traffic Conferences (Art. 12, para. 9,b).

It is interesting to see that under the regime of Bermuda 2 already one "tariff war" has broken out on the North Atlantic. Laker's low-cost, no-reservation Skytrain service between London and New York will be offered to the public for $135. one way Eastbound and $100. one way Westbound. Through IATA's ratemaking machinery six airlines (Air India, British Airways, El Al, Iran Air, Pan Am, TWA) have now filed a $256. return excursion fare between London and New York to match the Laker competition. This fare is $94. lower than the lowest scheduled excursion fare available at the present time. If approved, passengers will have the option of purchasing and paying their tickets 21 days before departure with flights assigned 10 days before the week of travel or travelling on a standby basis with seats assigned after 4 a.m. on the day of departure. The U.S. Justice Department has already challenged the filing of these six airlines as being "predatory" and "unfair".

APPENDICES

A. IATA Membership List

Source: The State of Air Transport Industry, 31st AGM, Oslo, September 29 - October 2, 1975.

Key:
- * member of Clearing House
- ** clears via Airlines Clearing House, Inc.
- 1 entirely privately-owned IATA active member (total - 21)
- 2 more than fifty percent privately-owned IATA active member (total - 4)
- 3 fifty or more percent State-owned IATA active member (total - 24)
- 4 entirely State-owned IATA active member (total - 39)

Totals: Active members: 88
Associate members: 24
Total number of members: 112

Active members

* 4	Aer Lingus (Ireland)
* 4	Aerlinte Eireann (Ireland)
* 4	Aerolineas Argentinas (Argentina)
* 1	Aeromexico (Mexico)
* 3	Air Afrique (Ivory Coast)
* 3	Air Algérie (Algeria)
* 4	Air Canada (Canada)
* 4	Air Ceylon (Sri Lanka)
* 3	Air France (France)
4	Air Guinée (Guinée)
* 4	Air India (India)
3	Air Liberia (Liberia)
* 4	Air Malawi (Malawi)
4	Air Mali (Mali)
3	Air Malta (Malta)
* 4	Air New Zealand (New Zealand)
* 1	Air Siam (Thailand)
* 3	Air Vietnam (Vietnam)
3	Air Zaire (Zaire)
* 4	ALIA - The Royal Jordanian Airlines (Jordan)
* 3	Alitalia (Italy)
** 1	Allegheny Airlines (U.S.A.)
* 1	American Airlines (U.S.A.)
4	Angola Airlines (Angola)
* 3	Ariana Afghan Airlines (Afghanistan)
* 3	Austrian Airlines (Austria)
* 1	Avianca (Colombia)
* 1	Braniff International (U.S.A.)
* 4	British Airways (U.K.)
* 1	British Caledonian Airways (U.K.)
* 4	British West Indian Airways (Trinidad)
* 1	C.P. Air (Canada)

4	Cameroon Airlines (Cameroon)
* 4	CSA - Ceskoslovenske Aerolinie (Czechoslovakia)
* 1	Cruzeiro (Brazil)
* 4	Cubana (Cuba)
* 3	Cyprus Airways (Cyprus)
** 1	Delta Airlines (U.S.A.)
* 4	DETA - Linhas Aéreas de Mocambique (Mocambique)
* 4	East African Airways (Kenya)
* 1	Eastern Airlines (U.S.A.)
1	Ecuatoriana (Ecuador)
4	Egyptair (Egypt)
* 3	El Al Israel Airlines (Israel)
* 4	Ethiopian Airlines (Ethiopia)
* 3	Finnair Oy (Finland)
** 1	The Flying Tiger Line (U.S.A.)
* 4	Garuda Indonesian Airways (Indonesia)
3	Ghana Airways (Ghana)
* 4	Iberia (Spain)
* 1	Icelandair (Iceland)
* 4	Indian Airlines (India)
* 4	Iran Air (Iran)
* 4	Iraqi Airways (Iraq)
* 3	Japan Air Lines (Japan)
* 4	JAT - Jugoslovenski Aerotransport (Yugoslavia)
* 3	KLM Royal Dutch Airlines (The Netherlands)
* 4	Kuwait Airways (Kuwait)
4	Lan Chile (Chile)
* 4	Libyan Arab Airlines (Libya)
* 4	LOT - Polish Airlines (Poland)
* 3	Lufthansa (West Germany)
** 2	Mexicana (Mexico)
* 3	Middle East Airlines (Lebanon)
** 1	National Airlines (U.S.A.)
* 4	Nigeria Airways (Nigeria)
* 4	Olympic Airways (Greece)
* 3	Pakistan International Airlines (Pakistan)
* 1	Pan American World Airways (U.S.A.)
* 2	Philippine Air Lines (Philippines)
* 4	Qantas Airways (Australia)
* 3	Sabena (Belgium)
* 3	SAS (Scandinavia)
* 4	Saudi Arabian Airlines (Saudi Arabia)
* 4	South African Airways (South Africa)
* 4	Sudan Airways (Sudan)
* 2	Swissair (Switzerland)
4	Syrian Arab Airlines (Syria)
* 2	TAP - Transportes Aereos Portugueses (Portugal)
* 3	THY - Turkish Airlines (Turkey)
* 1	Trans-Mediterranean Airways (Lebanon)
* 1	Trans World Airlines (U.S.A.)
3	Tunis Air (Tunisia)
* 1	United Air Lines (U.S.A.)
* 1	Union de Transports Aériens (France)
* 1	Varig (Brazil)
* 3	Viasa (Venezuela)
* 4	Zambia Airways Corporation (Zambia)

Associate members

Aerial Tours (Papua/New Guinea)
Aerochaco (Argentina)
Aerolineas Cordillera Ltda. (Chile)
Air Niugini (Niugini)
* Ansett Airlines of Australia (Australia)
AVNA (Aviation-Natal) (South Africa)
Chicago Helicopter Airways (U.S.A.)
Commercial Airways (South Africa)
Crowley Airways Pty. Ltd. (Papua/New Guinea)
East-West Airlines (Australia)
Eastern Provincial Airways (Canada)
* Ladeco (Chile)
Macair (Papua/New Guinea)
Mount Cook Airlines (New Zealand)
** New York Airways (U.S.A.)
* New Zealand National Airways (New Zealand)
Quebecair (Canada)
Suidwes Lugdiens (South West Africa)
TALAIR Pty. Ltd. (Papua/New Guinea)
* Trans-Australia Airlines (Australia)
Trans Brasil (Brazil)
Trans-West Air Charter (W.A.) Ltd. (Australia)
United Air Services (South Africa)
VASP - Viacao Aerea Sao Paulo (Brazil)

B. IATA Organization Chart

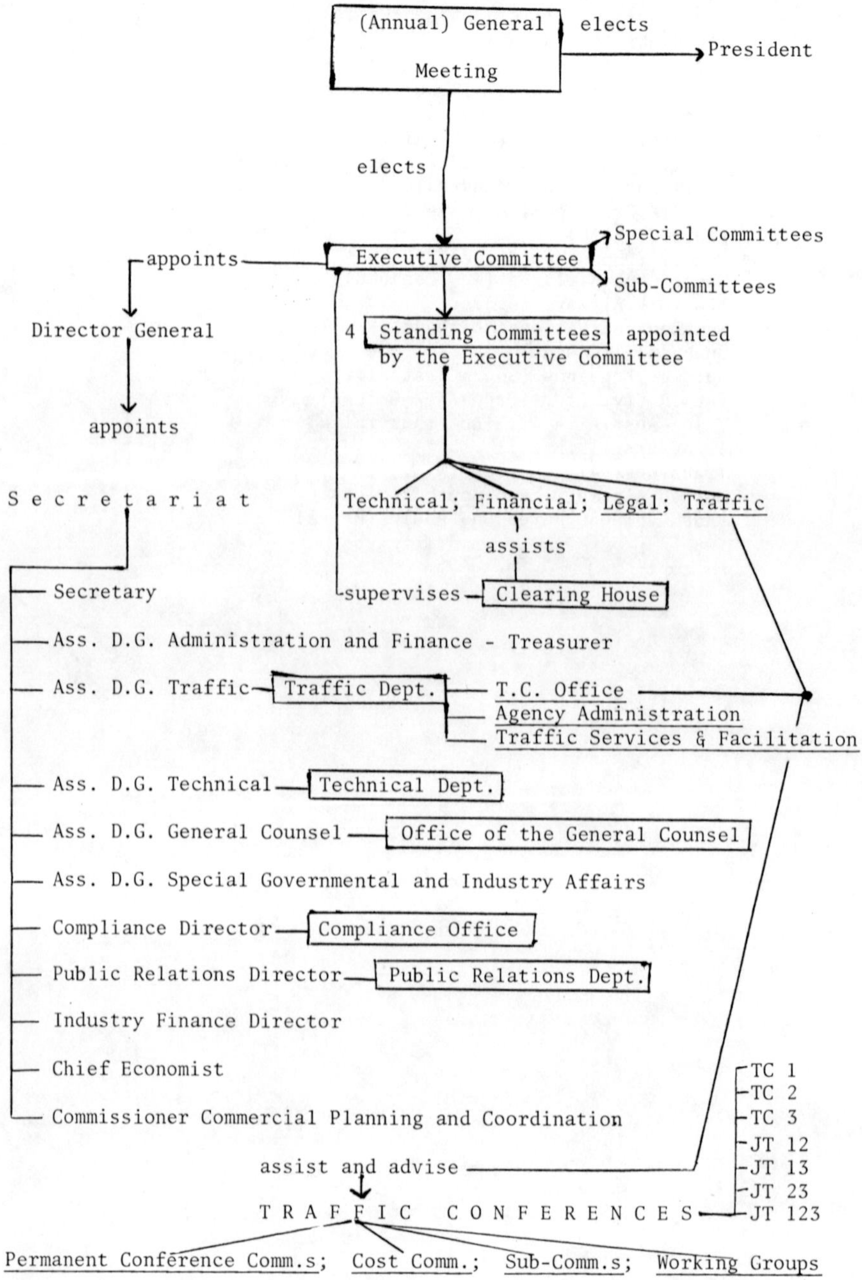

C. IATA Doc. AGM 30/24.E

FINAL RESOLUTIONS

I. RESOLUTION AUTHORIZING AN AMENDMENT OF THE ACT OF INCORPORATION AND OF THE ARTICLES OF ASSOCIATION

WHEREAS The Executive Committee of the International Air Transport Association recommended, at its 90th meeting held in Montreal on the 17th day of September, 1974, that the Association's Act of Incorporation and Articles of Association be amended to permit participation in the Association by air transport enterprises operating air services between territories of two or more States for public transportation of passengers, mail or cargo, other than scheduled air services as at present referred to in the Act of Incorporation and in the Articles of Association;

NOW THEREFORE BE IT RESOLVED THAT

1. the Association be and is hereby authorized to present a petition to the Canadian Senate and House of Commons requesting an amendment of the Act of Incorporation of the Association, that is Chapter 51 of 9-10 Georges VI of the Statutes of Canada, in order to delete the word "scheduled" in paragraphs (a) and (b) of Article I of the Act of Incorporation;
2. the Articles of Association be amended as follows:
   Delete Paragraphs (2), (3) and (5) of Article IV of the Articles of Association and substitute the following:
   "(2) The following are eligible for membership as Active Members:
      (a) Any "air transport enterprise", as defined in the Act of Incorporation, which is operating a scheduled "air service", as defined in the Act of Incorporation between the territories of two or more States as a designated air carrier under an inter-governmental air transport agreement (specifying the route or routes to be served by such carriers);
      (b) Any other "air transport enterprise", as defined in the Act of Incorporation, which is operating an "air service" as defined in the Act of Incorporation between the territories of two or more States.
   "(3) Any "air transport enterprise", as defined in the Act of Incorporation which is operating a scheduled "air service" as defined in the Act of Incorporation is eligible for membership as an Associate Member, provided it is not eligible for membership as an Active Member.
   "(5) Application for membership in the Association shall be submitted to the Head Office in the form and detail required by the Executive Committee for consideration and action by the Executive Committee. In the case of application for membership by an air transport enterprise referred to in paragraph 2(a), if the application is found in order and the applicant eligible for election to the Association, the applicant shall be duly admitted by the Executive Committee to Active membership; otherwise the application shall be rejected. In the case of application for membership of an air transport enterprise referred to in Paragraphs 2(b) or (3) above, the applicant shall be duly admitted by the Executive Committee to the appropriate class of membership, provided that it meets the qualifications for admission of such applicant which the Executive Committee

shall prescribe from time to time having regard to such factors as the length of time that the applicant has been established as an air transport enterprise and the extent of its operations; otherwise the application shall be rejected. The election to membership shall be effective upon payment of entrance fees and dues for the current year."

V. TERMINATION OF MEMBERSHIP

Amend Paragraph (2) by deletion of the word "scheduled" from sub-paras (b)(i), (ii) and (iii).

AND BE IT FURTHER RESOLVED that the Director General, the General Counsel and the Secretary of the Association be and are hereby authorized and directed to do and execute all things, deeds and documents necessary or desirable for the due carrying out of the foregoing.

AND BE IT FURTHER RESOLVED that participation in the Traffic Conferences by air transport enterprises referred to in paragraph 2(b) of the amended Articles of Association shall be limited to joint meetings of Traffic Conferences 1 and 2 held for the purpose of determining charter prices and/or fares and rates on charter flights and/or conditions of sale and service applicable to charter flights between any point in Traffic Conference 1 and any point in Europe over the Atlantic. This limited participation by air transport enterprises referred to in paragraph 2(b) of the amended Articles of Association shall not be extended beyond this area, nor shall this provision be amended or rescinded without approval of a General Meeting of the membership by a 4/5 vote of the Active members present in person or by proxy and voting.

D. Resolutions adopted by the Twenty - First Assembly of the International Civil Aviation Organization (ICAO).

A21-25: Consideration of Air Transport Problems on a Worldwide Basis

WHEREAS the international air transport industry is faced with very serious economic problems which have been reviewed by the Assembly on the basis of documentation presented by the Council and the Secretary General (e.g., Chapter I in the Annual Reports of the Council to the Assembly, The Review of the Economic Situation of Air Transport 1963-1973, the ICAO regional air transport studies and the Inventory of Major Problems Associated with Continued Development in the Air Transport Field);

WHEREAS in order to find solutions to these problems it is necessary to set long-term objectives on the basis of a considered approach by governments and airlines, and that ICAO play a more effective and continuous part in this work by providing guidance for governments and promoting the exchange of ideas and experience related to possible remedies and solutions at both the regional and worldwide level;

WHEREAS Assembly Resolution A15-18 recognized that it might be suitable for ICAO to treat economic problems on a worldwide basis between sessions of the Assembly, taking into account the results achieved by regional bodies, and invited the Council to consider the possibility of convening a special air transport conference to deal with problems in the economic field;

WHEREAS problems relating to the economics of airports and route air navigation facilities, to air transport statistics and to facilitation are dealt with through existing ICAO machinery at both the worldwide and regional levels;

WHEREAS other air transport problems relating to such matters as the regulation of non-scheduled operations and their relationship to scheduled services, international air transport fares and rates, cooperation between airlines, regulation of capacity, and tariff enforcement are dealt with regionally through such mechanisms as AFCAC, CACAS, ECAC, LACAC, regional meetings of Directors of Civil Aviation, and airline conferences, but on a worldwide basis only at the ordinary triennial sessions of the Assembly; and

WHEREAS the results achieved by regional bodies are not at the present time sufficiently used on a worldwide basis for the development of air transport;

THE ASSEMBLY DIRECTS the Council:

1. as a matter of urgency, to draw up a descriptive list of those major economic problems confronting international air transport that are not already being dealt with through existing ICAO machinery on a worldwide basis;
2. to send this list to all Contracting States and to appropriate worldwide and regional civil aviation bodies, both governmental and non-governmental, with the request that they give the items due consideration and communicate to the Secretary General their experience and suggestions for remedial action;
3. on the basis of the material received in response to (2) to prepare with the Air Transport Committee in consultation with the representatives of regional civil aviation bodies and other experts, as appropriate, and taking into account the economic situation of international air transport, a plan for consideration of these matters on the global level by means of either -
   a) convening a special air transport conference or an extraordinary session of the Assembly, making the necessary arrangements for such a conference or Assembly including the preparation and circulation of terms of reference, agenda, and documentation; or
   b) referring the matter to a regular session of the Assembly, placing the appropriate item or items on the agenda for the Assembly and preparing the necessary documentation.

A21-26: International Air Transport Fares and Rates Studies

WHEREAS the establishment of international air transport rates that are fair and reasonable and designed to promote the satisfactory development of air services is a matter of major importance to the economies of many States;

WHEREAS governments have a responsibility to the users of air transport for such fares and rates;

WHEREAS there is an increasing concern among national tourist and trade interests and their international organizations about the level and structure of international fares and rates;

WHEREAS the costs of operation of international air services and appropriate yields are of great concern to the airlines of the world;

WHEREAS the objective studies by ICAO of the international air transport fares and rates situation should be of real value to States;

WHEREAS the Assembly in Resolution A18-17 directed the Council to initiate an examination of the feasibility of the Organization undertaking studies of international air transport fares and rates, and, provided the outcome of this examination was favourable, to proceed with a first study if the necessary resources were available; and

WHEREAS the Council determined that it was feasible for ICAO to undertake studies of international fares and rates, and instructed the Secretary General to proceed with a first study, which has been published as Circular 123-AT/33;

NOTING that IATA and IACA have indicated their willingness to co-operate in such studies.

THE ASSEMBLY:

1. DIRECTS the Council to:
   a) instruct the Secretary General to issue annually a survey of the fares and rates in international air transport with a content similar to that of the first survey on this subject which has now been issued by a decision of the Council;
   b) undertake analyses of the degree to which regional differences in the level of international air passenger fares, variations in fares with the distance and other traffic variables reflect corresponding variations in operating costs;
   c) establish, within the triennium 1975 to 1977, a small panel of experts which, in the light of results being achieved under 1 (a) and (b) and of other relevant factors, would examine the machinery for the establishment of international fares and rates and make recommendations to the Council for submission to the Assembly concerning possible improvements of that machinery, taking into account not only the legitimate interests of the international air carriers, but also the legitimate interests of the users of international air transport; and
   d) supplement, as appropriate, and to the extent that resources permit, the activities described in 1 (a), (b) and (c) above with other studies of international fares and rates for which a real need is seen to exist. Such other studies shall be of a factual character and could deal with the principles on which fares and rates are based, including the impact on fares and rates of such key cost factors in international air transport as, *inter alia*, fuel, wages and salaries, environmental factors, charges for airport and en route facilities, etc.
2. DECLARES that the present Resolution supersedes Resolution A18-18.

A21-27: The procedure for the establishment of tariffs for scheduled air services

WHEREAS tariffs for scheduled air services should be established on the basis of uniform principles and procedures; and

WHEREAS ICAO has not yet developed any standard bilateral tariff clause and existing bilateral tariff clauses vary considerably from each other;

THE ASSEMBLY:

DIRECTS the Council to instruct the Secretary General to untertake a study of existing bilateral tariff clauses with a view to exploring the feasibility and relative benefits of either an international ICAO standard tariff clause or an international agreement embodying such a clause.

BIBLIOGRAPHY

A. BOOKS AND THESES

BONBRIGHT, Principles of Public Utility Rates, Columbia Univ. Press, New York, 1961.

BRANCKER, IATA and what it does, Sijthoff, Leyden, 1977.

BUERGENTHAL, Law-Making in the International Civil Aviation Organization, Syracuse Univ. Press, Syracuse, N.Y., 1969.

BURKHARDT, CAB - The Civil Aeronautics Board, The Green Hills Publishing Co., Dulles Int. Airport, Va., 1974.

CHAYES, EHRLICH and LOWENFELD, International Legal Process: Materials for an Introductory Course, Little, Brown & Co., Boston, 1968.

CHUANG, The International Air Transport Association. A Case Study of a Quasi-Governmental Organization, A.W. Sijthoff, Leiden, 1972.

CODDING, The Universal Postal Union. Coordinator of the International Mails, NYU Press, New York, 1964.

DERINGER, The Competition Law of the European Economic Community (Articles 85-90) Including the Implementing Regulations and Directives, CCH, Inc., Chicago, Ill., 1968.

DIRLEWANGER, Die Preisdifferenzierung im Internationalen Luftverkehr, Verlag Herbert Lang & Cie. A.G., Bern, 1969.

Encyclopaedia Britannica, Vol. 18, 1968.

Explorations in Aerospace Law, Selected Essays by John Cobb Cooper, Ed. by Ivan A. Vlasic, McGill Univ. Press, Montreal, 1968.

Freedom of the Air, Ed. by Edward McWhinney and Martin A. Bradley, Sijthoff, Leiden/Oceana Publications, Dobbs Ferry, N.Y., 1968.

FRIEDMANN, Ed. Anti-Trust Laws. A Comparative Symposium, Carswell Co. Ltd., Toronto, 1956.

GRAUPNER, The Rules of Competition in the European Economic Community. A Study of the Substantive Law on a Comparative Law Basis, Nijhoff, The Hague, 1965.

HEERE, International Bibliography of Air Law 1900 - 1971 Sijthoff, Leiden/Oceana Publications, Dobbs Ferry, N.Y., 1972.

JOHNSON, Rights in Air Space, Manchester Univ. Press, Manchester, 1965.

KELLER, Der Versuch einer Multilateralen Regelung des Internationalen Luftverkehrs und die Schweizerische Luftverkehrspolitik der Nachkriegszeit, Ravensburg, 1952.

KRONSTEIN, The Law of International Cartels, Cornell Univ. Press, Ithaca/London, 1973.

LAMB and SHIELDS, Trade Association Law and Practice, Little, Brown & Co., Boston/Toronto, 1971.

LASOK and BRIDGE, An Introduction to the Law and Institutions of the European Communities, Butterworths, 1973.

LOWENFELD, Aviation Law, Matthew Bender, New York, 1972.

MEYER, Freiheit der Luft als Rechtsproblem, Aeroverlag, Zürich, 1944.

MAGDELENAT, Le fret aérien. Aspects juridiques, Dissertation,

Aix-en-Provence, 1975.
O'CONNOR, Economic Regulation of the World's Airlines. A Political Analysis, Praeger Publishers, New York, 1971.
PILLAI, The Air Net. The case against the world aviation cartel, Grossman Publishers, New York, 1969.
SCHENKMAN, International Civil Aviation Organization, Dissertation, Geneva, 1955.
TREBING, Essays on Public Utility Pricing and Regulation, Institute of Public Utilities, Graduate School of Business Administration, Michigan State Univ., 1971.
VAN DEN ASSUM, International Air Charter Transportation: Its Legal Rules and Implications, unpublished thesis, McGill Univ., Montreal, 1975.
WASSENBERGH, Postwar International Civil Aviation and the Law of the Air, Nijhoff, The Hague, 1957.
__________ Aspects of Air Law and Civil Air Policy in the Seventies, Nijhoff, The Hague, 1970.
WEDGWOOD, International Rail Transport, Oxford Univ. Press, Oxford, 1946.
WOLFGANG, Die IATA. Eine Organisation des grenzüberschreitenden Luftlinienverkehrs und ihre Allgemeinen Beförderungsbedingungen, Lang, Bern/Frankfurt, 1973.

B. ARTICLES

BAKER, The Bermuda Plan as the Basis for a Multilateral Agreement, Lecture delivered at McGill Univ., Montreal, April 18, 1947.
BEBCHICK, The International Air Transport Association and the Civil Aeronautics Board, 25 JALC 5 (1958).
BERLE, The Freedoms of the Air, Dept. of State Publ. 2.348 - Conf. Series 70, US Govt. Printing Off., Washington, 1945; in French: 9 RGA 190.
BROWNE, The International Angle, 77 The Aeronautical Journal 29 (1973).
BRUNNER, Die Rechtsstellung der IATA Agenten, Journées d'étude "Problèmes juridiques de la navigation aérienne internationale", 6 Referate gehalten am 6/7 Nov. 1969 an der Universität Basel, ASDA/SVLR Publ. 1969.
BURDEN, Opening the Sky. American Proposals at Chicago. Dept. State Publ. 2.348 - Conf. Series 70, US Govt. Printing Off. Washington, 1945; in French: 9 RGA 214 (1946).
CAB Regulation of International Aviation, 75 Harvard L.R. 580 (1961-1962).
CAB Held to have Exclusive Jurisdiction to Grant Injunctive Relief Against Acts Alledgedly in Violation of Antitrust Laws, 63 Columbia L.R. 923 (1963).
COHEN, Crisis in the Conferences: A Case History in International Air Fares and Rates Negotiation, 27 JALC 150 (1960).
______ Confessions of a Former IATA Man, 34 JALC 610 (1968).
COOPER, The Proposed Multilateral Agreement on Commercial Rights in International Civil Air Transport, 14 JALC 125 (1947).
COULTAS, The Doctrine of Primary Jurisdiction: Determination of Express and Implied Immunity From the Antitrust Laws, 39 JALC 559 (1973).
CRIBBETT, Some International Aspects of Air Transport, Journal of the Royal Aeronautical Society 669 (1950).
de la PRADELLE, La Conférence de Chicago, 1er Novembre - 7 Décembre 1944, Sa Place Dans l'Evolution Politique, Economique et Juri-

dique du Monde, 9 RGA 107 (1946).
DETIERE, Competition between Scheduled and Charter Services, 11 ITA Bull. 247 (March 1973).
EDLES, IATA, The Bilaterals and International Aviation Policy, 27 Fed. Bar J. 291 (1967).
GARNAULT, La première Assemblée de l'OACI et le Projet d'Accord Multilatéral sur les Libertés commerciales de l'air, 1 RFDA 231 (1946-1947).
GARSEK, Summary Power of the Civil Aeronautics Board to Suspend Proposed Airline Rates, 39 JALC 267 (1973).
GAZDIK, Rate-Making and the IATA Traffic Conferences, 16 JALC 312 (1949).
______ Traffic Conference Machinery, 15 IATA Bull. 63 (June 1952).
______ IATA et la libre concurrence, Journées d'étude "Problèmes juridiques de la navigation aérienne internationale", 6 Referate gehalten am 6/7 Nov. 1969 an der Universität Basel, ASDA/SVLR Publ., 1969.
______ Antitrust Laws and International Airline Cooperation, 135 Recueil des Cours 481 (1972/1).
______ Co-Existence of Scheduled and Charter Services in Public Air Transport, 77 The Aeronautical Journal 32 (1973).
______ The Distinction between Scheduled and Charter Transportation, 1 Air Law 66 (1976).
GOLDKLANG, Transatlantic Charter Policy - A Study in Airline Regulation, 28 JALC 99 (1961-1962).
GOODWIN, The Role of the U.S. in the 1963 Transatlantic Air Fare Crisis, 307 JALC 82 (1964).
HAANAPPEL, The IATA Conditions of Contract and Carriage for Passengers and Baggage, IX European Transport Law 650 (1974).
________ Background of the Dutch-American Aviation Conflict, I Annals of Air and Space Law 63 (1976).
________ Deregulation of the United States System of Government Regulation of Domestic Civil Aviation in Light of the Overall Structure of International Civil Aviation, 9 Akron Law Review 651 (1976).
HAMMARSKJOLD, The Challenging Years Ahead for the World Air Transport Industry, Address before the American Institute of Aeronautics and Astronautics, Commercial Aircraft Design and Operations Meeting, Los Angeles, June 13, 1967.
HILDRED, International Air Transport Association, 1 Air Affairs 277 (1946-1947).
HOUSTON LAY and MENKE, International Charter Flight Strandings: Proposals for Multinational Regulation, 3 Cal. Western L.J. 333 (1973).
IATA: The First Three Decades. A Record of Thirty Years of International Cooperation by the Airlines of the World in the Interest of the Public, 9 IATA Bull. 11 (July 1949).
IATA: Seeking a New Image for Changed Times, Montreal Star, Jan. 24, 1976.
International Conference on Air Law, Montreal, September 3- 25, 1975, 1 Air Law 114 (1976).
Impact of Technology on IATA Ratemaking: Problems, Prognostications, Proposals, 39 Geo. Wash. L.R. 1167 (1970-1971).
KEYES, The Making of International Air Fares and The Prospects for their Control, 30 JALC 176 (1964).
______ The Transatlantic Charter Policy of the United States, 39 JALC 215 (1973).
______ Policy Innovations in the Domestic Passenger-Fare In-

vestigation, 41 JALC 75 (1975).

LAROSE-AUBRY, Annual General Meeting of IATA, 1 Air Law 135 (1976).

LATCHFORD, A Comparison of the Chicago Air Convention with the Paris and Habana Conventions, 12 Dept. of State Bull. 411 (1945).

LEE, The International Flying Convention and the Freedom of the Air, 33 Harvard L.R. 23 (1919).

LESTER, Sales Agency Contracts in the Field of Air Transport, 135 Recueil des Cours 433 (1972/I).

LICHTMAN, Regularization of the Legal Status of International Air Charter Services, 38 JALC 441 (1972).

LOWENFELD, A New Takeoff for International Air Transport, 54 Foreign Affairs 36 (1975).

MASEFIELD, The Air Charter Challenge, Flight International 548 (1973).

McCLURKIN, The Geneva Commission on a Multilateral Air Transport Agreement, 15 JALC 39 (1948).

McCOOK BOND, A Critical Comparison of the IATA Traffic Conferences and the Maritime Shipping Conferences, unpublished term paper, McGill Univ., Montreal, 1964

MOUSSU, L'application du traité de Rome au transport maritime à propos de l'arrêt de la Cour des Communautés européennes du 4 avril 1974, Annuaire de Droit Maritime et Aérien 149 (1974).

OACI. Rapport final de la Commission chargée d'établir un accord multilatéral sur les droits commerciaux dans le transport aérien civil international, 2 RFDA 74 (1948).

Papers presented to the Symposium on "The Effect of Federal Regulation on Air Transportation", The University of Akron, Ohio, Nov. 13-14, 1975; reprinted in 9 Akron Law Review 629 (1976).

PILLAI, Consumer Protection in Aviation Rate Regulation, 38 JALC 215 (1972).

Pillai v. Civil Aeronautics Board - CAB Regulation of International Air Fares, 57 Temple Law Quarterly 620 (1974).

Politics, Downturn Hit Far East, AWST, Jan. 13, 1975.

Public Law 92-259: New CAB Authority Over International Air Fares, 5 N.Y.U. Journal of International Law and Politics 281 (1973).

REIN, Current Policy Problems in International Aviation, 64 Dept. of State Bull. 15 (Jan. 4, 1971).

RENTZEL, U.S. Regulation of the C.A.B. The Position of the Civil Aeronautics Board in American Government Tradition and Structure, 13 IATA Bull. 21 (June, 1951).

RINCK, Interessengemeinschaften und Kartelle im Luftverkehr, in Festschrift für Otto Riese, Verlag C.F. Müller, Karlsruhe, 1964.

_____ The International Factors in German Air Transport, 33 JALC 102 (1967).

RUEGGER, L'Organisation de la Croix Rouge Internationale sous ses Aspects Juridiques/The Juridical Aspects of the Organization of the International Red Cross, 82 Recueil des Cours 377 (1953/I).

SCOUTT and COSTELLO, The New Mode: Starting a New Course for International Air Transportation, 39 JALC 1 (1973).

SHEEHAN, IATA Traffic Conference Machinery, 17 IATA Bull. 45 (Mid-Year 1953).

STABENOW, The International Factors in Air Transport under the Treaty Establishing the European Economic Community, 33 JALC 117 (1967).

TAUBER, Enforcement of IATA Agreements, 10 Harvard Int. L.J. 1 (1969).

The Ins and Outs of IATA: Improving the Role of the United States in the Regulation of International Air Fares, 81 Yale L.J. 1102

(1971-1972).
THORNTON, Governments and Airlines, 25 International Organizations 541 (1971).
VERDURAND, Transports Aériens Internationaux. Les Conséquences de la Conférence de Chicago, 9 RGA 224 (1946).
WALDE, Sequels to the Chicago Aviation Conference, 11 Law and Contemporary Problems 609 (1946).
WARNER, The Chicago Air Conference, Accomplishments and Unfinished Business, 23 Foreign Affairs 406 (1945); in French: 9 RGA 168 (1946).
______ How Can a Multilateral Agreement in International Air Transport Be Attained? in Studi in Onore di Antonio Ambrosini, Milano, 1957.
WASSENBERGH, The Special Air Transport Conference of ICAO, April 1977: A new basis for the trade in traffic rights for international air services? 42 JALC 501 (1976).
WOOD, The IATA Traffic Conferences: An Airline's Man View, Paper Presented to the Second Air Transport Conference of N.Y.U., held at N.Y. on May 24, 1962.

C. CASES

McManus v. CAB, USCA, 2nd Circ., Feb. 6, 1961, 7 AVI 17.260, and USCA, 2nd Circ., Nov. 16, 1962, 8 AVI 17.271.
American Airlines, Inc. v. CAB, USCA, D.C. Circ., March 4, 1965, 9 AVI 18.230.
Pan American World Airways, Inc. v. CAB, USCA, 2nd Circ., July 20, 1967, 10 AVI 17.399.
John Caceres, d/b/a Caceres Agency, et al. v. IATA, et al., USCA 2nd Circ., Jan. 13, 1970, 11 AVI 17.408.
Robert Hefler, d/b/a Party Time Tours v. IATA, et al., USDC, SDNY, May 22, 1970, 11 AVI 17.540.
NACA, et al. v. CAB, USCA, D.C. Circ., May 28, 1970, 11 AVI 17.571.
NACA, et al. v. CAB, USCA, D.C. Circ., March 9, 1971, 11 AVI 17.989.
ACAP, Pillai and Robertson v. CAB, USDC, D.C. Circ., July 12, 1972, 12 AVI 17.500.
E.A. McQuade Tours Inc. v. Consolidated Air Tour Manual Committee et al., USCA, 5th Circ., Aug. 21, 1972, Certiorari denied, 12 AVI 17.549.
American Importers Association v. CAB, USCA, D.C. Circ., Nov. 29, 1972, 12 AVI 17.656.
Thomas P. Noone Travel Agency v. IATA, et al., USDC, D. of Mass., Dec. 11, 1972 (unreported).
Saturn Airways, Inc. v. CAB, USCA, D.C. Circ., July 11, 1973, 12 AVI 17.986.
Pillai, Goldwyn and ACAP v. CAB, USCA, D.C. Circ., Aug. 22, 1973, 12 AVI 18.036.
The Committee of the European Communities v. The French Republic Court of Justice of theEuropean Communities, April 4, 1974, Case No. 167/73, Recueil 1974, p. 359.
USA v. CAB, USCA, D.C. Circ., April 23, 1975, 13 AVI 17.702.
Pan American World Airways, Inc. and Trans World Airlines, Inc. v. CAB, USCA, 2nd Circ., May 22, 1975, 13 AVI 17.856.
Pan American World Airways v. Department of Trade, Court of Appeal (U.K.), July 28, 29, 1975, I Lloyd's L.R. 257 (1976).
Laker Airways v. Department of Trade, Q.B.D. (U.K.), July 30, 1976; appeal dismissed; see 2 Air Law 31-34 (1977).

D. INTERNATIONAL AGREEMENTS

Convention Relating to the Regulation of Aerial Navigation, Paris, 1919, 11 LNTS 174.
Ibero-American Convention Relating to Aerial Navigation, Madrid, 1926.
Convention on Commercial Aviation, Havana, 1928.
Convention for the Unification of Certain Rules Relating to International Carriage by Air, Signed at Warsaw on October 12, 1929, TS 876.
Convention on International Civil Aviation, Interim Agreement on International Civil Aviation, The International Air Services Transit Agreement, The International Air Transport Agreement, Standard Form of Agreement for Provisional Air Routes, Chicago, Dec. 7, 1944, ICAO Doc. 2187.
Air Services Agreement between the Government of the U.S.A. and the Government of the U.K., Feb. 11, 1946. Annexes and Final Acts of the Civil Aviation Conference, held at Bermuda, Jan. 15 - Feb. 11, 1946, TIAS 1507.
Protocol to Amend the Convention for the Unification of Certain Rules Relating to International Carriage by Air, Signed at Warsaw on October 12, 1929, Signed at The Hague on September 28, 1955, ICAO Doc. 7632.
Multilateral Agreement on Commercial Rights of Non-Scheduled Air Services in Europe, Signed at Paris on April 30, 1956, ICAO Doc. 7695.
Treaty Establishing the European Economic Community, Rome, 1957.
Convention on the High Seas, Geneva, 1958, UN Doc. A/Conf. 13/L. 53.
Treaty on Air Transport in Africa, Yaoundé, 1961, ICAO Circ. 98 - AT/19 (1970).
International Agreement on the Procedure for the Establishment of Tariffs for Scheduled Air Services, Signed at Paris on July 10, 1967, ICAO Doc. 8681.
Protocol to Amend the Convention for the Unification of Certain Rules Relating to International Carriage by Air, Signed at Warsaw on October 12, 1929, as Amended by the Protocol done at The Hague on September 28, 1955, Signed at Guatemala City on March 8, 1971, ICAO Doc. 8932.
Multilateral Agreement on Commercial Rights of Non-Scheduled Air Services Among the Association of South East Asian Nations, Signed at Manila on March 13, 1971.
Agreement Relating to the International Telecommunications Satellite Organization "INTELSAT", and Operating Agreement Relating to the International Telecommunications Satellite Organization "INTELSAT", Signed at Washington on August 20, 1971, TIAS 7532.
Memoranda of Understanding on the operation of Charter Air Services between the U.S.A. and

1) Belgium, Oct. 17, 1972, TIAS 7479, as extended (TIAS 8265).
2) The U.K., April 2, 1973, TIAS 7594, as amended (TIAS 7832, 8047, 8102).
3) Germany, April 13, 1973, TIAS 7605, as amended (TIAS 7804).
4) France, May 8, 1973, TIAS 7617, as amended (TIAS 7815, 8236).
5) Ireland, June 28/29, 1973, TIAS 7662, as amended (TIAS 8306).

6) The Netherlands, July 11, 1973, TIAS 7771.
7) Austria, Nov. 6, 1973, TIAS 7751, as amended (TIAS 8250).
8) Switzerland, June 12/July 25, 1974, TIAS 7916.

Non-Scheduled Air Service Agreements between the Government of the U.S.A. and
1) The Government of the Socialist Federal Republic of Yugoslavia, Sept. 27, 1973, TIAS 7819, as amended (TIAS 8305).
2) The Government of Canada, May 8, 1974, TIAS 7824.
3) The Government of the Hashemite Kingdom of Jordan, Sept. 21, 1974, TIAS 7954.

Text of Agreed Principles for North Atlantic Charter Flights, Ottawa, Declaration, October 21, 1972, 68 Dept. of State Bull. 20 (1973).

Air Transport Agreement between the Government of the U.S.A. and the Government of Canada, Signed at Ottawa on Jan. 17, 1966, as Amended by Exchange of Notes, Signed at Ottawa on May 8, 1974, TIAS 7824.

E. DOCUMENTS

i) ECAC

ICAO Doc. 8185, ECAC / 4-1 (1961).
ICAO Doc. 9044, ECAC / INT. S/5 (SP) (1972).
ICAO Doc. 9062, ECAC / 8 (1973).
ECAC / ECO - II / 7, April 1974.
ECAC Press Rel., No. 26 E, May 24, 1974.
ICAO Doc. 9086, ECAC / INT. S/6 (SP) (1974).
ECAC Doc. INT. S/8 (1975).

ii) IATA

Act of Incorporation, 9-10 Geo. VI, Chap. 51, Assented to 18th Dec., 1945, Amended by 23 Eliz. II, Chap. 26, Assented to Feb. 27, 1975.
Aspects of World Airline Cooperation, Clearing House, IATA Publ., 1969.
An Analysis of International Air Charters Undertaken at the Request of the European Civil Aviation Conference, Prepared by IATA, Geneva, Switzerland, Feb. 1972.
Annual Report of Director General of IATA, 29th AGM, Auckland, Nov. 1973.
Report of Traffic Conferences, 29th AGM, Auckland, Nov. 1973.
Agreeing Fares and Rates, 2nd Ed. IATA Publ., June 1974.
Act of Incorporation, Articles of Association, Rules and Regulations, IATA Publ., 14th Ed., Sept. 1974, as amended.
The State of the Air Transport Industry, 30th and 31st AGM, IATA Publ., Montreal, 1974 and 1975.
Annual Report of Director General of IATA, 30th AGM, Montreal, Sept. 1974.
Report of the Executive Committee, 30th AGM, Montreal, Sept. 1974.
Report of Financial Committee, 30th AGM, Montreal, Sept. 1974.
Report of Traffic Committee, 30th AGM, Montreal, Sept. 1974.
IATA Doc. AGM 30/24 E (1974).
Report of Director General of IATA, 31st AGM, Oslo, Sept. 1975.
Review of Cartel and Restraint of Trade Legislation, unpublished IATA Study.
Manual of Traffic Conference Resolutions, IATA Publ., current ed.

iii) ICAO

Draft Multilateral Agreement on Commercial Rights in International

Air Transport, PICAO Doc. 1577 - AT/116, April 17, 1946, reissued as PICAO Doc. 1632, EC/2.
Records of the Commission on Multilateral Agreement on Commercial Rights in International Civil Air Transport, ICAO Doc. 5230 A2 - EC/10 (1948).
Proceedings of the International Civil Aviation Conference, Chicago, III, Nov. 1 - Dec. 7, 1944, Washington, 1948, Dept. of State Publ. 2820; 2 Vols. XVI - 774 pp. and XVII - 734 pp.
ICAO Doc. 6894 - AT/694 (1949).
Definition of a Scheduled International Air Service, ICAO Doc. 7278 - C/841, May 10, 1952.
ICAO Ass., 7th Sess., Resolutions and Indexes to Documentation, ICAO Doc. 7417, A7 - p/3, Aug. 27, 1953.
ICAO Ass., 7th Sess., Minutes of the Plenary Meetings, ICAO Doc. 7409, A7 - P/2, Sept. 1, 1953.
Air Mail Study, ICAO Doc. 8240 - AT/716 (1962), revising the Air Mail Study of ICAO Doc. 5348 - AT/654 (1948).
Non-Scheduled Services in International Air Transport, ICAO Doc. 8244 - AT/717 (1962).
Handbook on Administrative Clauses in Bilateral Air Transport Agreements, ICAO Circ. 63 - AT/6 (1962).
Handbook on Capacity Clauses in Bilateral Air Transport Agreements, ICAO Circ. 72 - AT/9 (1965).
A Review of the Economic Situation of Air Transport, ICAO Circ. 73 - AT/10 (1965).
Summary of Materials Collected on Cooperative Agreements and Arrangements, ICAO Circ. 84 - AT/14 (1967).
Scandinavian Airlines System Consortium Agreement and Related Documents, ICAO Circ. 99 - AT/20 (1970).
Review of the Economic Situation of Air Transport (1963 - 1973), ICAO Circ. 122 - AT/32 (1974).
Survey of International Air Transport Fares and Rates, ICAO Circ. 123 - AT/33 (1974).
ICAO Doc. A 21 - WP/21, EC/3, May 27, 1974.
ICAO Doc. A 21 - WP/60, EC/8, July 30, 1974.
ICAO Ass., 21st Sess., Res. A 21 - 25/26/27 (1974).
Tariff Clauses in Bilateral Agreements, ICAO Doc. AT-WP/1207, Attachment (1975).
Report of the First Meeting of the Panel of Experts on the Machinery for the Establishment of International Fares and Rates, ICAO Doc. FRP/1 - Report (1976).
Special Air Transport Conference, ICAO Doc. SATC, Report Folder (1977).

iv) U.S.A.

Sherman Act, Act of 2 July, 1890, 26 Stat. 209, as amended.
Clayton Act, Act of 15 October, 1914, 38 Stat. 730, as amended.
Shipping Act, Act of 7 September, 1916, 40 Stat. 903, as amended.
Civil Aeronautics Act, Act of 23 June, 1938, 52 Stat. 973.
Hearings on Monopoly Problems in Regulated Industries before the Antitrust Subcomm. of the Comm. on the Judiciary, House of Representatives, 84th Cong., 2nd Sess., 1956; Report of the Subcomm. (Celler Comm.) of the Comm. on the Judiciary, House of Representatives, 85th Cong., 1st Sess., 1957.
Federal Aviation Act, Act of 23 August, 1958, 72 Stat. 731, as amended.
Hearings on International Air Transportation Rates and S.1539 and S.1540 before the Comm. on Commerce, Senate, 88th Cong., 1st Sess., 1963.